THE CANADIAN NOVE

THE CANADIAN NOVEL

HERE AND NOW

Critical Articles with an Introductory Essay by

JOHN MOSS

Edited by John Moss

NC PRESS LIMITED
TORONTO, 1978

Here and Now is the first volume of the series, *The Canadian Novel*. Further volumes will include a study of the novel in French Canada and an examination of the early writing, fiction and nonfiction, in Canada.

Cover illustration: Jack Chambers, *Diego Sleeping, No. 2*, (1968-71). By permission of Nancy Poole's Studio.

Canadian Cataloguing in Publication Data
Main entry under title:

The Canadian novel

Contents:v.1. here and now. - -
ISBN 0-919601-16-5 (v.1)bd.
ISBN 0-919601-04-9 (v.1)pa.

1. Canadian fiction –History and criticism–
Addresses, essays, lectures. 1.Moss, John, 1940–

PS8187.C35   C813'.03   C78-001385-9
PR9192.2.C35

We would like to thank the Ontario Arts Council and the Canada Council for their assistance in the production of this book.

New Canada Publications, a division of NC Press Limited, Box 4010, Station A, Toronto, Ontario, M5W 1H8. (416) 368-1165.

CONTENTS

Alice Munro

Mordecai Richler

Rudy Wiebe

INTRODUCTION

I

The Canadian Novel: Here and Now is meant to be unique. Critical anthologies and guides through Canadian literature are available, but their purpose has generally been to foster a particular argument or approach, or to capitalize on material published elsewhere. Usually, they are broad in scope and either random or arbitrary in selection, so that their usefulness is limited. In this book, I have attempted to set the literature first; combining previously unpublished essays with articles already in print in order best to illuminate it for the reader. By a clearly defined concentration, and by offering several essays written by different critics on a single work or author, the book encourages comparison both of the novels discussed and of approaches to them. At the same time, it shows that any work is more amenable to some types of criticism than to others. Together, these essays celebrate Canadian writing by making its achievement more readily accessible.

Margaret Atwood, Robertson Davies, Margaret Laurence, Alice Munro, Mordecai Richler, Rudy Wiebe: the choice of these novelists was not capricious. This volume is about the Canadian novel here and now. These six are the most significant among us. They presently have the most impact on public and critical consciousness; they are the most influential of our contemporaries, seen from a contemporary perspective. There are others who might have been included, but few would deny the importance and quality of these who are.

The term "Canadian novel" is generic. It implies a certain unity amidst the diversity of form and content to be found in Canadian fiction. Yet what is brought forcefully home in the essays gathered here is how dissimilar are the novels of these six writers. It is Canada the writers have in common rather than particular patterns of response to it. Each has a voice and a vision that is recognizably Canadian, informed by the common traditions and common culture that make us a people, however variegated we may be. But each of them is quite unique. Canada does not define them as Canadians but through their work achieves definition.

A search for the distinctively Canadian characteristics among these writers is probably counter-productive. The study of literature should expand, not limit, our consciousness. Still, certain generalizations might be made. The landscape, the climate, the spaces and sparse population of Canada do not translate into a shared reality, but their impact does, perhaps, determine certain attitudes, just as surely as do our history and culture. The effect of the Canadian experience is a voice that tends to be ironic, and a vision that is representational, yet ambiguous. Our writers today work in a realistic mode, for the most part, and are not exceptionally innovative in form or style. They share with those who precede them in the Canadian tradition a strong sense of the dualism of their experience — in Canada, at least, there are two sides to everything. This leads, on the one hand, to marvellous ironies and, on the other, to the sometimes startling reconciliation of opposites. The only safe generalization about content is that they, and the six represented here in particular, pay Canada the special compliment of taking it for granted. It is this quality of self-assurance within a Canadian context that sets them apart from their immediate predecessors, that makes them recognizably our contemporaries.

II

For the critic, Alice Munro can be the most enigmatic writer in Canada today. She offers none of the usual puzzles, ambiguities, or clever allusions which the student of literature expects of contemporary writing and virtually depends upon for analysis. Her prose is clear and uncluttered. She exhibits meticulous control over narrative voice and situation. She effortlessly evokes mood and manipulates response. There are no stylistic fireworks, no surprises; simply competence elevated to virtuosity.

Munro is not a simple writer. Her evocations of the personal past are warm but haunting. The small details of time and place are disconcerting to the reader, because they are exactly right — and therefore belong to another world. Her small-town Ontario is not what actually was, but what has been precisely remembered. Her past, her worlds of girls and women, she opens for us not through confession or revelation but directly as experience shared in recollection. The effect is one of *déjà vu*.

This quality of sharing, the quality of heightened realism, or magic realism, or, as the late artist Jack Chambers called it, "perceptual realism," is the distinguishing characteristic of Munro's writing. It invites comparison rather than explanation — in the same way that among painters we say Chambers is like Danby is like Forrestall is like Pratt is like Colville, making connections according to the intensity of their perceptions although each is different in tone, in subject-matter, in technique. This quality in Munro's writing invites analysis of content rather than of form or style. Her major themes are of growing up, of the friction between personal integrity as a woman and repressive femininity, of innocence lost and self attained, of the devastating impact of passing time, and of time redeemed through memory. All of these attract critical inquiry far more than does her subtle genius with language and narrative technique. Her particular heightened realism — exact, direct, haunting — is her means of making the truth so palpably self-evident that the reader, the critic, is hard pressed to discover arguments to be pursued or explanations to be given, and yet is enthralled with the complexities her writing evokes.

Alice Munro seems to affirm the reader's existence. Margaret Atwood confirms the reader's doubts. The pleasures of recognition come in Atwood from seeing things to be as mean or feckless as we sometimes suspect they are. It is easy, then, to understand how the very effectiveness of her writing leads the reader away from the art, to a consideration of his own or of the author's situation in the world. This is, perhaps, appropriate, for Atwood above all is a social critic, although her medium is what might be called psychological realism.

Nothing is accidental in Atwood's plots nor in her use of language. With a deadpan colloquial style she conveys complex intellectual metaphors. There is nothing said or done that does not imply its opposite — behind every joke, the hurt; behind the simple image, profound complexity. Little of the ironic ambiguity in her work is resolved, except through tone of voice: the reader finds himself agreeing or disagreeing with attitudes, rather than being moved by ideas, themselves, or by plot or characterization.

Atwood has been taken as the spokesman of her times for representing in a strong satiric light the anxieties and aspirations of the present day. Marian MacAlpine in *The Edible Woman* survives consumerism, sexism, and her own bland personality by force of will. The narrator of *Surfacing* escapes word-game superficiality by discovering her integrated self as woman and human animal in the primeval prenatal past. Joan Foster in *Lady Oracle* endures romantic manipulations of herself and those around her, and becomes many people, each unreal. Each novel imposes a form of psychoanalysis upon its protagonist — in order to illuminate the conditions that made her. Atwood is a behaviourist at heart. Her characters are not responsible for their own conditions or conditioning, and at times come perilously close to illustrating social theories rather than having fictional lives of their own.

Ideas more fully integrated with the narrative than in Atwood's writing, infused with high Tory intelligence and an energetic sense of wonder, lead Robertston Davies on his search for a secular soul. Davies occupies his position in Canadian letters with a flourish. His plots affirm the dictum that fiction can be more flamboyantly dramatic than real life or much more subtle, but never merely the same. His fiction is the antithesis of Munro's perceptual realism. It resounds with the contrivances and excesses of romance. Yet, we are urged to accept, this is the way things are — the mtaure, urbane, erudite presence of the author within his fiction tells us so. In his early novels, as in his plays and essays, authorial displays of style and wit often obscured considerable substance. With *Fifth Business*, art prevails over artfulness and, being fully integrated into the novel; the Davies' personality, itself, becomes technique.

Davies is the most worldly of our contemporary writers, and of the six examined here, the most innovative. His novels are schematic, constructed to allow maximum exploitation of themes and concepts — the duality of experience, the beneficence of wonder, the sanctity of the psyche, the processes of individuation. Character, with the exception of Dunstan Ramsay, is less notable than the dramatic analysis to which it is treated. Voice, ultimately, carries the fiction; particularly in *Fifth Business* where Davies and Ramsay seem perfectly attuned to one another.

Under more conscious control, the authorial and narrative voices often diverge in the fiction of Rudy Wiebe. In this way, Wiebe transcends the limited perspective of the so-called reliable narrator. The author's presence is both directly and indirectly felt. He is a prose stylist, in a way that none of the others are, in his shaping of each sentence, each phrase, as an icon or artifact. His characters work out the moral dilemmas of their lives in conflicts which are authentic and yet are moral paradigms clearly enunciating the author's creed. Wiebe involves us in his fiction. We experience the worlds he populates with an uncanny sense of immediacy. Particularly in *The Temptations of Big Bear*, his most powerful work, his vision of the Plains Cree in the last century is transported into our immediate presence. It is an effect exactly opposite to that of historical romance, where it is the reader who is transported, while the reality stays safely removed.

It is interesting to compare Wiebe's fiction with Mordecai ᐧichler's. Both writers excel in the creation of character and both subordinate plot to the exploration of ideas. Both express their sense of having been shaped in communities apart from the Canadian mainstream. Richler writes of the urban Jew; Wiebe, of Mennonites, and of Indians and Métis. Both display acute moral consciousness. Society, for both, can be reduced to dialectical explication. Both are so conservative as to seem radical in terms of social change and personal ethics. Character is always a matter of choice and will, whatever the social context impinging upon it.

Richler writes with satiric flair, Wiebe with solemn thoughtfulness. Richler's style is journalistic, sometimes glib, and always urbanely clever. Irony permeates Richler's fiction, leading sometimes to absurdity, sometimes into touching confessional. Richler rails at the world and its ills. Wiebe illuminates culpability and attempts redemption. Richler chronicles contemporaneity, the city, himself. Wiebe chronicles our conscience. Both judge: Wiebe rages and possibly forgives; Richler scorns and, perhaps privately, weeps.

Mordecai Richler seems most at home writing about the worlds that made him, particularly the Jewish immigrant section of Montreal around St. Urbain Street, and the artistic expatriate community in London, England, in the Fifties and Sixties. Sometimes it seems as if there are ghosts to be exorcised, but first he must be reconciled with them — and to do that, he must array them within his fiction where they may be thoroughly considered. In *The Apprenticeship of Duddy Kravitz*, judgment predominates. In *St. Urbain's Horseman*, it is reconciliation that prevails.

Of the six novelists considered here, Margaret Laurence is the most influential at the present time. She is probably the most widely read, studied, and respected. Her work, along with Richler's in a much different way, embodies the popular conception of Canadian writing. More so than most, she is a story-teller. Memorable characters work out convincing situations that are at once dramatic and significant. Plot and personality are inseparable. The lives of Hagar, Morag, Stacey, Rachel, and Vannessa inform their narratives with shape, with meaning, with conviction. We know them because we have experienced their experience of themselves. They transcend their origins and seem to dwell in our imaginations.

Somehow, Laurence speaks to us of our own place, in our own idiom, the way no writer has before. She writes in what might be called the grand colloquial style. Simple direct language is embellished with pungent imagery, syntactical flourishes, rich arrangements of symbolism, and literate allusions. Style and form, though, always serve the presentation of characters in action. Motifs, themes, and meaning are all sustained, not illustrated. Even in *The Diviners*, her novel most self-consciously redolent with thematic significance, the story of Morag easily prevails over the powerful themes her life conveys.

With dramatic realism Laurence presents the struggle of her female protagonists to discover a balance or a reconciliation between the selves imposed upon them and the selves they are. The town of Manawaka, Manitoba, while not knowable with the precision of Munro's Jubilee, nor a definitive source, like Davies' Deptford, occupies a notable place in the Canadian imagination. It is there that the problems and the personalities of her main characters originate. Manawaka is not the heart of a region so much as it is a social condition, extended through time, which determines the drama of her characters' lives. As such, it is inseparable from our own.

III

There is not one approach to literature but many, a "polysemous" number, to use Northrop Frye's word for a multiplicity of acceptable meanings. Frye argues for intellectual tolerance as a prelude to his assertion that literature derives solely from literature. This precept, used to foster discipline and responsibility on the part of the critic, is obviously valid. Taken literally, it is simply inadequate to our experience. Literature as perceived is not autonomous: we do not read as an act separate from our continuing experience of ourselves. Literature as created is not accidental and intuitive but involves acts of will and the refining effects of intelligence. Each work is a process that links creation and response, not an artifact that separates them. Seen as process, it is easy to understand why a novel will sustain many readings from many perspectives. In this book, the dynamic quality of each novel and the flexibility of the novel form are both given emphasis, for there are as many approaches taken as there are essays presented.

The most noticeable and at the same time the most elusive difference among them is in tone. They vary from the casual authority of Wilfred Cude's brief essay on *Lady Oracle* to the nearly austere formality of J. R. (Tim) Struther's definitive treatment of Alice Munro's aesthetic sources. Some, like those of Ellen Warwick and Gordon Roper, both on Davies, take on the attitudes of formal argument. Others, such as my own, lean more towards considered opinion. Some are cool and eloquent, while Tom Marshall's is so relaxed and colloquial as to seem intimate. There are no correct tones for an essay, beyond those of enthusiasm and sincerity.

In scope and in depth of field, these essays vary greatly. Cheryl Cooper pursues a single dominant motif within the text of *The Diviners*, to show how major images, themes, the form itself, are integrated towards wholeness or closure which, in retrospect, encompass all of Laurence's earlier Manawaka works. Frank Pesando relates aspects of apocalyptic mythology to an even broader spectrum of Laurence's writing. He places particular emphasis on her African phase, which produced the powerful short stories in *The Tomorrow Tamer*, but follows through with a discussion of several of her Canadian novels, most particularly, *The Stone Angel*. Clara Thomas, while concentrating on *The Diviners*, ranges with eclectic aplomb through history, literature and literary myth, biography, and the entire Laurence canon. Gordon Roper includes Carl Jung in his intriguing analysis of *Fifth Business* and Catherine McLay makes effective use of the radical psycho-theories of R. D. Laing in her discussion of Margaret Atwood. Some essays stay relatively close to the descriptive surface while others plunge deep in pursuit of an enigma to be resolved. Others range afield in search of comparisons to be made and sources to be established. The purpose always, though, is to illuminate the text, to make it more accessible.

An essay may be interpretive as is for instance, John Lauber's revealing analysis of Atwood's *The Edible Woman*. This approach gives a reading and argues that that reading best accounts for the effectiveness, the characteristic qualities, of a work. Another approach, one too rarely seen in Canadian criticism, is the evaluative, where the critic assesses quality — what does a work mean to be, to what extent does it achieve its implicit intent, and is that intention, in fact, worthwhile, measured against the achievement of other works in the same genre. An excellent example is Wilfred Cude's article on *Lady Oracle* which applauds Atwood's novel because it exploits to well the contemporary possibilities of the comic tradition from which it draws form and substance.

A third approach, falling between these two, finds the critic giving a close textual reading in order to show how the novel works. It does not pretend to be definitive in either interpretation or evaluation, but rather aims directly at appreciation. An essay such as Miriam Packer's on *Lives of Girls and Women* relates major elements of form and theme, story and character, in order to clarify the novel's effectiveness. It is from this perspective that the critic most closely approaches being a representative reader.

The essential difference, of course, between critic and reader is that the critic must articulate his responses, must objectify what may initially have been very subjective and must test with intellect to discover what the work brought to him and he to the work. All criticism is in some measure comparative. The critic's taste and ability to judge have been refined by his experience of literature and the world. His appreciation of a specific work will be within the context of this experience. In order to structure his responses, the critic may arrange them according to archetypes evoked, or knowledge of the genre or the tradition or the author's other works — according to some system which may be known equally as well by his own readers. The critic's personal responses, ultimately, are irrelevant. It is his function as critic to communicate intellectually and without ambiguity, what in itself is not intellectual but aesthetic and highly ambiguous.

Probably the most fruitful context for comparison is within an author's own canon, because it is the least arbitrary. Ellen Warwick traces the changes in Davies' fiction from romantic satire to psychological romance. Davies provides the perimeters of her analysis and argument. In contrast, Gordon Roper uses Jungian theory in his treatment of Davies, although perhaps Freud could be as effective, or R. D. Laing for that matter. It is to Roper's credit that he convinces us this is not so, that Jung is the key. Laurence particularly invites comparative studies within her work. as every student knows who at essay time has turned to her for source and inspiration. Mordecai Richler's fiction similarly invites comparisons. In both Tom Marshall's essay and my own, we more or less take for granted that our readers are familiar with Richler's major works, or will become so.

Rudy Wiebe is a case somewhat apart. His novels are not only open to comparison, but seem to demand such treatment. In her essay on his Mennonite novels, Hildegard Tiessen examines the singular motif of "peace," drawing for her interpretation of the texts on a specifically Christian definition of the term. She does not establish biblical parallels, but rather elucidates the moral and theistic premises upon which the novels are built. Allan Dueck stays within the context of Wiebe's later novels in his comparative analysis of what might be called Wiebe's historical meditations, *The Temptations of Big Bear* and *The Scorched-Wood People*. It is rewarding for the reader to compare Tiessen and Dueck, to realize that Wiebe's work is an organic whole, bound by his profound moral consciousness and his commitment to a particular evolving style. Before his separate works can be fully appreciated against some broader literary or even social and historical context, it is necessary to see them in relation to each other. Individually, of course, they stand up well on their own, and are as readily open to textual analysis as are any of the other novels discussed in this book.

The critics here invariably hold the literature to be their primary source and concern. In this, they seem to follow Frye's dictum. Yet the novels themselves lead in myriad directions and show diverse influences. It is the discipline of the critic which keeps the literature foremost, not the limitations of the art. Criticism must communicate precisely, on an intellectual plane, to be understood. The novel, by contrast, is a process — form placed upon chaos — written to be experienced, appreciated and enjoyed. Critical understanding at its best will contribute to that potential.

These essays do not read like the works of a corporate personality. The literature itself will not tolerate such rigid treatment. Of those which have previously been published, several have been extensively revised and expanded. The periodical drawn upon most heavily is The *Journal of Canadian Fiction*. I would like to extend a special thanks to David Arnason and John Robert Sorfleet who shared responsibilities with me during my tenure as that magazine's Managing Editor. I would also like to thank the critics in this volume who have graciously assigned royalties to the *Journal of Canadian Fiction*, and the other journals which have given permission to have works from their pages reprinted.

This book is about contemporary Canadian novels written in English and is addressed to the English Canadian reader. Canadian writing in French is equally rich and diverse. Another volume in this series will attempt to make it more readily accessible to English-speaking readers. Others will consider major works in the Canadian tradition and the writers who have brought that tradition to its present level of achievement. Ultimately, the purpose of this volume is to reveal and to celebrate the best novels that have been created among us, here and now.

John Moss,
Queen's University, 1978.

MARGARET ATWOOD

ALICE IN CONSUMER-LAND: THE SELF-DISCOVERY OF MARIAN MacALPINE

John Lauber

Of course everybody knows *Alice* is a sexual-identity-crisis book, that's old stuff . . . What we have here, if you only look at it closely, this is the little girl descending into the very suggestive rabbit-burrow, becoming as it were pre-natal, trying to find her role," he licked his lips, "her role as a Woman . . . Patterns emerge. One sexual role after another is presented to her but she seems unable to accept any of them, I mean she's really blocked. She rejects Maternity when the baby she's been nursing turns into a pig, nor does she respond postively to the dominating-female role of the Queen and her castration-cries of 'Off with his head!' . . . and right after you'll recall she goes to talk with the Mock-Turtle, enclosed in his shell and his self-pity, a definitely pre-adolescent character . . . So anyway she makes a lot of attempts but she refuses to commit herself, you can't say that by the end of the book she has reached anything that can be definitely called maturity.[1]

As Fischer Smythe lectures to the patiently listening Marian Mac-Alpine, the reader may feel that a handy capsule interpretation of *The Edible Woman* has just been offered. "Sexual-identity-crisis book" — the cliché seems to apply, and many of the details fit. Marian indeed tries on a variety of roles (career-woman, submissive fiancée, competent nurse), but cannot finally commit herself to any of them. The pre-adolescent Mock Turtle, "enclosed in his shell and his self-pity," clearly is Duncan, who provides Marian with an alternative to, and finally an escape from, her lover Peter. The dominating-female role is played by Mrs. Bogue, the office manager of Seymour Surveys. Marian has no children, but her friend Clara does, and those children are presented in terms of stink and excrement — they're quite sufficiently pig-like. And it's certainly true that Marian has reached no very definite state by the conclusion of the novel, although she's rejected a good many things.

But Fish's speech is not really a précis of the novel. It's a masculine view, implying that the heroine's confusions are her own fault, that she ought to commit herself to one of the offered roles, and that "maturity" can be defined as such commitment. It reveals the speaker's own obsessions, and parodies the Freudian approach both to literature and to life. Not all the details fit, and Fish is not even speaking directly to Marian (he shuts his eyes as he lectures). Any temptation to accept that easy label "sexual-identity-crisis book" (which here carries the implication that only female identity is in doubt) and to treat *The Edible Woman* as a "feminist" work should be resisted. It is that, but also much more. Masculine identity seems as problematic as feminine (how can we consider one in isolation?), and the novel insistently asks whether and how anyone can achieve identity in the artificial society it presents. The setting may be recognizable as Toronto in the mid-sixties, but the issues are no more limited to that time and place than is the consumer society itself. Indeed, the nature of that society and the possibility of personal fulfillment within it, in spite of it, *are* the issues.

Possessing a job, an apartment, and a lover, Marian seems to be the fully emancipated modern woman, but in fact she's adrift; she has no tradition, no freedom, and no future. There is no moral or social authority she can accept (all the characters have cut themselves off from parents and place of origin), there is not even a suitable role-model (as her roommate Ainsley would put it) at hand. The only "wisdom" available is contained in Ainsley's paperbacks on psychology and anthropology. Marian's freedom is limited by an undefined and therefore all-inclusive guilt; if she is not forbidden to do some particular thing, she feels forbidden to do everything. The job holds out only the prospect of an inadequate pension after a lifetime of unrewarding work. The responsible positions are held by men and the work itself, preparing questionnaires and conducting market surveys, is an outrageous invasion of personal privacy.

Utterly normal both to outward appearances and in her own self-estimation, Marian seems to accept the conditions of her life and to pride herself in her ability to cope. The word "cope" holds a place of honour in her vocabulary; she seems so much more able to cope that the three Office Virgins (she has a man and they haven't) or than Ainsley with her idea of fulfilling her femininity by having a baby outside of marriage, or than Clara, with two infants and carrying a third. To cope, with one's emotions or one's dishes, means to be in control, and for Marian loss of control threatens her identity, even her existence. Listening to one of Duncan's monologues, she feels "all this . . . rather liquid confessing . . . seemed foolhardy to me, like an uncooked egg deciding to come out of its shell: there would be a risk of spreading out too far, turning into a formless puddle" (p. 99).

The other women in the novel offer other images of femininity: the antiquated, genteel landlady; the alternately dominating and wheedling office manager, Mrs. Bogue; but these are images that can serve, not as possible alternatives but as Awful Warnings. While Ainsley appears to be a genuinely liberated woman, finding her own way to fulfill her deepest needs, her freedom is bogus; her authorities, books and lecturers, tell her what those needs are. For them, biology is destiny; a woman can fulfill her femininity only by having a baby. Ainsley shows her contempt for conventionality by planning to have the baby without having a husband, yet before the end of the novel she too is husband-hunting because another Authority has told her that a boy (she's sure her baby will be a boy) needs a strong Father-Image to avoid becoming a homosexual. Ainsley's movement toward conventionality (for the most up-to-date reasons) ironically counterpoints Marian's growing rejection of it.

Twice in the novel, Marian is solemnly accused of "rejecting her femininity": once by the radical Ainsley and once by the conservative Peter. Their words are identical, and their meaning essentially the same. This biological version of woman's destiny reaches its climax in Fish's archetypal vision (derived from his study of "Womb-Symbols in D.H. Lawrence") of dark earthgods and goddesses, of big-bellied Venuses representing "warmth and vegetation and generation . . . teeming with life . . . about to give birth to a new world in all its plenitudes" (p. 200). Fish's language parodies itself; his vision is really not a great deal more sophisticated than the magazine advertisement Marian reads at the hairdresser's: "'Girls! Be successful! If you want to really Go Places, Develop Your Bust'" (p. 210). For Marian, biology is not enough.

The predominant masculine image is of the male as hunter — not as provider, but as destroyer. Commercialized (as in the Moose Beer billboards of shiny, neatly dressed hunters and fishermen with their prey) and perverted, the image has outlasted the circumstances that once justified it. So Peter, a smooth young lawyer in a big-city law office, likes to imagine himself a rugged, plaid-shirted outdoorsman, and treasures his collection of guns and knives and hunting recollections as proofs of masculinity. (His closest friend is nicknamed Trigger!) It is Peter's hunting story that initiates Marian's collapse:

> "Trigger said, 'You know how to gut them, you just slit
> her down the belly and give her a good hard shake and all
> the guts'll fall out.' So I whipped out my knife and took her
> by the hind legs and gave her one hell of a crack, like a
> whip you see, and the next thing you know there was blood
> and guts all over the place. All over me, what a mess, rabbit

guts dangling from the trees, god, the trees were red for
yards." (p. 69)

The story shocks not because the action was cruel (the rabbit must
have been already dead) but because of the insensitivity of the teller
to nature and to his audience. It's no wonder that Marian, listening,
identifies herself with the female victim.

The male, of course, can also be a hunter in his relations with
women. Len Slank offers a brilliant study of the psychology of a pro-
fessional seducer. Len fears pursuit, and therefore pursues: "You've
got to hit and run. Get them before they get you and then get out" (p.
66). (Ironically, Ainsley begins her pursuit of him only a moment
after this speech.) Len's sexual affairs are brief, not merely from fear
of involvement, but more importantly from his distaste for the
women he has, in his own word, "corrupted." Believing that most
women are "corrupt," Len searches endlessly for "innocence" (sexual
inexperience), which he immediately destroys. His attitude can be
formularized:

> You are innocent; therefore I am attracted to you.
> I am attracted to you; therefore I wish to seduce you.
> I have seduced you; therefore you are corrupt.
> You are corrupt; therefore I shall leave you.

And the process begins again.

But the sexual act can be corrupting only if sex itself is perceived as
unclean, and in fact Len is revolted by the physical process of sex and
its possible consequences of impregnation, gestation, and birth:
"'Birth,' he said, his voice higher and more distraught, 'birth terrifies
me. It's revolting. I can't stand the thought of having' — he shud-
dered — 'a baby'" (p. 157). Forced to confront his worst horrors when
he learns that Ainsley is pregnant by him and refuses abortion, he
collapses — comically and pitifully.

Clara's attitude toward biological necessity, in contrast, is the
healthy one. After her third delivery, answering Marian's routine
"How do you feel?", she says:

> "Oh, marvellous . . . I watched the whole thing: it's
> messy, all that blood and junk, but I've got to admit it's sort
> of fascinating. Especially when the little bugger sticks its
> head out . . . It's like when you were little and you waited
> and waited and finally got to open your Christmas presents."
> (p. 128)

Paradoxically, the female not only is hunted but hunts (as the male suspects). When Marian tells the Office Virgins of her engagement to Peter, their instant question is "How did you catch him?" Ainsley hunts Len, first as a biological father for her child, then as a Father-Image. She hunts by seeming not to, by appearing to be an inexperienced girl, a helpless victim: "her inert patience was that of a pitcher plant in a swamp with its hollow bulbous leaves half-filled with water, waiting for some insect to be attracted, drowned, and digested" (p. 75). This is precisely what happens to Len: the seducer is seduced, proving the truth of his own self-justification: "But you've got to watch these women when they start pursuing you" (p. 66).

The two leading male characters, Peter the lawyer, and Duncan the graduate student, seem like matter and anti-matter; they might cancel each other out if they ever met. Peter is "ordinariness raised to perfection" (p. 61), handsome and with the appropriate costume for every occasion (when he is being casual, his socks match the paint-stains on his shirt); Duncan is almost grotesquely emaciated, and his clothes never seem to change. Peter is shooting up in his profession; Duncan has lost himself in a muddle of unfinished papers and meaningless books. Peter has expensive hobbies, photography and model-making; Duncan irons, or sits in the laundromat watching clothes whirl in the dryer (his substitute for television).

Yet they are alike in their entire self-absorption. Peter is fascinated with techniques for taking self-portraits and in the décor of his bedroom, furnished with his guns, his cameras, his graduation portrait, and a full-length mirror. He decides to marry because all his friends have, and a wife might be useful — after a while people begin thinking an unmarried man is "queer." "Queerness" is Peter's dread, and is associated for him with "arts-crafts types" who engage in "unmanly" activity. Marian is convenient and dependable, and he can act out his fantasies with her. (Most of the men in this novel are "acting out" in their relations with women.) They make love on a sheepskin rug in his bedroom, in an open field, even in his bathtub, fantasies he has borrowed (not even his fantasies are his own) from "outdoorsy male magazines" or "men's glossies, the kind with lust in penthouses" (p. 60).

Duncan's complete egotism is revealed in a striking image at his first appearance in the novel: he "sat holding the cigarette before him, with his hands cupped, like a starved buddha burning incense to itself" (p. 51). A brilliant combination of physical appearance and posture, complacency, and complete narcissism. He is the idol of his own creation and his own worship. Even his talk, endless self-revelations that may or may not be true, is an offering of incense to himself. He lies sometimes for aesthetic pleasure, sometimes to inspire pity. Marian, for him, is a new listener to sympathize and to admire his cleverness, and only then a woman to make love to. In fact, Duncan is a pure narcissist, really unable to "make love" to anyone else; as he caresses Marian, she has "an uneasy suspicion . . . that what he was really caressing was his own dressing gown, and that she merely happened to be inside it" (p. 144).

Preferring winter to summer, snow to foliage — "in the snow you're as near as possible to being nothing" (p. 263) — praising the mining-town of his birth because on its rock and slagheaps, nothing can grow, Duncan seems an incarnate death-wish. Physically he is like a corpse; his skull-like features arouse both fear and pity. (As he stands before the mummies, his favourite exhibit in the museum, Marian feels that if she touched him, he might crumble.)

A shrewd psychologist, Duncan is perfectly aware of the impression he makes and uses it to play on Marian's last illusions, her pride in her own sexual competence and her concept of herself as the Nurse bringing the Gift of Life. He entices her into bed, once, with his tale that he is a virgin who needs to be introduced to sex, and so to be initiated into life. Since one can't imagine Duncan getting enjoyment from any physical act, the pleasure must lie in the deceit and the resulting sense of power. The whole performance seems to be for the moment he can tell Marian that she is not the first, that she has been taken in. His sexual life, like Len Slank's, must necessarily be a series of one-night affairs.

Section I, about one-third of the novel, is narrated in the first person, presenting the heroine in apparent control of her life, coping adequately with her job and her affair. She gets little satisfaction or pleasure from either, but she doesn't expect pleasure. A cautious and meticulous person, afraid of attracting attention to herself and choosing her clothes "for protective colouration" (p. 14), afraid of public opinion in the person of her landlady, she is thoroughly conventional, even in her sexual freedom.

But when Peter asks her to set a time for their wedding, "I heard a soft flannelly voice I barely recognized, saying, 'I'd rather have you decide that. I'd rather leave the big decisions up to you'" (p. 90). That flannelly voice is the voice of society, of its traditional expectations about woman's role, incorporated within her own personality and responding automatically, before her conscious mind can act. Her growing dissatisfaction with that role, with her work, leads her to unpredictable and irrational acts. In the shock of hearing Peter's

story about gutting a rabbit, Marian identifies with the female victim
and finds herself weeping. She, the rabbit, and even a roll of toilet
paper in the ladies' powder room, are imagined as "helpless and
white and furry and waiting passively for the end" (p. 70). This identification dominates the remainder of the book.

When Marian, like a hunted creature, takes refuge in an impro-
vised burrow beneath a bed in Len Slank's apartment, the scene is
comic in its violation of social proprieties and in its appealingly absurd logic; if the talk is dull, the music too loud and the lights too
bright, why *not* take shelter under a bed? But it indicates an alarm-
ing dissociation both of Marian from her society and, internally, of
her mind from her body, her intellect from her emotions, her conscious from her unconscious. Fantasy becomes reality as Marian
breaks away, runs down the street, and is recaptured. Without conscious direction, her body has tried to escape from Peter, but the loss
of control is terrifying and she returns to him, as "a rescuer from
chaos, a provider of stability" and a rescuer from Seymour Surveys.

Duncan-Peter seem to be her alternatives, and her serious involvement with Duncan begins immediately after the engagement. (There
was no need for an escape or alternative before). After their accidental meeting at the laundromat: "We stood facing each other irreso-
lutely . . . Then, as though someone had pulled a switch, we drop-
ped our laundry bags . . . I found myself kissing him" (p. 100). The
kiss is no more predictable than her answer to Peter: the latter from
her social self and this from her rebellious body.

This rebellion dominates the long second part (nearly two-thirds)
of the novel. It is against social convention and the conclusion —
marriage to Peter — to which it is leading her. It is also a conflict between Marian's social self (what has been expected of her and what
she has accepted) and her true self (her inarticulate desires, needs,
and revulsions). "Marian was sitting listlessly at her desk" (p. 107),
Part II begins, signalling the change from first-person to third-person
narration. The change is necessary because she can no longer understand her own motives or predict her actions. As she drifts toward
the party at which she is to meet Peter's friends, and the wedding, the
rebellion of her body intensifies, leading to an increasing involvement with Duncan, a refusal to eat — first steaks and chops, then a
wide and illogical variety of foods — and at last a successful flight
from Peter and his party.

As her rational consciousness loses control, Marian's life moves
from order to disorder, activity to passivity, conventionality to un-
predictability. The involvement with Duncan is quite unplanned, the

touches and kisses seeming to occur quite independently of her conscious desires. In her apartment, as the careful pattern of her life breaks down, dirt appears everywhere, the sink overflows with unwashed dishes, and the refrigerator fills with rotting food. Her prized ability to cope apparently lost, Marian can only respond helplessly.

"She was becoming more and more irritated by her body's decision to reject certain foods. She had tried to reason with it . . . had coaxed it and tempted it, but it was adamant, and if she tried to use force, it rebelled" (pp. 177-8). Here is an almost schizophrenic split between two elements of the person, resulting from the effort of one (the socially conditioned mind) to deny the existence of the other. Marian's revulsion against meat, her sudden realization that her steak is "A hunk of muscle. Blood red. Part of a real cow that once moved and ate" (p. 151) rather than a cookbook diagram, results from Trigger's story and her identification with all helpless, hunted, slaughtered creatures. (The novel doesn't endorse such exaggerated sensitivity, which would make life impossible; one of the signs of Marian's recovery is her ability to eat a steak again.)

The reality of meat has been hidden by its packaging. Unreality is the basic principle of the consumer society. The hunters and fishermen on the billboards are tidy and unbloodied; "the fish also was unreal, it had no slime, no teeth, no smell; it was a clever toy, metal and enamel" and the dead deer cannot be "ugly or upsetting; it wouldn't do . . . to have a deer with its tongue sticking out" (p. 150). Unreality extends to the products themselves. A sandwich is "a slice of plastic cheese between two pieces of solidified bubblebath with several flaps of pallid greenery" (p. 127). Toilet paper is printed in "flowers and scrolls and polka dots . . . as though they wanted to pretend it was used for something quite different, like Christmas presents. There really wasn't a single human unpleasantness left that they had not managed to turn to their uses" (p. 174).

The "intellectual" world of Duncan and his roommates Trevor and Fish offers no real alternative to the consumer society. The search for truth "collapses in a welter of commas and shredded footnotes" (p. 96), or in essays with titles like "Sado-Masochistic Patterns in Trollope," "Pre-Raphaelite Pornography," or "Womb-Symbols in Beatrix Potter." The titles reveal the same obsession with sex that is found in the commercial world, and here, too, the obsession doesn't at all indicate sexual fulfillment — quite the opposite! Trevor is a latent homosexual, Fish (the follower of D.H. Lawrence) is still a virgin at thirty. As Duncan sees: "Production-consumption. You begin to wonder if it isn't just a question of making one kind of garbage into

another kind . . . what *is* the difference between the library stacks
and one of those used-car graveyards?" (p. 143)

All of these themes are combined and resolved at Peter's party.
Marian reaches a climax of unreality as she packages herself, getting
an elaborate coiffure, a "daring" new dress, a girdle, heavy make-up
(applied by Ainsley), and even Ainsley's gold earrings. To get the ap-
proval of Peter (who wishes she would always look like that), she
has turned herself into a product:

> "She held both of her naked arms out towards the mirror.
> They were the only portion of her flesh that was without a
> cloth or nylon or leather or varnish covering, but . . . even
> they looked fake, like soft, pinkish-white rubber or plastic,
> boneless, inflexible . . ." (p. 229)

Ainsley tries to blackmail Len into marrying her, fails, but catches
the interest of Fischer Smythe, who is happy to provide the Father-
Image. Peter's friends, the "soap-men" and their wives, are present;
this is the milieu in which Marian will live. Peter himself is busy
photographing everyone, hunting with a camera. Marian suddenly
panics:

> Peter was there . . . He had a camera in his hand, but
> now she saw what it really was . . . he raised the camera
> and aimed it at her; his mouth opened in a snarl of teeth.
> There was a blinding flash of light.
> "No!" she screamed. She covered her face with her arms.
> (p. 244)

This drunken fantasy shocks her into awareness of reality; she is
the prey, and must escape. Peter's camera is his substitute for the gun
he no longer uses, and to be "shot" would mean a kind of death:
"Once he pulled the trigger she would be stopped, fixed indissolubly
in that gesture . . . unable to move or change" (p. 245). So she
escapes (the imagery carrying on the theme), making her way
"through the thicket of people . . . behind the concealing trunks and
bushes of backs and skirts" (p. 245).

No one pursues, and the escape is only to the laundromat and
Duncan (she is not yet ready for freedom). Whether Duncan is to rescue her or she to rescue him is not clear, but he seems to offer safety.
To go to bed with him, to give sexual therapy, would finally separate
her from Peter, give her a refuge for the night, and reassure her of her
own continuing usefulness and reality. Sex under such conditions
could hardly be pleasurable, and the scrawny, unresponsive Duncan

is a most unattractive lover, but Marian struggles to carry out her self-imposed mission and preserve at least one self-image.

At breakfast the next morning she can eat nothing at all. Her withdrawal from food reaches its inevitable conclusion; the night with Duncan was not a beginning but the end of one phase of her life. (Free from Peter, she will have no more need for Duncan.) As Duncan reveals that his plea for sexual initiation was a lie that he has used before, "The starched nurse-like image of herself that she had to preserve as a last resort crumpled like wet newsprint" (p. 264)

There are no more false identities left, only herself. Freed from them, free also from the illusion that safety can be found with either Peter or Duncan, Marian begins her recovery.

"I was cleaning up the apartment" (p. 277) is the opening sentence of Part III, the action and the first person both announcing the heroine's regained control. She begins by coping in the most literal and physical way, washing the grimy windows and the dirty dishes and throwing away the spoiled food from the refrigerator.

More profoundly, she has already coped with Peter by preparing a "reality-test" — ironically, through baking a cake, a traditionally feminine action. That cake, shaped and decorated to resemble a woman (the "edible woman" of the title) is the central image of the novel. With its ruffled red dress, its "smiling, lush-lipped pink mouth" (p. 268), its pink shoes and pink fingernails and fantastically elaborate coiffure, it's a caricature of Marian at her most artificial, as she prepared herself for the party. Symbolically, it represents woman as simply an object for male consumption (as Peter and Duncan both tried to consume Marian, as Len thought he was consuming Ainsley). To be consumed means to be assimilated to the man's life and personality, to meet his requirements; it means to lose one's individuality; to make one's self into an object and to be treated accordingly, as the cake is. "That's what you get for being food" (p. 270). Marian's refusal to eat had grown out of her unwillingness to be eaten; subconsciously, and correctly, she had identified herself with the hunted, with the objects of consumption.

Marian offers Peter the cake as a substitute for herself when he comes to demand an explanation for her behaviour. Not surprisingly, he is embarrassed by the cake (recognizing its significance) and quickly leaves. Once dealt with, he is reduced to insignificance in Marian's mind: "She could see him . . . posed jauntily in the foreground of an elegant salon . . . impeccably dressed, a glass of rye whiskey in one hand; his foot was on the head of a stuffed lion and he had an eyepatch over one eye. Beneath one arm was a strapped revolver" (p. 272). The frightening image of Peter the Hunter has been exorcised, dissolving into the silliness of a Hathaway Shirt or Canadian Club advertisement.

With Peter disposed of, Marian attacks the cake, ending her withdrawal from food (and symbolically repossessing herself). But Duncan is left. He comes by his own invitation (Marian has forgotten him), is offered the remainder of the cake, finishes it without recognition of its symbolism, and politely thanks her. Marian watches "with a peculiar sense of satisfaction to see him eat, as if her work hadn't been wasted" (p. 276). It hasn't; Duncan deserves the cake as much as Peter. Momentarily Marian doubts herself as he tells her that her fear of Peter "was just something you made up," but as he placidly eats, his authority vanishes with her awareness of his lack of perception. She sits comfortably smiling at him (p. 281).

Part III is necessarily brief. Marian has gained self-understanding and has integrated the conflicting forces within herself. She is again able to cope — by implication, more effectively — and to tell her own story. She is able to order her apartment and to confront Peter and Duncan; she has eaten a steak; she has given up her job with Seymour Surveys. "You're back to so-called reality, you're a consumer," is Duncan's characteristically deflating comment, but he has already had to admit, "You look jaunty and full of good things" (p. 280).

Figuratively and literally, winter has ended. Even near the end of Part II, during Marian's last walk through the snow with Duncan, the imagery foretells spring and renewed life. As they walk beside a ravine, "Level with her eyes there were treetops, a maze of branches, the ends already pale yellow, pale red, knotted with buds" (p. 260).

Comedies have happy endings, and most of the characters of *The Edible Woman* get at least what they think they want. Marian recovers her self-control and ability to cope. Duncan is free to return to the snow and solitude. Peter is bound to succeed, and he may get Lucy, the most glamourous of the Office Virgins, who would make him a more satisfactory wife anyhow — she wants nothing better than to be consumed. Ainsley and Fischer have each other, or to be more exact, Fischer has his earth-goddess and Ainsley her Father-Image (both were more interested in symbols than realities). Even the helpless Clara, with her third and presumably final pregnancy over, is beginning to cope. Unlike the "black humour" of writers like Joseph Heller and Thomas Pynchon, Atwood's comedy is fundamentally optimistic. (The novel approaches black humour most closely in its final picture of Len, taking shelter after his crackup with Clara and Joe, and reverting to childhood as he squabbles with Clara's tots).

Certainly there is absurdity enough in the society presented, and there are powerful forces working to create and maintain it in their own interests, but absurdity is not final, "they" are not all-powerful. True sanity is possible (although it may have to be reached through what is ordinarily considered madness) and the heroine appears to achieve it. Marian does not change her society (how could she?) or escape from it; the proof of her sanity is that she has learned to live effectively within it.

The healing withdrawal through dissociation achieved by Marian (and by the narrator of *Surfacing*) closely resembles the schizophrenic dissociation described by the psychiatrist R.D. Laing. For Laing, too, this withdrawal is potentially curative, if allowed to run its course undisturbed, leading to a deeper understanding of the self and a truer sanity than the "normal" possess. But when Laing asks "Can human beings be persons today? . . . *Are persons possible* in our present situation?" he seems to believe that Western capitalistic society is so thoroughly corrupt and corrupting that political, economic and social revolution is necessary before anyone can achieve true personality.[2] Atwood's answer is that attaining personhood is difficult but possible.

The wit of *The Edible Woman* is concentrated in its brilliant images: concepts instantly become physical realities. Joe, Clara's husband, remarks that the feminine role demands passivity, and instantly "Marian had a fleeting vision of a large globular pastry, decorated with whipped cream and maraschino cherries, float-suspended in the air above Joe's head" (p. 235). The image suggests passivity and domestic function, woman as an object of consumption, overrichness and over-decoration in the consumer society. It clearly foreshadows Marian's cake, the "edible woman."

Lucy, man-hunting in expensive restaurants, is described as:

> . . . "trailing herself, like a many-plumed fish-lure with glass beads and three spinners and seventeen hooks, through the likely-looking places, good restaurants and cocktail bars with their lush weed-beds of philodendrons, where the right kind of men might be expected to be lurking, ravenous as pike, though more maritally inclined" (p. 113).

The plumes, the beads, the spinners and the hook imply the colour and elaboration of Lucy's outfit, and its intention. Implied also is her entire lack of interest in men as individuals (one fish is as good as another). The paradoxes of the female role are clearly stated; woman must be passive and active, she is the fisherman and she is the bait, and she can capture only by yielding up herself.

The Edible Woman is a successful comic novel (rare enough in any literature) which offers constantly the pleasures of surprise and incongruity — through the wit and sheer unexpectedness of its striking yet relevant images, through the startling yet somehow logical reversals of intention and action by its characters, and through reversals of normal expectations as to how people should talk, feel, and behave. It instructs us in certain realities of the world we live in, providing both the satisfaction of recognition and the shock of novelty and combining them as it transforms the familiar into the novel.

Yes, this world in which advertising and packaging obscure almost every reality, in which even consuming loses its pleasure because the items consumed have lost their identity, is the world we live in. Yes, these are the stereotypes — poor as they are! — of femininity and of masculinity, and of relations between the sexes, which control our lives. This is how reality is hidden from us and how we are confused as to the nature of our own bodies. This is how we are manipulated. But the novel hints that at least a relative freedom can be achieved.

Notes

1 Margaret Atwood, The Edible Woman (Toronto: McClelland and Stewart, 1969, reprinted in New Canadian Library, 1973), p. 194. All references are to this edition.
2 R.D. Laing, The Politics of Experience (London: Penguin Books, 1967), p. 20.

THE DIVIDED SELF: THEME AND PATTERN IN
SURFACING
Catherine McLay

> . . . [In such a person] the totality of experience is split in
> two main ways: in the first place there is a rent in his rela-
> tion with his world, and in the second, there is a disruption
> of his relation with himself. Such a person is not able to
> experience himself "together with" others or "at home in" the
> world but, on the contrary, he experiences himself in
> despairing aloneness and isolation; moreover, he does not
> experience himself as a complete person but rather as a
> "split" in various ways, perhaps as a mind more or less
> tenuously linked to a body, or two or more selves, and so
> on.   —R.D. Laing[1]

In her second novel, *Surfacing*, Margaret Atwood explores a contemporary problem, the search for unity in a self which has become
divided. Atwood, in an interview with Graeme Gibson, has defined
Surfacing as a "ghost story" in the tradition of Henry James where
"the ghost that one sees is in fact a fragment of one's own self that has
split off." Her first novel, *The Edible Woman*, she has called an
anti-comedy.[2]

The two novels are, however, not as dissimilar as these comments
and their surface appearances seem to indicate. Both are essentially
what Doris Lessing has termed "Inner-Space Fiction."[3] In both, the
heroine is engaged in a search for self and for the truth underlying
appearance. She passes through a period of negation in which she
denies not only her society but her closest friends and, ultimately,
herself.

While *The Edible Woman* is comic, with an undersurface of
nightmare, *Surfacing* probes more deeply into the heroine's search
for a sense of place, a psychic home, and for satisfying personal relationships. Above all, she seeks the unity of reason and emotion,
mind and body. Her final return to society is an affirmation of her
need to be human and to live with other human beings in an im-
perfect world.

Surfacing begins as a straightforward narrative of a physical journey. The heroine returns to her childhood home, a remote island in
the Quebec bush, to search for her missing father. She is accompanied
by Joe, with whom she has been living, and the couple, David and

Anna. She also brings in memory several other characters who influence her actions more truly; her mother, her father, her brother and her "husband."

In her quest, however, she is essentially alone. Her mother is dead, her father missing, and her brother on the opposite side of the earth: "nothing he's done since we grew up is real to me." Her "husband" is a married man who has been her lover. The three friends are as detached. She remarks of Anna "she's my best friend, my best woman friend; I've know her two months," and of Joe "I'm fond of him, I'd rather have him around than not." Of the three she observes: "I've driven in the same car with them before but on this road it doesn't seem right, either the three of them are in the wrong place or I am."[4]

Almost immediately, the physical journey becomes a journey into the mind. Atwood's poems "Journey to the Interior" and "A Pursuit" use landscape in a similar manner, and indeed in *Survival*, her commentary on themes and patterns in Canadian literature, Atwood notes that landscapes of poems are often "interior landscapes . . . maps of a state of mind" and defines Canada itself as "a state of mind, as the place you inhabit not just with your body but with your head."[5] In *Surfacing*, the heroine is seeking her "place" in the psychic sense, her "home ground."

Difficulties present themselves at the outset. Her old home is in Quebec, in "foreign territory" where people speak a language not hers. The road too is wrong; it "ought to be here" but there is a detour. "Nothing is the same, I don't know the way any more." As they approach the French Canadian village, she expects to be filled with nostalgia and waits for "the cluster of nondescript buildings to be irradiated with inner light like a plug-in crèche." But the children are gone away to the cities, the little church is neglected, and "what I mean is dead."

The trip by boat to the island is an image of the search — through a maze where "it's easy to lose your way if you haven't memorized the landmarks." From a plane, or in an aerial photograph, one can see "the water radiates like a spider"; but "when you're in a boat, you can only see a small part of it, the part you're in." The whole physical landscape, the winding waterways, the sheer cliffs, the decayed logs and pine stubble, the mirroring waters, jungle-like swamps, birches dying of tree cancer: all these evoke the narrator's state of mind. She is lost, helpless, walking in circles.

While "nothing is out of place" in the house itself, the narrator is as "out of place" as truly as her companions. She is unable to call out

"We're here" as they arrive, for she is afraid to "hear the absence"; and indeed she is not "here." The place where she is is inaccessible; she wants to reach out to Joe, to "tell him how to change so he could get there, the place where I was" but she is unable to, for he too has come to seem one of the "enemy."

Even more significant, then, is the disruption in personal relationships reflected through the narrator. This barrier is underlined by the use of pronouns. The narrator is given no name and is referred to as "I." She later explains: "I no longer have a name. I tried for all those years to be civilized but I'm not and I'm through pretending." Her father, her mother, her brother and her "husband" also have no names. The pronouns "he," "she," or "they" are used interchangeably for these figures of the past and for Joe, David and Anna, without an apparent shift in time or reference. Occasionally "they" includes the narrator herself as a child. But throughout, the world is divided into two groups, "I" and "they," "me" and "not-me," a child's earliest recognition of the division between the self and the world.

The failure of relationships is generated by the narrator's sense of aloneness. In none of her relationships is there a sense of commitment; she has deliberately chosen freedom from commitment in her selection of friends and in her response to her family. This is most clear in Joe whom she describes in a detached manner as being "like a buffalo on the U.S. nickel, shaggy and blunt-snouted, with small clenched eyes and the definite but insane look of a species once dominant, now threatened with extinction" (p. 8). This wry comedy effectively distances us from the real Joe, as does her comment on their decision to live together: "It was like buying a goldfish or a potted cactus plant, not because you want one in advance but because you happen to be in the store and you see them lined up on the counter."

Joe too is alienated. He has frequent nightmares and spends much of his time "off in the place inside himself." His artistic creations also suggest disturbance: "overgrown pots" which he "mutilates, cutting holes in them, strangling them, slashing them open." They come to her to look like "fragmentary memories or murder victims." Her response to him is evasive, and she sums him up: "He's good in bed, better than the one before; he's moody but he's not much bother, we split the rent and he doesn't talk much, that's an advantage" (p. 42). In a moment of unusual insight, she recognizes that her choice of Joe reveals something basic about herself: "Perhaps it's not only his body I like, perhaps it's his failure, that also has a kind of purity" (p. 57).

Her relationship with Anna is even less demanding. Although she has known Anna for two months, she has little sense of her as a person. Indeed she remarks of all three: "my friends' pasts are vague to me and to each other also, any one of us could have amnesia for years and the others wouldn't notice" (p. 30). Anna's make-up is a form of disguise behind which she hides from the world. The narrator is surprised to discover that, "shorn of the pink cheeks and heightened eyes, her face is curiously battered, a worn doll's, her artificial face is the natural one" (p. 43). Anna's talk is usually irrelevant chatter. When she does attempt to break through the surface to ask "Are you okay?" or remark of the father: "I'm sorry he wasn't here," the narrator evades her sympathy and even questions the intrusion on her privacy, "as though it's her grief, her catastrophe." And when Anna wants to exchange confidences (largely, it is true, about her own ailments) her overtures are refused. Anna distracts the narrator from morbid thoughts and introversion. The narrator does not want to seek out the real human being. David seems even less real. An instructor in communications, he fails to communicate, most of all with his wife.

Their relationship, however, illuminates the narrator's concept of marriage, the closest of human relationships. David and Anna, she believes, have succeeded where she has failed:

. . . They must have some special method, formula, some knowledge I missed out on; or maybe he was the wrong person. I thought it would happen without my doing anything about it, I'd turn into part of a couple, two people linked together and balancing each other, like the wooden man and woman in the barometer house. (p. 40)

For a successful marriage, Anna claims, "you just had to make an emotional commitment, it was like skiing, you couldn't see in advance what would happen but you had to let go." For the narrator "it was more like jumping off a cliff. That was the feeling I had all the time I was married; in the air, going down, waiting for the smash at the bottom" (pp. 47-8).

Gradually the narrator comes to realize that this marriage is not ideal; it is an armed truce. Anna's admission that her husband does not know she wears make-up is the first glimpse of subterfuge and deceit. Sex is used not as a means of communication but as a weapon. David taunts Anna by telling her every time he makes love to other women. He taunts her too with his body, rewarding or denying her according to a set of rules which keeps changing: "He watches me all the time, he waits for excuses." When she retaliates by making love with Joe, he complains: "I get the impression she wants out, she's waiting for the chance to leave. But I haven't asked, we don't talk much except with other people around" (p. 138). Through the thin partitions of the cabin, the narrator hears the sound of their love-making, the cry of "pure pain, clear as water, an animal's at the moment the trap closes" (p. 82). Ultimately she realizes that they do have a commitment; through hatred they have achieved "a balance almost like peace." Like the barometer couple, "glued there, con-demned to oscillate back and forth, sun and rain, without escape," they alternate back and forth, without communication.

The dislocation in human relationships marks also the narrator's past. As Atwood has remarked in Survival: "part of you is where you've been. If you aren't too sure where you are . . . [you may] retrace your history to see how you got there."[6]

The narrator's relationship with her parents is central. Her initial reaction to their loss defines the demands she has made upon them. While she has left home on pretense of marriage, to return only when she chooses, she denies them the right to change, indeed to be human:

> . . . They have no right to get old. I envy people whose
> parents died when they were young, that's easier to remem-
> ber, they stay unchanged. I was sure mine would anyway, I
> could leave and return much later and everything would be
> the same. I thought of them as living in some other time, go-
> ing about their own concerns closed safe behind a wall as
> translucent as jello, mammoths frozen in a glacier. All I
> would have to do was come back when I was ready . . .
> (p. 9)

She believed her parents immortal. When her mother died, she remarked, "I was disappointed in her," and her father's disappear-ance enrages her:

> All at once I'm furious with him for vanishing like this,
> unresolved, leaving me with no answers to give them when
> they ask. If he was going to die he should have done it
> visibly, out in the open, so they could mark him with a
> stone and get it over with. (p. 58)

The failure of communication with her mother is implied in their final conversation in the hospital where the mother lies, dying of cancer:

> . . . She peered at me with bright blank eyes. She may not
> have known who I was; she didn't ask me why I left or

where I'd been, though she might not have asked anyway, feeling as she always had that personal questions were rude.

"I'm not going to your funeral," I said. I had to lean close to her, the hearing in one of her ears was gone. I wanted her to understand in advance, and approve.

"I never enjoyed them," she said to me, one word at a time. "You have to wear a hat. I don't like liquor." She must have been talking about Church or cocktail parties. (p. 22)

She looks at her mother's diary, hoping that "there might be something about me." But the pages, except for the dates, are blank. Her mother has gone, leaving no trace but the leather coat hanging still on its nail beside the window: "there's nobody in it . . . Leather smell, the smell of loss" (p. 174).

Gradually the narrator comes to see her mother in a different light, as a separate person and not merely an adjunct of herself. She begins to wonder how she occupied herself "between the routines of lunch and supper" and recalls her in the garden or feeding the birds "quiet as a tree," or vanishing into the forest by herself. Her mother, she now recognizes, is "either ten thousand years behind the rest or fifty years ahead"; she is the embodiment of nature, emotion, the body, the feminine, which the narrator has rejected, and her gift, when it comes, must be interpreted in this manner.

The father is equated with reason. His influence has been stronger and more complex; he represents in her the dominance of the mind. A botanist and tree scientist, he learned to love the Quebec hinterland where he took his family seven months of every year and where he retired alone after the death of his wife. A rationalist on the model of his favourite authors, Thompson, Goldsmith, Cowper and Johnson who "learned the secret of the golden mean, the balanced life," he rejected industrialism and returned to individualism, believing that "with the proper guide-books you could do everything yourself" (p. 33). The father's legacy is of the mind, but she interprets it as a gift of faith in human communication and human continuity beyond death, enabling her to complete her quest.

The brother is vital as a complement to the sister: they form two halves of the divided self. From an early age he has been attracted to science, to the rational, and to violence. He kept snakes, frogs and crayfish in a secret laboratory in the woods where he could perform scientific experiments upon them. He reduced life to simple opposites: "There had to be a good kind and a bad kind of everything." He was attracted to cruelty, throwing the bad leeches into the fire and watching their tormented writhing, or attacking her doll and throwing the mutilated body into the lake. It was he who told passers-by that the children were wrapped in blankets in the car because "the Germans shot our feet off." When the children fought, "both sides got punished as in a real war." But the girl always retreated: "I never won . . . The only defence was flight, invisibility" (p. 135). And these retreats define her later reaction to the encroachment of society.

The children's scrapbooks vividly illustrate the contrast between them. The boy's are filled with violence. The girl's are filled with magazine illustrations of smiling ladies with toeless shoes or Easter eggs and people-shaped rabbits all "smiling or laughing hilariously." The narrator now sees that they bear a close relationship to the illustrations for fairytales she paints for a living. Now she sees them as escapism:

> I didn't want there to be wars and death, I wanted them
> not to exist; only rabbits with their coloured egg houses, sun
> and moon orderly above the flat earth, summer always, I
> wanted everyone to be happy. But his pictures were more
> accurate, the weapons, the disintegrating soldiers, he was a
> realist. (p. 131)

The world is no longer orderly and meaningful but chaotic and threatening. Society is dominated by "the enemy," which expands to include all those around her.

The enemy at first is the Americans who set up a camp outside the town during the War and now return for sport. The two "Americans" in the novel violate the privacy of others with the "eye rays" of their binoculars or chase loons to relieve their boredom. The dead body of the heron, suspended from the tree branch like a "lynch victim," typifies their destructiveness: "I wondered what part of them the heron was, that they needed so much to kill it" (p. 119). The discovery that these men come from Toronto does not dispel the stereotype; it broadens it to include Canadians too, men, even her own family.

Anna now becomes for the narrator merely a mechanical doll. David is unreal, "an imposter, a pastiche, layers of political handbills, pages from magazines . . . Second-hand American was spreading over him in patches, like mange" (p. 152). Even Joe ". . . was one of the killers, the clay victims damaged and strewn behind him, and he hadn't seen, he didn't know about himself, his own capacity for death" (p. 147). Her brother has always been of the enemy and now she sees of her father: "his job was wrong, he was really a surveyor, he learned the trees, naming and counting them so others could level and execute" (p. 186). She comes to see all others as outside of herself, destroyers she herself longs to destroy.

This widening separation is marked by the increasing problem of communication by language. The first evidence is in French-English relationships. Here communication is largely non-verbal, the exchange of ritual vegetables between her father and Paul or of mechanical smiles, "our faces petrified in well-intentioned curves, mouths wreathed in parentheses." Paul responds "like a priest or a porcelain mandarin," his face "a closed suit-case." To them, French Canadians seem unreal, like their own *habitant* carvings. The narrator's school-French, with its folk-songs or passages of Racine and Baudelaire, is inadequate. Even common transactions are marked by hesitation. She thanks Paul for the tea: "'*Délicieux!*' Doubt seizes me, *thé* may be *feminine*" (p. 20). The comic scene between Madame and the narrator's mother, as they await their husbands on the porch, underlines this failure to establish communication. It is in Quebec that the narrator discovers "people could say words that would go into my ears meaning nothing. To be deaf and dumb would be easier" (p. 11).

Talk becomes a cover to distract from more important concerns. She appeals silently to Anna: "*Help . . . talk!*" and Anna remarks "What's for dinner?" Like the couple in Atwood's poem, "Playing Cards," David and Anna occupy themselves with "double solitaire." The radio blares to cover the need for conversation. Language ultimately becomes threatening; the land agents "chitter and sizzle like a speeded-up tape, . . . language ululating, electronic signals thrown back and forth between them" (pp. 184-5). Society, recognizing the importance of language, has defined sanity as having "someone to speak to and words that can be understood." But the narrator rejects language as "the voice of reason." It marks the separation of mind and body; it "divides us into fragments." She retreats to a world of nature with "the names of things fading but their forms and uses remaining" (p. 150); here "the animals have no need for speech, why talk when you are a word" (p. 181).

Lies underline failure to communicate through language. Many of them are minor. The narrator asks Anna to accompany them in the canoe "for extra weight, which is a lie as we'll be too heavy already." and plans to persuade them to leave the island because there is not enough food. Others suggest the barriers in certain relationships. When she refuses David's advances, he tells her "I respect you for it, I really do" and when she fears involvement with Joe she uses a possi-

ble pregnancy to ward him off, for this "frightens them all." The central lie of the novel, however, is told not only to her parents and to
Joe, but to herself and to us as well; it is the whole tale she has constructed of her wedding, her husband and her lost child.

Her final admission of the truth, of her affair with a married man,
the abortion, and her flight from the past, marks the beginning of her
salvation. She turns to Joe because for him "truth might still be possible." While she adds "what will preserve him is the absence of
words," she finally comes to admit that communication through language is necessary. Her response when he calls her name is an admission that she must re-enter the human world:

> . . . If I go with him we will have to talk . . . we can no
> longer live in spurious peace by avoiding each other, the
> way it was before, we will have to begin. For us it's neces-
> sary, the intercession of words; and we will probably fail,
> sooner or later, more or less painfully. That's normal, it's the
> way it happens now. (p. 192)

These problems of language and communication which affect personal relationships are also closely related to the division in the novel
between mind and body, language being associated solely with mind.
R. D. Laing observes:

> . . . Some persons do not have a sense of that basic unity
> which can abide through the most intense conflicts with one-
> self, but seem rather to have come to experience themselves
> as primarily split into a mind and a body. Usually they feel
> most closely identified with the "mind."[7]

He continues: "*The body is felt more as one object among other
objects in the world than as the core of the individual's own being.*"[8]
This is the dilemma of the narrator. Sometime in the past, she
believes, she has allowed herself to be divided:

> . . . Woman sawn apart in a wooden crate, wearing a
> bathing suit, smiling, a trick done with mirrors, I read it in a
> comic book; only with me there had been an accident and I
> came apart. The other half, the one locked away, was the
> only one that could live; I was the wrong half, detached, ter-
> minal. I was nothing but a head. (p. 108)

Detached from the body, she is incapable of feeling. In high
school, she used to prick her arm with a compass point for, like the
rats in the texts, she preferred "any sensation to none."

The narrator's sense of dislocation is conveyed by the recurrent image of the frog. She felt sympathy for these amphibians when her brother put hooks into their backs or secreted them in glass bottles in his laboratory. She released them from the jars also during the fishing expedition with David and Joe. "Bottles distort for the observer too: frogs in a jam jar stretched wide, to them watching I must have appeared grotesque" (p. 106). This image is closely related to her pre-natal memory of her brother's near-drowning. As she explains: "I believe that an unborn baby has its eyes open and can look out through the walls of the mother's stomach, like a frog in a jar" (p. 32). Like a frog, she lives in two separate worlds, the world of the self, and the world of others which she looks out on from behind glass barriers. Like a frog, she must submerge to find truth.

Searching for her father, she plunges beneath the surface "through the lake strata, grey to darker grey, cool to cold" (p. 141). Here she discovers his dead body, "a dark oval trailing limbs. It was blurred but it had eyes, they were open, it was something I knew about, a dead thing . . . The lake was horrible, it was filled with death" (p. 142). But the descent is not merely physical; it is a descent into the subconscious, the undersurface of the mind.

The narrator is set apart, in a sub-marine world like the narrator of the poem "This is a Photograph of Me": "I am in the lake in the centre/of the picture, just under the surface." The father's body recalls to memory that striking "image I'd kept from before I was born" of her brother drowning, "face upturned, eyes open and unconscious." But it also recalls something more deeply submerged: the memory of the child she has aborted: "[it was] in a bottle curled up, staring out at me like a cat pickled; it had huge jelly eyes and fins instead of hands, fish gills, I couldn't let it out, it was dead already, it had drowned in air" (p. 143). These images have in common drown-ing and the recurring emphasis on eyes, unconscious and unseeing.

This last memory is purgative. She now admits: "I never saw it. They scraped it into a bucket and threw it wherever they throw them, it was travelling through the sewers by the time I woke up, back to the sea" (p. 143). And it is this recognition which allows her to resurface, to admit the truth of the past; the scrapbook of her mind has been a "faked album" with the wrong parts pasted over. For "a paper house was better than none and I could almost live in it, I'd lived in it until now" (p. 144).

The conceiving of another child is expiation for the life she has allowed to be sacrificed. It ensues from her discovery of her mother's gift to her which she has been seeking. While her father's gift has been "complicated, tangled," her mother's, she knows, "would be simple as a hand, it would be final." It will also be indirect, a mediation. It takes the form of a crayon drawing from her own childhood which her mother has left for her. Its message is essentially feminine, "a woman with a round moon stomach; the baby was sitting up in her gazing out" (p. 158). Her response is a release of pent-up feeling: "nothing has died, everything is alive, everything is waiting to become alive" (p. 159).

In *Survival*, Atwood has commented on the Canadian habit of introducing babies at the end of novels "to solve problems for the characters, which they obviously can't solve for themselves."[9] The baby here seems to function in this manner. But in her interview with Gibson, Atwood remarks that a baby keeps a woman in touch with her body, with the physical element of life, in a manner not available to the man.[10] In *Surfacing* the baby is related directly to the narrator's need to prove herself real, and it is a positive response to the problems of being human. In the act of conception, Joe is secondary, manipulated by her life force — a Shavian touch. It is she who sets the stage as in the prophecy, with "the moon on my left hand and the absent sun on my right." Her reward is the renewal of life: "I can feel my lost child surfacing within me, forgiving me, rising from the lake where it has been prisoned for so long." The child is not divided, for "the two halves clasp interlocking like fingers" (pp. 161-2).

Ultimately, the child heals the division in the mother. But at this point, it engenders a deeper separation. In rejecting guilt, the narrator rejects also the human world and reason which she equates with guilt. She turns to the animal world, to nature, and she embraces its gods which are indigenous,[11] for these are "the only ones who had ever given me anything I needed; and freely."

The Christian God she early rejected as without power. Once "I prayed to be made invisible and when, in the morning everyone could still see me, I knew they had the wrong God" (p. 73).

The gods which belong to the country are native, Indian gods her father has bequeathed through his rock paintings:

> . . . The Indians did not own salvation but they had once known where it lived and their signs marked the sacred places, the places where you could learn the truth . . . His later drawings weren't copied from things on the rocks. He had discovered new places, new oracles, they were things he was seeing the way I had seen, true vision; at the end, after the failure of logic. (p. 145)

She offers these gods her clothes and, in reward, "feeling was beginning to seep back into me. I tingled like a foot that's been asleep." (p. 146). But they demand also the renunciation of all that is human and rational. Walls and doors are barriers, "I can't see through them," lamps obscure truth, "I can't see what's happening outside." The mirror is a trap, for she wants "not to see myself but to see." The photographs record "a place I could no longer reach" with their pictures of ancestors in "face-front firing squad poses," and "successive incarnations of me preserved and flattened like flowers pressed in dictionaries."

As a result she destroys all records of the human past, the blankets, sheets, dishes and books, and closes the door "with a click behind me." Immersing herself in water so that her "false body floated on the surface," she emerges to build a lair and is accepted as a part of nature by the loon and her "ancestor," the frog. She moves back through the layers of the past, the phases of evolution, first to the animal with "no need for speech," then to "a tree leaning." Finally she is "not an animal or a tree, I am a thing in which the trees and animals move and grow, I am a place" (p. 181).

She has visions: first her mother as she had been in life, attuned with nature and feeding the birds; and then her father, who now too desires unity with nature and wants "the borders abolished . . . the forest to flow back into the place his mind cleared" (p. 186). But as she stares at him, she comes to see that he is not her father but "what my father saw, the thing you meet when you've stayed here too long alone." Indeed its footprints are familiar: "I place my feet in them and find that they are my own." Now she must choose between life and death. The self can no longer exist alone, divided from others. The gods themselves "prefer life" and "I owe them that." But in turning back to humanity, she loses them and their certainty. They represent "only one kind of truth" and she concludes: "From now on, I'll have to live in the usual way, defining them by their absence; and love by its failures, power by its loss" (p. 189).

In accepting her own humanity, her own guilt, the narrator comes to see others no longer as the enemy but fallible, like herself. David and Anna she recalls "with nostalgia, as I remember people I once knew." Her "husband" was human too, "only a normal man, middle-aged, second-rate, selfish and kind in the average proportions." Her brother is someone who took life's other choice: "to immerse oneself, join in the war," rather than be destroyed. Her parents no longer superhuman, "dwindle, grow, become what they were, human, something I never gave them credit for" (pp. 189-90).

Accepting the limitations of others, she must accept her own; she must also recognize her own power to act and to be held responsible. The child within her, retracing the history of the race from goldfish to frog to animal to human being, will be "no god," but may be a new Adam, "the first true human" (p. 191). And Joe, returning to the island to take her back to society, becomes a mediator between her and her fellow human beings; he is "an ambassador offering me something: captivity in any of its forms, a new freedom?" (p. 192). In accepting him, she accepts the necessity of language, "the intercession of words," and the need for trust: "to trust is to let go." The self is no longer divided into "I" and "they," self and other, mind and body, but achieves what Atwood has called "some kind of harmony with the world."[12]

Notes

[1] R.D. Laing, *The Divided Self* (New York: Random House, Pantheon Books, 1960), p. 15.
[2] Graeme Gibson, "Margaret Atwood" in *Eleven Canadian Novelists* (Toronto: Anansi, 1973), pp. 20-1 and 29.
[3] Doris Lessing, *Briefing for a Descent into Hell* (St. Albans, England: Panther Books, 1971).
[4] Margaret Atwood, *Surfacing*, (Toronto: McClelland and Stewart, 1972), p. 8. All further references appear parenthetically in the text.
[5] Margaret Atwood, *Survival* (Toronto: Anansi, 1972), p. 49, 18.
[6] *Ibid.*, p. 112.
[7] *The Divided Self*, p. 67.
[8] *Ibid.*, p. 71.
[9] *Survival*, p. 207.
[10] Gibson, p. 28.
[11] See Atwood's discussion of this with Gibson, pp. 30-1.
[12] Gibson, p. 27.

BRAVO MOTHBALL! AN ESSAY ON *LADY ORACLE*

Wilfred Cude

"This was the reason I fabricated my life, time after time," sighs the narrator and protagonist of Margaret Atwood's *Lady Oracle*, "the truth was not convincing."[1]

At first glance, Joan Foster seems to be yet another manifestation of a figure as old as the genre of the novel, the incurable innocent who must twist reality into conformity with romance. Like the inflexible Knight of the Doleful Countenance who brought chaos to Cervantes' La Mancha and like the relentless Tom Sawyer who turned Twain's Mississippi frontier on its collective ear, Joan pleads her mission as justification for whatever inconvenience she might on occasion cause.

Don Quixote, his mind gone spongy through absorbing the fabulous derring-do of Amadis of Gaul, racks up a windmill and frees a whole covey of rogues to scurry across the countryside in the name of chivalry. Tom Sawyer, his wits a trifle addled through following the intricacies of the novels of Dumas and Scott, brings a swarm of bullets around himself and his friends in the name of high adventure. And Joan Foster, her imagination undernourished by a debilitating mental diet ranging from Disney movies to *True Confessions* magazine, leaves behind her a swath of emotionally mangled people in the name of harmless escapism.

Lady Oracle exposes the sinister side of Canada's own opiate of the masses, the Harlequin Romances, in a manner at once hilarious, penetrating, and profound.

As with Cervantes and Twain, the literary axe Atwood has chosen to grind is of less consequence than what she cuts with it. Joan Foster is secretly Louisa K. Delacourt, creator of *The Lord of Chesney Chase*, *The Secret of Morgrave Manor*, *Love Defied*, and twelve other soppily sentimental historical romances; and machining out these "Costume Gothics" has been the one occupation she has consistently pursued all her adult life. In communing with herself, an activity that arises naturally out of her tendency to live multiple lives, she primly rationalizes the production of an art "neatly packaged like the other painkillers" merchandised at the corner drugstore. "The truth was that I dealt in hope, I offered a vision of a better world, however preposterous." She reassures herself, "Was that so terrible?" The answer, Atwood intimates, is a resounding "yes."

No matter how she tries to convince herself of the propriety of bringing pseudo-peace to frazzled housewifely souls "collapsed like soufflés in a high wind," Joan does not want her association with Hermes Books made public. "Mercury," she observes in quite another context, "was the god of thieves and trickery as well as speed." She knows that her art is childishly insubstantial. "My Costume Gothics were only paper; paper castles, paper costumes, paper dolls, as inert and lifeless finally as those unsatisfactory blank-eyed dolls I'd dressed and undressed in my mother's house." Her problem is that she cannot prevent herself from cranking the stuff out.

The truth is that Joan Foster is most herself as Louisa K. Delacourt, and all the other Joan Fosters are afraid the world will find out. What would her husband Arthur, the radical standard-bearer in anyone's hopeless cause, think of his wife exploiting the people? What would her lover, Chuck, the way-out "Master of the Con-Create Poem," think of his cult figure piece revealed as just another hustler? What would the reputable publishing firm of Morton and Sturgess, the establishment organization that had catapulted the unknown Ms. Foster to instant fame as the poetess of the season, think of their discovery being exposed as a notorious literary hack?

The novel opens with Joan hiding out in Italy after contriving a fake suicide, hoping to extricate herself from the clutches of a CBC dropout endeavouring to blackmail her. To understand how an intelligent, talented, and beautiful woman can get herself into such a dumb fix, it is necessary to understand the Miss Flegg Syndrome. Joan is stricken by this noxious infirmity at the tender age of seven, and she never really recovers. Enrolled in dancing school by her mother, who wants her to sweat off a little chubbiness, she becomes enthralled by the child's tinsel vision of the ballerina. She covets the lead role in the "Butterfly Frolic," the grand finale of Miss Flegg's end-of-season recital, and dreams of herself as transformed by a gauzy skirt and cellophane wings. Transformed she is, but, alas, not into a butterfly. Miss Flegg recoils in horror from the white grub that Joan most resembles, and hastily recasts the programme to accommodate the heavy fact they cannot disguise: at the end of "her gay, her artistic, her *spiritual* 'Butterfly Frolic,'" Joan will lumber on in a white furry costume carrying a sign marked "Mothball," and the lovely little butterflies will scatter. "It would be cute," she smilingly lies to the rotund little blob of anguish so cruelly singled out.

Of course, none of the kids is taken in by that guff. And, of course, Joan is humiliated and resentful. But — surprise, surprise — at the moment of her entrance, she actually triumphs as the hit of the show. "I felt naked and exposed," she recalls, "as if this ridiculous dance was the truth about me and everyone could see it." She stomps, flails about, and whirls menacingly at the butterflies; the cutesy moppets scatter and flee in very convincing terror. The dénouement is much to the taste of the fathers, dragooned by their females into reluctant attendance, and they accord Joan a standing ovation: "Bravo, Mothball!"

In this uproarious passage, with an economy and control to be found only in the finest writing, Atwood introduces the principal themes and motifs of the work: the pressures of creativity, the nature of art, the many guises of beauty, the sensitivities of the ugly, and the difficulties that one sex has in appreciating the values of the other.

The most important symptom of the Miss Flegg Syndrome is that the victim has no recognition of the lethal quality of the malady. At the novel's end, having contributed to her mother's early death as an alcoholic, having wrought considerable havoc in the lives of her husband and two lovers, having contrived the incarceration of two friends, and having laid open the face of a visiting reporter with a Cinzano bottle, Joan surveys the wreckage and murmurs: "I keep thinking I should learn some lesson from all of this." Yea, verily. The mothball incident impresses upon her Miss Flegg's technique for coping with harsh reality. Convinced that Miss Flegg has discovered the way, Joan embarks upon a career of bringing the message to the world.

Oppressed by her mother's resentment of her chubbiness, she gorges herself to obesity and literally drives her mother to drink. Prodded in late adolescence by a singular combination of a bequest from a beloved aunt and blood poisoning induced by a wayward arrow, she deflates herself down to a gorgeous shape, which has the pleasing side effect of further reducing her mother as well. And so it goes. Finding herself in bed with a Polish émigré in London, she permits him to deflower her. Finding herself bored in Merrie Olde England, she drifts into writing her Costume Gothics. Finding herself intrigued by an intent but stolid student radical, she drifts into a relationship with him, and must therefore dump the Polish émigré. At this point, the pattern of her life is set, and she is fast in the grip of the Miss Flegg Syndrome. The Polish émigré is devastated, Mother tumbles down a flight of stairs in a drunken stupor and dies, but Joan can't help that. She returns to Canada and carries on, marrying the radical in one life, writing Costume Gothics in another, and occasionally wondering if duplicity is all that it is cracked up to be.

Her response to her doubts is to clone even more, producing sufficient bad poetry through automatic writing to become a literary sensation, capitalizing upon fame to acquire a kinky poet as a lover, attracting with her success the attentions of a blackmailing creep. Only then can she decide that enough is enough. She arranges a fake suicide with the help of two friends, and runs off to Italy in disguise, but the friends are jailed for her murder, and they blab to their lawyer. He sends a reporter in hot pursuit of the oddest Canadian story of the year, and Joan, her brain inflamed by her current Costume Gothic, greets the poor slob by clubbing him down. The plot has gone full circle; years ago in London, she had done almost the same thing to the man who was to become her husband. If one discounts psychic damage, Arthur had just had his cheek scratched by her nails. Compared with what could be awaiting the reporter, to whom Joan feels attracted, he might even be the luckier of the two.

Possibly the most noteworthy feature of *Lady Oracle* is Atwood's dextrous evolution of a traditional comic victim of illusion into something very close to a tragic character. Ultimately, Joan Foster is not deluded by romance: she is deluded by reality. Naively assuming that there can be no authentic mystery or delight in our sordid universe, she sets out to make up the deficiency with some gaudy fantasy. She does this in her life as she does in her art: her one burning ambition, "the one thing I really wanted to do" is to "change the past." This brings us home to the menace of the Miss Fleggs of the world. Joan is so fascinated by Miss Flegg's adroit avoidance of ugly fact that she does not adequately remark how her teacher resorted to lies and cruelty. In defence of a creativity that was itself essentially tawdry, Miss Flegg stooped to hurt the feelings of a child, and what is beautiful about that?

This is the unspoken question that haunts the book, the genuinely gothic element that informs the struggle of Joan Foster to come to terms with her bizarre situation. Because she takes her past to be ugly, she lies constantly to conceal what she cannot contemplate. "The truth was out of the question, as usual," she flatly declares, cheapening the present in a vain effort to remake the past.

It is no accident that she comes so easily to the fabrication of chintzy historical romances: that is really what she is all about. Reflecting upon her fragmented self, she brushes against the thought: "Perhaps I have no soul." Wrestling with her latest Costume Gothic, a work that first unconsciously parodies and then consciously mirrors her life, she pauses to entertain a new idea: "Maybe I should try to write a real novel." These thoughts are fleeting, for she has given herself unreservedly over to mediocrity. She accepts a gaggle of clots as the men in her life; she accepts the bitterness of a dried-up spinster as the philosophy of her life; she accepts the hokum of a spiritualist chapel as the religion in her life. Why does she cling with such tenacity to her current project, *Stalked by Love,* Costume Gothic number sixteen? It is the story of her life.

Joan's childhood obesity, her convoluted relations with men, even her desperate dependence upon escapist literature, derive from her refusal to assess herself honestly. "I was a sorry assemblage of lies and alibis," she admits in a rare moment of candour, "each complete in itself but rendering the others useless." This is basically what Leda Sprott, the spiritualist medium who re-emerges as the Reverend Eunice P. Revele officiating at Joan's wedding, attempts to tell her after the ceremony. "You should stop feeling sorry for yourself. You do not choose a gift, it chooses you; and if you deny it, it will make use of you in any case, though perhaps in a less desirable way."

This scene echoes the mothball scene, the elder charlatan instructing the novice in the devious ways of the world, except that here, in the seclusion of Leda's kitchen, the novice is exposed to the nastiness of the lie. "I told them what they wanted to hear," Leda explains of her audiences; "you may think it's harmless, but it isn't." Now, who should know this better than Joan Foster? Had she not been her own best audience, she could have been a butterfly, but she was too enamoured of duplicity to venture what honesty might bring her. "Butterflies die too," she grumps, justifying her reliance upon cliché. This is the novel's most powerful irony, that she deprives herself of the very tangible beauty that is her own existence.

She will not look back at her past, so she cannot see its wonder. Her father, the *Maquis* hit man turned gentle doctor; her first lover, a real, live Polish nobleman; her husband, a sincere idealist; her second lover, a wild madcap of a fellow — any of these, viewed with compassion and insight, has infinitely more potential than the plasticized Redmonds of her novels. "Why do you refuse to believe in your own beauty?" her first lover pleads. The answer, at first ridiculous and at last painful, is a grating commentary on our times: she refuses because she craves escapism.

Perhaps I have made a very funny book appear quite sombre, but it is sombre, in the way that *Don Quixote* and *Huckleberry Finn* are. *Lady Oracle* must be measured against the comic novel, within the context of laughter that moves the reader to thought. I have always found the Atwood folk intensely irritating. They are the quintessence of Canadian spiritual poverty: moral masochists engrossed in self-inflicted agony, fatuous seekers wallowing in self-pity, pretentious hypocrites mouthing about commercialism and napalm but fundamentally oblivious to the misery endured by the greater part of mankind. For me, the weakness of *The Edible Woman* and *Surfacing* is not the portrayal of such people, but the lack of any marked indication that they are less than they should be. In distancing herself from her characters, in presenting us with a means of appraising both them and ourselves, Atwood, in *Lady Oracle*, has highlighted spiritual and intellectual dimensions hitherto murky in her work. Bravo, Mothball!

Notes

[1] Margaret Atwood, *Lady Oracle* (Toronto: McClelland and Stewart, 1976). All further references from this work.

ROBERTSON DAVIES

ROBERTSON DAVIES' *FIFTH BUSINESS* AND "THAT OLD FANTASTICAL DUKE OF DARK CORNERS, C.G. JUNG"

Gordon Roper

Dunstan Ramsay, the narrator of Robertson Davies' novel *Fifth Business*, in mid-life says of his closest friend and enemy, Boy Staunton:

> If his social life interested me, his private life fascinated me. I have never known anyone in whose life sex played such a dominant part. He didn't think so. He once told me that he thought this fellow Freud must be a madman, bringing everything down to sex in the way he did. I attempted no defence of Freud; by this time I was myself much concerned with that old fantastical duke of dark corners, C.G. Jung, but I had read a great deal of Freud and remembered his injunction against arguing in favour of psychoanalysis with those who clearly hated it.[1]

As the narrator of his own spiritual history in *Fifth Business*, Dunstan is a master of indirection and of understatement; this is his single allusion by name to Jung, in a book whose form and substance is overwhelmingly Jungian.

But Jungian in what sense? Jung explored so many dark corners in his long and far-reaching career. In his pursuit of knowledge and understanding of the soul of man he ranged through mythology and fairy tale, alchemy, anthropology, clinical cases of neuroses, art and literature, politics, the present and future, and religions east and west. His collected work alone forms eighteen volumes in the Bollingen Series XX, and he published many other papers, essays, lectures, and studies, notably in *Modern Man in Search of His Soul* (1933), *Man and his Symbols* (1964), and his remarkable spiritual autobiography, *Memories, Dreams, Reflections* (1961).

Robertson Davies, like his character Dunstan Ramsay, read widely in Freud's writings, and then even more widely in Jung's. In the decade before he wrote *Fifth Business*, Jung had become his "Wise Old Man." His deepening commitment to a Jungian angle of vision rarely emerged in his writing in the 1960s, since most of that writing was scholarly or occasional. But how the spiritual wind was blowing as he started to write *Fifth Business* was evident in a talk he gave to students in February, 1968:

Great as Freud was, and unassailable as his position is among the great liberators of the human mind, his actual technique seems more suited to the consulting-room than to the university lecture room; his mind dealt more strikingly with problems of neuroses than with matters of aesthetics, and his cast of mind was powerfully reductive. After the Freudian treatment, most things look a little shabby — needlessly so. Jung's depth psychology, on the other hand, is much more aesthetic and humanistic in its effects on artistic experience. The light it throws on matters of literature and on the temperament of the writer is extremely useful and revealing.[2]

Today most lay readers know something of Jung and his depth psychology, but that knowledge is not apt to be extensive or precise. So before looking at what light depth psychology can throw on *Fifth Business* let me — as a lay reader — attempt to provide a working sketch of what was in Jung's temperament and thought that may have provided a matrix for Robertson Davies' book.

Although his training was medical and scientific, Jung by temperament was unusually open to the power of the unknown. He felt strongly that the greatest force that shapes the lives of men — call it God, Fate, Destiny, Nature, or the Unconscious — was infinite and ungraspable. Yet something drives men to know and to understand. As a way of looking into the darkness, Jung placed his faith in the tireless observation of and speculation about the individual. In his *Memories, Dreams, Reflections*, he wrote:

My life has been permeated and held together by one idea and one goal: namely, to penetrate into the secret of the personality. Everything can be explained from this central point, and all my works relate to this one theme.[3]

Jung assumed that the individual was made up of an interacting body and psyche (or soul or spirit). The psyche, like the body, has had centuries of development, a development which each individual inherits from the collective past and individuates within his own capacity. Jung's most revolutionary concept was that the psyche in each individual — the total personality — is made up of three components. The only component we know directly is our ego, that small spark of consciousness, or awareness of the self and what is perceptible to us through our senses. This spark floats in a sea of unconsciousness of two distinguishable kinds. The sea closest to our consciousness Jung termed the "personal unconscious," and assumed that it was made up of memories, feelings, or states of mind which once were within the consciousness but now have slipped or were pushed outside. Beneath the personal unconscious lies the greater, unknown force of the "collective unconscious," common to all men in the primitive past and working still in each individual in forms Jung called "archetypes" which sometimes erupt in consciousness as "archetypal images," or "archetypal ideas or felt situations." Archetypal images manifest themselves to us in dreams, myths, and legends, and fairy tales, works of art, or religious symbols.[4]

Jung also assumed that as biological life is a form of energy, so too is psychic life. Psychic energy he called the "libido," and the law of its dynamics, he believed, was a constant flow between opposing poles, or "opposites."

> Old Heraclitus, who was indeed a very great sage, discovered the most marvellous of all psychological laws: the regulative function of opposites. He called it *enantiodromia*, a running contrariwise, by which he meant that sooner or later everything runs into its opposite.[5]

Thus if the consciousness represses strongly the unconscious forces within the personality, the unconscious will surge back into the consciousness in the form of oppressive dreams, violent sudden emotion, or bodily pain, or illness. The invasion will continue until the conscious part of the personality somehow recognizes the opposing force and comes to some accommodation with it, a balancing which often requires outside help to achieve.

Jung's hypothesis of the polarity of psychic forces led him to posit tensions between parts of the personality — the conscious, and the personal and collective unconscious. He observed that as the individual grows, the conscious part, or ego, tends to develop those functions (or roles, or qualities) which come easiest to it, and which are encouraged by the physical and social world outside of it. Indeed, it develops a special side of itself, the persona (or mask) which it interposes between itself and the world, and which the world mistakes as the whole personality of that ego. Meanwhile as consciousness grows in the individual's earliest years, the ego tends to suppress or to drive into the personal unconscious those functions which oppose its development. This suppressed part of the personality, gathering force in the personal unconscious, Jung called "the shadow." By "shadow" he meant that it was the dark or more primitive side of consciousness, not that it was immoral or evil.

As our ego grows, our shadow grows. And under certain conditions the shadow will erupt into our consciousness. Then we find ourselves feeling or doing something which startles us because it seems out of character. After, we may say "I was not myself," or "I was beside myself." Or the shadow may manifest itself when we meet someone of the same sex and feel a sudden, intense enmity, envy, or contempt for him. Since Jung assumed that our perception of all outside of us is highly (if not fully) subjective, he believed that when we responded to others in this unreasonable way what really happened was that the shadow part of our personality was projecting an image of itself onto that other person, to which our repressing ego reacted. An ego which refuses for long to recognize the existence and force of its shadow is inviting disruption. A healthy ego expands its consciousness by recognizing its shadow and by accepting its reality. This is one way of coming to know one's Self.

Jung also identified another pair of opposites — the ego and the anima (or animus). From his observation of thousands of clinical cases and of individuals outside clinics, he concluded that in each male personality is hidden a female force and that in each woman a male force. He believed that these pairs of opposing forces were laid down deep in the collective unconscious. In men, this compelling attraction to the opposite sex — a yearning for completion, or for wholeness — projected itself as an "anima" image; in women, as an "animus" image. In men the force of the anima makes itself first felt to the individual in his image of his mother, the female image which he projects from within his collective unconscious to satisfy his deepest needs — and probably an image that bears little resemblance to his mother's actual personality.

When the bearer of this image fails him, as fail she must, he is driven in search of his anima to other women, finding one aspect in one particular woman and other aspects in other women, for at different times in his life his anima will express itself in different figures, some appearing to him as beneficent, some as malign, some as enigmatic. Some will be highly attractive, some highly repulsive, some a mingling of the highly attractive and repulsive. The man who approaches psychic wholeness is he who, along with other things, has found a satisfying anima in one individual woman — the Great Mother archetypal image, who is mother of himself and of his children, mistress, companion, spiritual guide, and burier of the dead.[6]

These concepts of the shadow and of the anima helped Robertson Davies to shape his characters and their interactions in *Fifth Business*. The structure of the novel as a whole was shaped, I believe, by

his interpretation of the concept at the heart of Jung's view of man —
the concept of the growth of the individual personality towards
wholeness, a process Jung called "individuation." In his spiritual
autobiography, *Memories, Dreams, Reflections*, Jung wrote: "The
central concept of my psychology [is] the process of individuation."
In the same book he wrote:

> Individuation means becoming a single, homogeneous be-
> ing, and, in so far as "individuality" embraces an innermost,
> last, and incomparable uniqueness, it also implies becoming
> one's own self.[7]

"Self" here appears to mean what it usually does in Jung's writing,
the whole personality, made up of consciousness (with the persona or
mask turned towards the public), the private unconsciousness, and
the collective unconsciousness.

> Conscious and unconscious do not make a whole when
> one of them is suppressed and injured by the other. If they
> must contend, let it be at least a fair fight with equal rights
> on both sides. Both are aspects of life. Consciousness should
> defend its reason and protect itself, and the chaotic life of
> the unconscious should be given the chance of having its
> way too — as much as we can stand. This means open con-
> flict and open collaboration at once. That, evidently, is the
> way human life should be. It is the old game of hammer and
> anvil: between them the patient iron is forged into an inde-
> structible whole, an "individual." This, roughly, is what I
> mean by the individuation process.[8]

Coming to know the self, or getting to one's inner centre and
making contact with the living mystery of the unconscious, alone
and unaided, is difficult and dangerous; indeed, it is impossible for
some.

Jung believed that the individual life unfolded itself in stages —
early years, and maturity. Each stage had its own nature and appropriate functions. Youth extends from puberty to middle age, which
begins between thirty-five and forty. He described the stages:

> Take for comparison the daily course of the sun — but a
> sun that is endowed with human feeling and man's limited
> consciousness: In the morning it rises from the nocturnal sea
> of unconsciousness and looks upon the wide, bright world
> which lies before it in an expanse that steadily widens the
> higher it climbs in the firmament. In this extension of its

field of action caused by its own rising, the sun will discover
its significance; it will see the attainment of the greatest
possible height and the widest possible dissemination of its
blessing, as its goal. In this conviction the sun pursues its
course to the unforeseen zenith — unforeseen because its
career is unique and individual. At the stroke of noon the
descent begins. And the descent means the reversal of all the
ideals and values that were cherished in the morning.[9]

After he had started to write *Fifth Business*, Robertson Davies
commented on this change in the middle years of life:

What is the nature of this change? It is part of intellectual
and spiritual growth. As Jung explains it, in the early part of
life — roughly the first half of it — man's chief aims are personal and social. He must grow up, he must find his work,
he must find out what kind of sex life he is going to lead,
he must achieve some place in the world and attempt to get
security within it, or else decide that security is not important to him. But when he has achieved these ends, or come
to some sort of understanding with this part of existence, his
attention is turned to matters that are broader in scope, and
sometimes disturbing to contemplate. His physical strength is
waning rather than growing; he has found out what sex is,
and though it may be very important to him it can do little
to surprise him; he realizes that some day he is really going
to die and that the way he approaches death is of importance to him; he finds that without God (using that name to
comprehend all the great and inexplicable things and the
redemptive or destructive powers that lie outside human
command and understanding), his life lacks a factor that it
greatly needs; he finds that, in Jung's phrase, he is not the
master of his fate except in a very modest degree and that he
is in fact the object of a supraordinate subject. And he seeks
wisdom rather than power — though the circumstances of
his early life may continue to thrust power into his hands.[10]

Later in his talk, Davies continued:

The values that are proper and all-absorbing during the
first half of life will not sustain a man during the second
half. If he has the courage and wisdom to advance coura-
geously into the new realm of values and emotions he will
age physically, of course, but his intellect and spiritual

growth will continue, and will give satisfaction to himself and to all those associated with him. And such courage and wisdom are by no means rare; they may show themselves among many people who never have thought along these lines at all but who have a knack of living life wisely; and they also are to be found among those who regard self-awareness as one of the primary duties of a good life.[11]

As *Fifth Business* bodies forth so powerfully, the afternoon and evening of life can bring disaster to the individual who cannot adapt. As Jung warned, adaptation does not come easily; it comes only after the severest shocks. To adapt, the individual must turn inward; he must expand his conscious grasp of the unconscious that is master of his Fate. His consciousness grows by coming to recognize his shadow in his own personal unconsciousness. It grows by coming to cope with the more powerful and less graspable anima in the collective unconscious. And the anima is only one of the "archetypes" with which he must somehow integrate.

Jung thought of archetypes in various contexts as "the original components of the psyche," or "the great decisive forces" that bring about all events in individual and collective life. He likened them to biological instincts, and to primordial patterns of psychic energy flow.

The language of the archetypes is symbolic. They speak to our consciousness from nature and from our cultural past, through certain shapes — mandalas, circles or crosses. They speak through certain actions, such as journeys, ascents, or descents, or metamorphoses and rebirths, or they speak through certain natural places or scenes, or our fantasies of Gardens, Paradises, or Hells. They make their presence felt in our dreams, through our senses, in rituals and celebrations, in myths, legends, fairy stories, folk lore, in religions, in music, dance, sculpture, painting, story or poem. Archetypal images are multitudinous; the symbolic forms in which they present themselves are unendingly various and shifting. But some basic symbols seem to occur most frequently. Besides the shadow and the anima, Jung identified as basic the Great Mother; the Father in his many forms, the Hero in all his guises as God-man, vanquisher of monsters, saviour of all people; the Wise Old Man who counsels and directs us in crises. Jung also identified other figures, such as the Rich Young Prince, the Sleeping Princess, the Devil in his many roles (often variants of the Father, Hero, or Wise Old Man), the Magus, or Magician, and the Witch or She-Devil.

Whatever their symbolic form, archetypes are always felt by the effects of their unmistakable force — what Jung called their "numinosity" — in our consciousness. Our ego must recognize them as the symbolic language of our Fate speaking to us, and must somehow align itself with their force if it is to grow towards wholeness of Self.

> You can know all about the saints, sages, prophets, and other godly men, and all the great mothers of the world. But if they are mere images whose numinosity you have never experienced, it will be as if you were talking in a dream, for you will not know what you are talking about. The mere words you use will be empty and valueless. They gain life and meaning only when you try to take into account their numinosity — i.e., their relationship to the living individual. Only then do you begin to understand that their names mean very little, whereas the way they are *related* to you is all-important.[12]

Jung made a vital distinction between his use of "symbol" and "sign." For him a symbol must have numinosity. It expresses itself in an unpredictable variety of forms, and its "meaning" is in the way it affects the individual consciousness. Conversely, consciousness cannot assign fixed meanings to symbols without reducing and distorting their force and so misapprehending them. It cannot decode them, for it cannot grasp a key to the code. It can establish a code of signs, a short-hand system of referents to what it knows. The cross is a sign to many Christians, but it is not a symbol in the Jungian sense unless it has a numinosity to the individual — be he Christian or non-Christian. Robertson Davies is fully aware of Jung's distinction between the nature of symbol and sign, and the reader who decodes *Fifth Business* according to a system of fixed signs will be working against its grain.

The grain of *Fifth Business* is, I suggest, that of modern myth. Jung believed that myth was a symbolic dramatization in story form which the forces of the collective unconscious bring into being in the imaginations of men, and perpetuate so long as the psychic energy expressed through it moves its auditors. He assumed that serious writers could create from the unconscious new myths or variants of the old which would speak eloquently to contemporary readers. In matter and manner, *Fifth Business* is a modern myth, and has been responded to as such by many readers.

At the most immediate level, *Fifth Business* is a memoir written by Dunstan Ramsay to the Headmaster of Colborne College, the prep school from which Ramsay has retired after years of teaching history. His writing is triggered by a farewell article in the college paper which stereotypes him flippantly as a Mr. Chips. This cheapening of his public image as a history master also violates his inner sense of himself: his commitment to life, his training as a scholar, and his years of passionate questing into mythology and the mysteries of sainthood. As a man (and as a teacher) he must tell the truth about his whole life, especially about that hidden life which has been so much more adventurous and strange than his public life.

What he writes here at seventy-two, from high in the Swiss mountains, reveals that by temperament he is introverted, an individual of intense, complex feeling, driven by something within to break through the shell imposed upon him by his Scots Presbyterian upbringing. To protect himself, he has learned long ago to walk alone, to deal out personal revelations cautiously, hedging them with indirection and understatement. From mid-life his view of himself and the world around him had been ordered by his reading of Jung, although characteristically he only mentions this reading once, almost casually. Now at seventy-two, from near St. Gall, with his companions Liesl and the artist-magician Paul, he has achieved some sense of wholeness; from here he tells his story.

Dunstan orders his story, it seems, to dramatize how two interlocking constellations of characters play their parts in his unfolding physical and spiritual life. One constellation asserts forces primarily on his outer, public life, and at the end of the story enables him to recognize himself as "Fifth Business," his shadow side. This constellation includes Boyd (Boy) Staunton, Boy's first and second wives, Leola and Denyse, and Paul Dempster, son of Mrs. Mary Dempster. The other constellation dramatizes his inner search for his anima: his mother, Mrs. Mary Dempster, Leola, Diana Marfleet, and finally, Liesl. Two priests, one in his village and one in his private life, add their direction: Father Regan dogmatically warns him against pursuing a "fool saint"; Father Blazon acts as his Wise Old Man, and directs the pursuit of the spirit inward. Mary Dempster, in her changing aspects, is the major interlocking force between the two constellations.

Dunstan's journey is at once an inner and outer one. Let me, at the risk of distortion, suggest the central thrust of his inner journey: his search for his anima. After his secret involvement with Mrs. Dempster, his mother attaches him to Mrs. Dempster as helper and watchdog. When he is fourteen he undergoes a traumatic experience with his mother. And bereft of a mother he seeks that image in Mrs.

Dempster. Mrs. Dempster becomes more deranged, and outrages the villagers by her charity to a tramp in the gravel pit. She is tied up within her home, but Dunny (Dunstan) seeks her aid when he believes his brother has died, and she performs her second miracle. Mrs. Ramsay tries to retain possession of "her wee laddie", but Dunny evades her force by slipping away from home to join the army.

In the second chapter, Dunny encounters two more anima figures. He is violently wounded at Passchendaele in November, 1917. Before he loses consciousness, he sees a vision of a Madonna with the face of Mrs. Dempster. He regains consciousness in an English hospital in May, 1918, terribly scarred and without a left leg. After this season in the dark he is "reborn," and initiated into manhood by his nurse, Diana Marfleet. When he realizes his attraction to her may lead to a possession by another mother, a wife-mother, he extricates himself, and she rechristens him Dunstan (after St. Dunstan) on Christmas Day. When he returns to his village with a Victoria Cross awarded by his King, he is given a village hero's welcome. He also finds that his friend and rival, Percy Boyd Staunton, has claimed the village princess, Leola, to whom Dunny was attracted in a teen-age way. His mother and father have died in the influenza epidemic in 1918, and he feels freed. He also learns that Paul had run away with a circus when he was ten and Mrs. Dempster has been taken to live with an aunt near Toronto.

After his University years he becomes a history master at Colborne College in Toronto, and his search for his anima takes two paths. He visits Mrs. Dempster, and finally has her placed in an asylum, as the sad, best thing he can do to help her. Meanwhile, his association with her, and what to him were her three miracles, has led him to devote all of his private time to research into the lives of the saints. This leads him to a village in the Tyrol in search of knowledge about St. Uncumber, and there he meets Paul, now a magician in a small travelling show. When Dunstan is in Toronto, he keeps in touch with Boy Staunton and his wife Leola, for whom Dunstan has little feeling other than pity now. On another European research trip to the Bollandists he meets the Jesuit, Father Blazon, who turns out to be his Wise Old Man. Father Blazon counsels him in Jungian language not to seek the meaning of sainthood in Mrs. Dempster or in the Lives of the Saints, but within himself:

> I do not suggest that you should fail in your duty toward
> her; if she has no friends but you, care for her by all means.
> But stop trying to be God, making it up to her that you are

sane and she is mad. Turn your mind to the real problem:
who is she? Oh, I don't mean her police identification or
what her name was before she was married. I mean, who is
she in your personal world? What figure is she in your personal mythology? If she appeared to save you on the battlefield, as you say, it has just as much to do with you as it
had with her — much more probably. Lots of men have visions of their mother in time of danger. Why not you? Why
was it this woman? Who is she? That is what you must discover, Ramezay, and you must find your answer in psychological truth, not in objective truth.[13]

In Chapter Five, "Liesl," Dunstan again meets with Paul while on a
research trip in Mexico. Paul is now Magnus Eisengrim, masterly
artist at his craft, and is managed by a strangely repulsive-attractive
woman, Liesl. After an infatuation with Faustina, the young trouper,
he comes to know Liesl in a rousing bedroom scene. She convinces
him that he has "a whole great piece of life that is unlived, denied, set
aside" and urges him to live his unlived life, to shake hands with his
own devil. He does more than just shake hands. Finally she hurls at
him:

> Here you are, twice-born, and nearer your death than
> your birth, and you have still to make a real life.
> Who are you? Where do you fit into poetry and myth?
> Do you know who I think you are, Ramsay? I think you are
> Fifth Business.

and she proceeds to tell him in detail what "Fifth Business" means.[14]
He discovers that he is indeed Fifth Business in his room with Paul
and Boy on the night of Boy's death. At Eisengrim's performance at
the Royal Alexandra the next night, it is Liesl, speaking through the
Brazen Head, who answer cryptically the question "Who killed Boy
Staunton?" and it is Liesl who writes to Dunstan, after his heart attack, to invite him to join her and Paul in the mountains of Switzerland, and so in the end it seems Dunstan finds his anima.

Dunstan's outer journey is made largely through the effect on him
of his relation to Percy Boyd Staunton and Paul Dempster. Staunton
(who later rechristens himself "Boy") from village days has been to
Dunstan his opposite. Boy is an extrovert, with a single-minded
genius for acquiring money and power. His father has become rich
by village standards; Boy becomes much richer. To Dunstan he
seems an envied Rich Young Prince; he marries Leola, the village

Princess. He models himself on that Ideal Prince of the 1920s, the Prince of Wales. Dunstan admires the young Prince's father, the King. Boy gives his sexual drive free rein, while Dunstan, scarred by his physical and psychic wounds, subdues his in pursuit of the spirit. Boy treats women as objects; Dunstan sees them as individuals.

Apparently Boy has suppressed completely any awareness of his relation to Mrs. Dempster. But Dunstan and he feel a bond, a responsibility for each other. Boy helps Dunstan with financial advice and guides him to a modest financial security. Dunstan is disturbed by Boy's enigmatic behaviour in the "Gyges and King Candaules" episode. He worries about Boy's spiritual unawareness and urges him to come to know himself, although, at the same time, Dunstan himself is unaware of how his own shadow projects its images onto Boy. It is Father Blazon who begins Dunstan's enlightenment about his relation with Boy, and later it is Liesl who advances that enlightenment.

Boy continues to believe in his image of himself as the Rich Young Prince well into his middle years. But when his ideal collapses in the Abdication of 1936, Boy falls into a private hell. His family disintegrates (in a way told by his son David in The Manticore). Leola attempts desperately to save herself by turning to Dunstan; he runs away (as he later says), although after her attempt at suicide he does return to try to help clean up the emotional mess. Leola dies, and Boy apparently feels little loss; when Mrs. Dempster dies later, Dunstan loses one of "the fixed stars in my life." Boy marries (or is married by) Denyse, a woman "of masculine mind" without recognizing that she will devour him. He thinks of death; it comes through Paul, now the great magician, whom he meets in Dunstan's college rooms after a performance.

Dunstan's shadow — his Fifth Business side — breaks through his conscious image of himself to tell Paul how Boy became related to both their lives in village days. Boy is found dead in his submerged car in Toronto Harbour, with a stone in his mouth, the stone that Dunstan has treasured since Boy threw it in a snowball years before. So Boy is killed, by the four principals and Fifth Business. Dunstan collapses, but his acceptance later of Liesl's invitation to join her and Paul in Switzerland suggests that he has come to know his shadow side and to live with it, as in his inner journey he has arrived at a harmony of forces. So he attains some fused inner and outer state of wholeness in the mountains at St. Gall.

This is one reading of the myth of individuation which seems to structure Fifth Business — a structure enriched by many archetypal images, ideas, and situations, and enhanced by interwoven signs.[15]

Presented in this reductive way, it may suggest that Robertson Davies has worked consciously from a scheme of fixed Jungian concepts. But such a conclusion would go contrary to his mode of working and to Jung's mode of thought. As Jung wrote in Part II of his "Aion":

> Therefore, in describing the living process of the psyche, I deliberately and consciously give preference to a dramatic, mythological way of thinking and speaking, because this is not only the more expressive, but also more exact than an abstract scientific terminology, which is wont to flirt with the notion that its theoretical formulations may one fine day be resolved into algebraic equations.[16]

Davies' way of thinking and speaking is also intuitive, dramatic, and mythological. For some years Jung's angle of vision has coincided with his own, and Jung has 'become for him a spring of wisdom. From that spring the archetypal forms flow, and the writer's task is to body them forth in words so their effect will be felt by the reader. The process of bodying forth is that of the unconscious and the conscious working together, often in a way that the consciousness cannot control or recognize. When he is expressing myths the writer does not know what he is doing; when he is inventing signs, he does know. *Fifth Business* is made up of both myth and sign. These working together give it a strange power. And this was Davies' aim, for, like his magician Paul, he desires to move his audience to wonder. When Dunstan and Paul talk in Mexico City after Paul's performance, Paul says:

> You see what we are doing . . . We are building up a magic show of unique quality . . . You know that nowadays the theatre has almost abandoned charm; actors want to be sweaty and real; playwrights want to scratch their scabs in public. Very well; it is the mood of the times. But there is always another mood, one precisely contrary to what seems to be the fashion. Nowadays this concealed longing is for romance and marvels. Well, that is what we can offer, but it is not done with the back bent and a cringing smile; it must be offered with authority . . .

Dunstan asks him: "What do you want? To be feared?" and Paul replies:

> To be wondered at. This is not egotism. People want to

marvel at something, and the whole spirit of our time is not to let them do it . . .[17]

Like Paul, Robertson Davies offers his *Fifth Business* with authority arising from a brilliant performance and from a wisdom that is old and forever new. Perhaps Davies also has done in words something similar, and for similar reasons, to what Jung did when he built his house on the lake shore near Zurich when he was nearing fifty:

> I had to achieve a kind of representation in stone of my innermost thoughts and the knowledge I had acquired. Or to put it another way, I had to make a confession of faith in stone. That was the beginning of the "Tower," the house which I built for myself at Bollingen . . . so in 1922 I bought some land . . . It was situated in the area of St. Meinrad, and is old church land, having formerly belonged to the monastery of St. Gall.[18]

Notes

[1] Robertson Davies, *Fifth Business* (Toronto: Macmillan, 1970), p. 213.
[2] Robertson Davies, "The Conscience of the Writer," a talk given to students at Glendon College, York University, on February 15, 1968, and printed in *One Half of Robertson Davies*, (Toronto: Macmillan, 1977), p. 126.
[3] C.G. Jung, *Memories, Reflections, Dreams*, recorded and edited by Aniela Jaffe, (New York: Alfred Knopf, 1961), p. 206.
[4] See Jung's discussion of the nature of the psyche in *Collected Works* (hereafter referred to as CW) 9, parts I and II, (Princeton: Bollingen Series XX, Princeton University Press).
[5] C.G. Jung, "Two Essays on Analytical Psychology," CW 7, paragraph 111.
[6] For Jung on the shadow and anima, see particularly CW 9, 11.
[7] C.G. Jung, *Memories, Dreams, Reflections*, p. 209.
[8] C.G. Jung, CW 9, 1, paragraphs 522-523.
[9] C.G. Jung, "The Stages of Life," CW 8, paragraph 778.
[10] Robertson Davies, "The Conscience of the Writer," pp. 127-128.
[11] *Ibid.*, p. 128.
[12] C.G. Jung, *Man and his Symbols*, (Garden City, N.Y.: Doubleday, 1954) (reprinted New York: Dell, 1968), p. 88.
[13] Robertson Davies, *Fifth Business*, pp. 198-208.
[14] *Ibid.*, pp. 259-267.
[15] To be discussed elsewhere. This essay is the first part of a chapter on *Fifth Business* in a study of all of Robertson Davies' work, scheduled for publication in the Twayne World Authors Series by the Twayne Publishing Company, New York.
[16] C.G. Jung, CW 9, part II.
[17] Robertson Davies, *Fifth Business*, p. 244.
[18] C.G. Jung, *Memories, Dreams, Reflections*, p. 223. The following paragraphs are also of interest.

THE TRANSFORMATION OF ROBERTSON DAVIES
Ellen D. Warwick

In the Deptford novels, according to one reviewer, Robertson Davies had developed "a shelf of interlocking books."[1] "Interlocking" is apt. Davies explores many of the same characters, events, settings and themes in *Fifth Business, The Manticore,* and *World of Wonders.*[2] Although each can be read independently, most readers will delight in having their perceptions enlarged and enriched by touring a fictional world, first with Dunstan Ramsay, then David Staunton, and finally Magnus Eisengrim as guides.

While each book covers some of the same imaginary terrain, the author's methods change from one volume to the next. So different are his techniques that "interlocking" assumes added meaning. Perhaps one *must* read all the books if any assessment is to be valid. Indeed, a reader may detect in the trilogy what might be called "the transformation of Robertson Davies." This writer, who had been known as a satirist, has produced what can only be termed romance. In *Fifth Business,* Paul Dempster changes Faustina from Gretchen into Venus, magically, in an instant. Real life transformations occur more slowly. Few critics have focused on Davies' growth and change as a novelist.

In a 1960 article, "The Mask of Satire," Hugo McPherson examines Davies' world in the three Salterton novels. Linking some of the early difficulties to the habits of a playwright and essayist, McPherson describes Davies' growing strength and skill as a novelist. Noting the author's talent for satire, wit and ribaldry, he sees him nonetheless as a serious writer whose constant theme is the plight of the Canadian imagination in "this chilly cultural climate." McPherson puts these novels in the genre of *satirical romance.*[3]

Elspeth Buitenhuis, in her 1972 study of Davies, examines all his works to that time including his essays, criticism, plays and masques.[4] Judging the novel to be his most successful form, she not only accepts the classification of satirical romance, but expands greatly upon it. One of her main conclusions is that Davies is split in his approach, walking a tightrope between satire and romance, between head and heart, between the Apollonian and Dionysian ideals. The forces of restraint, balance, and reason are at war with intuition, passion, and the ultimately untameable irrational. Buitenhuis thinks Davies has moved from a strict Apollonian approach in the early Marchbanks books to a more Dionysian emphasis in *Fifth Business.*

It is now possible to take the analysis one step further. With the completion of the Deptford trilogy, Davies has continued the shift from satirical romance to romance proper. Most critics have agreed that Davies' earlier books are weakest in their characterization. The author's fondness for types is too obvious, as is his tendency toward balanced pairs. A reader begins to expect the domineering parent versus the benign kindly one, the narrow philistine coupled with the creative artist. Davies' women, with the exception of Monica Gall, are especially flat and unsatisfactory. Moreover, the author's voice, without proper warning or identification, frequently intrudes upon a character.

Fifth Business is a breakthrough. Much of its success arises from its satisfying characterizations, particularly that of its principal, Dunstan Ramsay. The reader comes to know him with an intimacy offered by no other Davies' creation, in part because Dunstan is given adequate time to develop. In previous novels, the action spans a few weeks, months, or, at most, a few years; in *Fifth Business*, the hero matures from boyhood to wise old age, a period of some fifty years. More important, Dunstan himself is narrator, a role that allows an "inside" view. In this, Davies' first attempt at first-person narration, the voice of the author is wedded to the consciousness of the main character. That the marriage is a happy one may spring from Dunstan's strong resemblance to his creator.

With great economy, the first pages present Dunstan as a sympathetic main character, establish his main conflict, and prepare the reader to accept him as a reliable narrator. Dunstan is precise, remembering events with great clarity. Even as a boy he was unusually perceptive: he accurately assesses how to best Percy without engaging in physical combat. Sensitive, he feels for the injured Mrs. Dempster; reticent, he believes he is watching a "scene" as she cries. With quick wit and some craftiness, he explains his tardiness at the dinner table. Possessed of an overly active conscience, he ponders his guilt in the early arrival of the baby, Paul Dempster.

Besides this careful delineation of the main character, the opening section also links Dunstan Ramsay, Boy Staunton, Mrs. Dempster and the stone that will initiate Dunstan's guilt-ridden search for salvation. At the end, these elements will again unite when Mary Dempster's son takes the paperweight from Dunstan's desk and gives it to Boy, precipitating another "accident." After these four short pages of recall, Dunstan Ramsay surfaces as an elderly schoolteacher, writing a report to his Headmaster. The reader is now more than willing to reject Lorne Packer's view of him as fussy, doddering, "with tears in his eyes and a drop hanging from his nose." Rather, his self-estimate appears honest and objective; a meticulous, respected scholar who has gone beyond the musty world of books and "risen to the full stature of a man" knowing beauty and mystery in life; altogether, a trustworthy narrator.

Davies' love of pairing does not desert him, but Dunstan is so believable that the constant contrasts with Boy Staunton serve only to enrich the portraits of each. Speaking of his lifelong friend and enemy, Dunstan comments: "You see how it was: to him the reality of life lay in external things, whereas for me the only reality was of the spirit . . ." And so events of the story prove. Boy falls for the vacuous Leola, Dunstan for strong, understanding Diana. The status-conscious minister, Rev. George Maldon Leadbeater, appeals to Staunton, while Ramsay learns to appreciate the almost Franciscan Joel Surgeoner. Boy's mature love affair is with the grasping, ambitious Denyse; Dunstan's, with the intuitive, other-worldly Liesl. When Boy dies, probably on the fifty-first anniversary of Dunstan's near-death in wartime, the coincidence is barely marked. Both characters have developed so organically that chance, acceptable in real life, is accepted here.

Satire and irony, Davies' stock-in-trade, depend to a certain extent upon author and reader sharing knowledge that is denied a character. Thus, while first person narration grants immediacy and closeness, it may also destroy the distance necessary to see a character with humour. Davies has solved this problem in a masterly fashion. First, Dunstan, as principal character, is somewhat isolated. He can view those surrounding him with a detached, ironic gaze. His perspective on Boy is devastating, mainly because the reader is never allowed inside Boy's mind — and Dunstan convinces us the trip would not be worth it. Secondly, Dunstan as narrator is a different self than the younger man he describes. The passing of time lends him the distance needed for humour.

Throughout, Dunstan can interrupt, correcting, commenting and smiling at his immature self, as when he recalls his break-up with Diana Marfleet. Perhaps his later affair with the grotesque Liesl, one of the few incidents in the novel that fails, never comes to life precisely because both Ramsay and Davies view her with too *much* detachment. Unlike Diana, she remains only the serio-comic personification of an idea; in this case, the demonic side of Ramsay's nature that must be recognized. For the most part, however, Ramsay as both principal and narrator maintains a balanced distance toward people and events.

In *Anatomy of Criticism* Northrop Frye points out that in romance the hero's origins are often obscure: cruel, false parents seek his destruction while true ones remain disguised. Davies' preoccupation with themes of domineering and ambiguous parents receives its most romantic treatment in *Fifth Business*. Dunstan Ramsay knows he must escape his parents, particularly his overpowering mother. Although Mary Dempster comes to stand for several things in his life, he most often sees her as an idealized maternal figure. With a boy's curiosity he peeks to watch her feeding Paul. Agonized and guilty, he enlists in the army when his mother demands a choice between herself and "that woman." Barely noting his own mother's death, he is chief and sole mourner at Mary's bier; the undertaker mistakes him for her son. That night, as if again to force a choice, Mrs. Ramsay appears to him in horrible nightmares. And, of course, Dunstan links Mary with the Divine Mother when her image merges with that of the Madonna at Passchendaele who "miraculously" saves his life. Dunstan not only becomes one of the "twice-born"; in his novel, he rejects the false mother and chooses a new, truer source of abundant life.

Mrs. Dempster connects with another romantic theme in the novel: Dunstan's love of magic and the marvelous. "Some of the oddity and loneliness of the Dempsters was beginning to rub off on me," Ramsay notes (p. 27). In the solitude of the library he discovers two books, one on conjuring, the other on saints. Radically influencing the lives of both Dunstan and Mary's son Paul, these books represent a theme that Ramsay considers throughout: "that religion and *Arabian Nights* were true in the same way."

Of Mary Dempster, Father Blazon asks Dunstan, "Who is she in your personal mythology?" (p. 159). Dunstan's long quest for an answer leads him to consider various kinds of truth. Even as a boy he likes imagination better than reason; as a young war hero he ponders the truth of symbol when he meets the king. Surgeoner tries to show him the relation between parable and fact, much as he, himself, tries to teach schoolboys the relation between myth and history. Ramsay's lifelong love of magic is part of his search for a truth beyond objective fact that will feed "a hungry part of the spirit."

At one point Davies comes close to articulating the romantic quest of his hero. At the Basilica in Mexico City, aesthetic, magical, psychological and religious truths coalesce around the picture of the Virgin of Guadalupe, an image strongly reminiscent of Mary Dempster as Madonna. Dunstan ponders, "Why do people all over the world, and at all times, want marvels that defy all verifiable fact?"

His tentative conclusion is "that faith was a psychological reality, and that where it was not invited to fasten itself on things unseen, it invaded and raised bloody hell with things seen. Or in other words, the irrational will have its say, perhaps because 'irrational' is the wrong word for it." Ultimately the higher wisdom that Ramsay's fool-saint represents remains inexplicable except through symbol. Thus, it is appropriate that Mary should die mad, with no last words for Dunstan, just a silent squeeze of his hand. As Father Blazon warns, too much "scientizing" can do no good. It is enough that "belief has coloured your life with beauty and goodness" (p. 222).

Several themes, then, tend toward a romantic, Dionysian approach. The structure of *Fifth Business*, however, is a model of classical, Apollonian balance. As noted earlier, the author uses a favourite device by beginning and ending in the same way: Ramsay, Staunton, Dempster, stone, accident. Furthermore, the six parts divide rather neatly. In each of the first three, a "miracle" of Mary Dempster's is recorded. In each of the last three, Dunstan moves closer to discovering the place his fool-saint occupies in his life. In addition, various events in the first half are balanced by repetition in the second: Dunstan discovers a book about saints in Part I; Dunstan writes a book about saints in Part IV. The affair with Diana in Part II links nicely with that with Liesl in Part V. Dunstan begins his search for the Madonna of Passchendaele in Part III and finds her in Part VI.

In the last few pages of *Fifth Business*, almost as an afterthought, Dunstan tells the Headmaster of a strange incident at the Royal Alexandra Theatre that occurred shortly after Boy's burial. The addendum provides the lead-in to *The Manticore* which begins with David Staunton, Boy's son, describing his behaviour at the theatre the same evening. This second Deptford novel, though an elaboration and continuation of the first, is a change for Davies. He leaves the genre of the satirical romance and moves into romance proper.

In some ways the new first-person narrator resembles his old school-master, Dunstan Ramsay. David, too, is reticent: "my nature is a retentive, secretive one" (p. 39). The reader is soon acquainted with his sensitivity, his lawyer-like passion for, and memory of, detail, his over-developed conscience. And, as the novel progresses, it becomes evident that, like Dunstan, David has felt the need to move into a realm uninhabited by a strong, domineering parent.

Still, David never comes through with the same depth and wholeness as Dunstan. A series of communications with a Jungian analyst supposedly bares David's soul. Unfortunately, what emerges is a shadow of a man, a dim abstraction passed through the filtres of psychoanalysis.

David could be credible as an emotionally disturbed adult working his way toward wholeness. But even on this level he is less than convincing. Part of the problem is that the reader does not witness enough of his distress before the trip to Zurich to believe that he truly needs such drastic treatment. The incident in the theatre seems simply the action of a man justifiably disturbed by his father's unusual death. Moreover, during analysis David is not shown groping toward the maturity he achieves at the end. When the analyst interrupts, correcting both David's and the reader's perspective, she claims he is becoming "a much pleasanter, easier person." The comment remains a statement; the reader feels that progress has been only asserted, not shown. David's cure is too automatic, too obviously the appropriate ending. Even the layman knows that therapy is tortuous and rarely produces dramatic change.

The analysis device ultimately seems tacked on, a clever way of telling a story. The reader begins to focus on the superimposed scheme rather than on the story itself. One is tempted to read a treatise on Jung rather than to view David within the confines of the work itself.

Nonetheless, David *is* more than a cardboard cut-out, or, one is tempted to say, shrunken head. He has validity and life, if not in the abundance that Ramsay possesses them. A reader may resist him simply because he is not as sympathetic as Dunstan. In the first pages David is defensively haughty, and impatient when the examiner and analyst fail to comprehend his remarks. Frequently, he calls attention to his wealth putting him in a sphere different from the common run. Although he rightfully defines his drinking as a symptom rather than a cause, his dismissal of alcoholism as a "middle-class predicament," albeit amusing, is overbearing. Then too, the novel takes its time before presenting David in the exculpating circumstances of childhood. Davies has created a character that one may dismiss not because he lacks credibility, but because insofar as he is real, he is unlikeable.

The distance that in *Fifth Business* gave room for irony and satire is much less evident in the second Deptford novel. David lacks Dunstan's perspective. Indeed, as a character undergoing analysis, he is caught in a pit of buried emotions. His detachment is not the healthy attitude of irony, but the defensive posture of the maimed. There are humourous moments in *The Manticore* (the scenes in Deptford with

Grandfather Staunton are marvelous) but they are much less frequent than in previous Davies novels.

In his analysis of the quest-romance, Frye mentions its analogy to
the worlds of dream and ritual examined by Jung and Frazer. The
similarity between Frye's stock romantic figures and the cast surrounding David in the Jungian *The Manticore,* is fascinating. The
cruel, destructive parents suggest Boy, Denyse, and possibly Netty.
The wise old man, often a magician, is represented by Ramsay,
Knopwood, and the blind Pargetter. Dr. von Haller even uses the
Jungian term "magus" when speaking of these men. The sybilline,
wise, mother-figure brings to mind Liesl or Dr. von Haller herself.
The latter, in fact, appears as a sybil in David's dream of the manticore. Judy is the romantic young heroine; Myrrha Martindale is the
siren or witch. Pledger-Brown seems to be the faithful companion;
Dick Unsworth is the traitor.

In *The Manticore* Davies continues exploring the romantic theme
of false versus true parents. In *Fifth Business* Dunstan suspected that
he may have been instrumental in stirring the "uxorious fire" that
produced David. The "greedy novel-reader and romancer" Carol
thinks Dunstan is David's father in physical fact. David calls Pargetter his "father in art." And while making sexual advances to Judy, he
is troubled by visions of parental authority that include not only
Boy, but also Father Knopwood. It is significant that the girls at
Bishop Cairncross School produce an opera entitled *Son and
Stranger.* The phrase sums up the relationship between Boy and
David. Dr. von Haller tells David outright that his historical father
bears little relationship to the archetype of fatherhood lying in his
depths. Dunstan clearly states the false father theme when he explains to David at the end of the novel that "every man who amounts
to a damn has several fathers, and the man who begat him in lust or
drink or for a bet or even in the sweetness of honest love may not be
the most important father. The fathers you choose for yourself are
the significant ones" (p. 261).

The romantic theme of magic also appears, but with the emphasis
shifted to a modern conception of the mysterious, the world of psychological truth. Not only the illusionist but also the Jungian analyst
can say that things are seldom what they seem. Liesl, although she
does not appear until the last section of the book, is a figure uniting
the old and new magic. Presiding over the workroom that produces
many of the effects of Eisengrim's show, she is equally familiar with
the worlds of Freud, Adler and Jung. The re-birth ritual she arranges
for David in the cave is a blend of psychological, religious and mag-

ical elements, a coming together of the same truths that Dunstan pondered in the Basilica of Guadalupe. Furthermore, Liesl articulates an ideal — Frye tells us that romance always embodies an ideal — toward which David must strive: "It isn't everybody who is triumphantly the hero of his own romance . . . The modern hero is the man who conquers the inner struggle."

In *The Manticore*, the romantic quest becomes the search for psychological wholeness, accomplished through the modern magic of analysis. Once again, Frye provides guidelines: "The complete form of the romance is clearly the successful quest, and such a completed form has three main stages: the stage of the perilous journey . . . the crucial struggle . . . and the exaltation of the hero."[6] *The Manticore* is divided into three stages. "Why I Went to Zurich" implies journey. The peril becomes evident when David's suspicion of psychiatry and fear of being discovered in analysis are revealed. "David Against the Trolls" recounts his analysis proper, his crucial struggle to come to grips with his past. "My Sorgenfrei Diary," although it does not exactly exalt the hero, at least prepares him for future glory by showing the transformation scene in the cave.

This last section does raise the question: is David successful in his quest? Davies seems to intent on linking David with characters from *Fifth Business*, and then setting up a situation that leads to a sequel, that any consideration of "Sorgenfrei Diary" on its own falls short. The section is too poorly integrated with the rest of the novel to evaluate it structurally as anything but an overly-long addendum. Nonetheless, the ritual in the cave and the Christmas Day ending with the presentation of the three gifts, do connote some success for David.

Frye points out that the romance has six distinguishable phases. While David's story does not divide so neatly, the similarities can be seen. The first phase, the birth of the hero, is not included. Still, the reader knows that David as hero is marked. "It is not easy to be the son of a very rich man," he begins, pinpointing one cause of his singularity. Also, as mentioned earlier, his origins, like the romantic hero's, are mysterious. "Who is my father?" is the question David must answer. The second phase, the Golden Age, comes in the summers at Deptford, a place David labels his "Arcadia." The vacations with his grandparents, however strange and pastoral, are times of innocence he recalls with nostalgia.

The quest is the third phase, corresponding to the part of David's notebook where he begins talking about his relationship with his father, the Toronto part of the story. In the fourth, the hero tries to maintain some integrity against the assault of experience. A common image is the monster tamed by the virgin. David's sexual experience with Myrrha Martindale belongs here as does his dream of the sybil holding the manticore by the golden chain.

A reflective, idyllic view of his experience marks the fifth phase. This suggests the maturing David who gains perspective on himself, who discovers and respects his *persona* living on the lip of the volcano. The last stage is contemplative; its central image the old man in the tower absorbed in occult or magical studies. David has left analysis and visits Liesl in her castle-like home with the seventy-year-old magus, Dunstan Ramsay, as a companion. It is impossible to claim that *The Manticore* follows the phases of romance in any strict, one-to-one fashion. It is just as difficult, however, to avoid seeing the parallels between Frye's outline of romance and Davies' book.

In the third Deptford novel, Davies confirms his transformation from an Apollonian writer into a spinner of romantic tales. Gone are the tight structural underpinnings of *Fifth Business*. Gone too are the psychological/mythological patterns that mark *The Manticore*. Instead, *World of Wonders* leaves plot and usual characterization behind in favour of exploration into the marvelous, the grotesque, the nostalgic. Scene after scene glows with such unreal gilding that a reader concludes this is no recognizable terrain but, indeed, a world of wonders.

The most striking contrast between the final novel and its predecessors lies in the story's structure. In *Anatomy of Criticism*, Frye points out that "The essential element of plot in romance is adventure, which means that romance is naturally a sequential and processional form. . .At its most naive, it is an endless form in which a central character who never develops or ages goes through one adventure after another until the author himself collapses."[7] While the quotation does not apply unequivocally, *World of Wonders*, in its structure, comes closest of all the trilogy to the sequential form of romance.

Narrated for the most part by Magnus Eisengrim, the story is divided into three parts. The first deals with Paul Dempster's childhood as part of a circus travelling through Canada. The second takes up his career as a member of a theatrical troupe in England and his home country. The last very brief section is a coda tying up the loose ends of the trilogy. Nowhere is there a climax, a completion. In *Fifth Business*, Ramsay discovers the meaning Mary Dempster held in his life. In *The Manticore*, David Staunton uncovers the roots of his psychological problems and experiences stirrings of recovery. *World*

of Wonders, however, comes to no resolution. The tale remains a
highly entertaining adventure story that simply ends.

As narrator and main character, Eisengrim both resembles and differs from historian Dunstan Ramsay and lawyer David Staunton.
Like them, he is an older man with a secretive personality. A loner
who views the modern world with critical detachment and regret, he
too possesses specialized, somewhat arcane knowledge that sets him
further apart. However, Eisengrim lacks the wholeness of Dunstan or
even the shadowy validity of David. After his appearance as victim
in the brutal, cruelly vivid sodomy incident, Paul Dempster literally
disappears into the bowels of Abdullah, a mechanical monster he
operates in the circus. Dempster's disappearance as a character is
almost as complete. Though he emerges from time to time wearing
masks labelled Cass Fletcher, Jules LeGrand, Mungo Fetch and Magnus Eisengrim, he never again quite captures the reader's imagination
or belief. Instead, he functions as a disembodied voice who conjures
up the endless parade of characters and anecdotes that provide the
real charm of the tale.

Insofar as Eisengrim does develop as a character, the change high-
lights perhaps his basic difference from the other two narrators: his
lack of a sense of sin. Magnus undergoes a reversal of the usual
romantic phases, for he moves from experience into innocence. From
boy prostitute, which produces agonizing guilt, Magnus goes on to
become an old-style actor's double, acquiring not only Sir John's gait
and mannerisms but his world-view as well. Eisengrim crudely calls
it a "kiss my arse with class" attitude while Milady sweetly dubs it
the Guvnor's "romantic splendour." Whatever, the outward manner
signals an inward elevation in Eisengrim. Appropriately enough,
after his apprenticeship with the Tresizes, Magnus journeys to the
fairy-tale land of the Swiss Alps. Here, he enters a child's world of
mechanical toys and finds his final vocation in the domain of magic
and illusion. During this process of distancing from the real world,
Eisengrim seems to lose the fearsome conscience that marked his
boyhood and that still characterizes both Staunton and Ramsay. Little shame, remorse or even simply humanity occur to the sixty-two-
year-old narrator of *World of Wonders.* Instead, he appears preter-
naturally above such considerations in his treatment of Ingestree,
Faustina and Liesl. Still aware of conventional morality, Dunstan at
least tries to explain the hilarious *ménage à trois* at the Hotel Savoy;
Magnus seems to accept the incongruous three-in-a-bed with the un-
questioning simplicity of a child.

World of Wonders echoes some of the romantic themes that occur in the earlier books, particularly the idea of false versus true parents and the related notion of being born again. Amasa Dempster is Eisengrim's father in body only, while various others, including Ramsay, Professor Spencer, Zingara, and especially the Tresizes, become parents in spirit. And, as Eisengrim grows into innocence, Sir John mentions the theme of rebirth that appears in all the Deptford books: "Quite right, m'boy; born again and born different, as Mrs. Poyser very wisely said" (p. 202).

The concept that most animates *World of Wonders*, however, is a romantic preoccupation with the elements suggested in the title; the mysterious, the invisible, the marvelous. In the tawdry world of the circus, the freaks and misfits that surround Eisengrim serve as continual reminders of an inexplicable evil or grotesque reality which can never be reasoned away. Faith surfaces here as well: in a ludicrous fashion, when Happy Hannah quotes Scripture; in a touching fashion, when Eisengrim does so. Imprisoned in the innards of Abdullah, Magnus compares himself to Jonah in the belly of the great fish. He experiences spiritual desolation but never despair: "Such was the power of my early training that I never became cynical about the Lord — only about his creation." In the world of the theatre, Eisengrim discovers another reality, a golden, nostalgia-drenched realm created by art. The cramped backstage areas, the discomforts faced by the travelling troupe, the politicking and petty disagreements of the actors, none of these destroy the magic the stage holds for him. ". . .the theatre I knew was the theatre that makes people forget some things and remember others, and refreshes dry places in the spirit." Again, Liesl, the androgynous woman-monster articulates the romantic ideal and, in so doing, makes clear the theme of *World of Wonders*; indeed, of the whole trilogy. She explains Spengler's Magian World View, one that Eisengrim's life has embodied: "It was a sense of the unfathomable wonder of the invisible world that existed side by side with a hard recognition of the roughness and cruelty and day-to-day demands of the tangible world. . .It was poetry and wonder which might reveal themselves in the dunghill, and it was an understanding of the dunghill that lurks in poetry and wonder."

The Deptford novels, the second Davies trilogy, are finished. With his fondness for the magic number three, will the author attempt yet a third? Ramsay, the old sage, sits in his tower at the Savoy, pen in hand, noting, arranging, explaining. "Ramsay says. . .". Davies also "says" and, having observed him change from Apollonian satirist to Dionysian romanticist, one can only wonder what further transformations may occur.

Notes

1 William Dennedy, review of *The Manticore, New York Times Book Review*, November 19, 1972, p. 26.
2 All references are to: Robertson Davies, *Fifth Business* (New York: Signet, New American Library, 1971); *The Manticore* (Toronto: Macmillan of Canada Curtis Books, 1972); *World of Wonders* (Toronto: Macmillan of Canada, 1975). *World of Wonders* also available in paperback in the Penguin edition (1977).
3 Hugo McPherson, "The Mask of Satire," *Canadian Literature*, IV (Spring, 1960) pp. 18-30.
4 Elspeth Buitenhuis, *Robertson Davies* (Toronto: Forum House, 1972).
5 *Ibid.*, p. 58. The resemblance is obvious to any student of Davies, but Miss Buitenhuis is the first to note this in print.
6 Northrop Frye, *Anatomy of Criticism* (Princeton: Princeton University Press, 1957), p. 187.
7 *Ibid.*, p. 186.

MARGARET LAURENCE

IN A NAMELESS LAND: APOCALYPTIC MYTHOLOGY IN THE WRITINGS OF MARGARET LAURENCE

Frank Pesando

In the extreme climactic regions of this earth there is not the extended pause between birth and death that typifies the more temperate zones. The Northern territories and the arid countries of the south have this in common: growth must be rapid if there is to be growth, for cold and drought kill with equal speed. The wheat which grows inches in a day and the cactus flower which passes from bud to seed in forty-eight hours share a common struggle against time. The wheat must reach maturity before the frost kills its roots, and a blooming flower drains the cactus of its precious fluid. Both plants and both regions provide visual testimony to the quick mutability of life.

This phenomena of sudden change is described in detail by Margaret Laurence in *The Phophet's Camel Bell*. For Laurence, the harshness of the Sudan, where human decay is both prevalent and rapid, suggested a fundamental weakness in the theory of a benevolent deity. During her prolonged stay in Somaliland, the street beggars she repeatedly encountered, the child prostitute, and the families dying of hunger and thirst during the Jilal became more than merely a reproach. As the full implications of the things she had seen began to penetrate, Laurence came to recognize the threat posed by them.

> All at once I was aware of them, the ranks of beggars whining their monotonous plea outside the shops. The old and withered among them smiled with senile serenity, forever hoping for the miracle forever denied, the grace of Allah forever withheld. Their tattered remnants of robes fluttered like ancient prayer flags for a mosque, and the claws that held the wooden bowls were separated from skeleton only by skin as crinkled and brittle as charred paper. One dragged himself along with two blocks of wood strapped to his hands, because he had no legs.
>
> Many of the begging throng were children, the marks of their profession plain upon them — running sores on twig-like bodies, a twisted shoulder, a stunted stump of a leg dragged heavily, patiently, through the dust. They were the misshapen ones, the weak in a land where life came hard even to the strong.[1]

In her fictional writings Margaret Laurence would return to this vision of the crowded, dust ridden streets of Africa, where the European is faced with a throng of beggars and forced to recognize his helplessness before them. Thus, in "The Merchant of Heaven," Mr. Lemon's determination to ease the lives of the poor shatters quickly.

> He soon came to be surrounded by beggars wherever he went. They swamped him; their appalling voices followed him down any street. Fingerless hands reached out; half-limbs hurried at his approach. He couldn't cope with it, of course. Who could? Finally, he began to turn away, as ultimately we all turn, frightened and repelled by the outrageous pain and need.[2]

The beggars recur, but not always in human form. In *The Stone Angel*, Hagar will recall a moment from her childhood when she and a group of other young girls tiptoed past the rubble of the town dump, lifting their skirts to avoid the decay "like dainty-nosed czarinas finding themselves in sudden astonishing proximity to beggars with weeping sores." A moment later, they encounter the first of Hagar's visions.

> We saw, with a kind of horror that could not be avoided, however much one looked away or scurried on, that some of the eggs had been fertile and had hatched in the sun. The chicks, feeble, foodless, bloodied and mutilated, prisoned by the weight of broken shells all around them, were trying to crawl like little worms, their half-mouths opened uselessly among the garbage.[3]

Lottie kills them, crushing their skulls under her heels. Many years later, when Hagar and Lottie are plotting to break up the affair between their children, Hagar recalls this scene:

> "Remember those chicks that day at the dump ground, Lottie, when we were girls? I always marveled that you could bring yourself to do what you did. I haven't thought of it in years, but I used to wonder — didn't it make you feel peculiar?" (p. 213)

Lottie doesn't remember.

Lottie is still capable of the act. In this second instance, their children, Arlene and John, are likened to starving creatures and the Prairie that surrounds them is compared to the wasteland which had surrounded the chickens. Once again Lottie will crush the creatures while Hagar watches. The desire to ruin a love affair which they view as impractical and unsightly is merely an extension of the desire to destroy the mutilated chickens, whose very existence seemed to threaten. The crippled birds become crippled children.

The throng of beggars is not the only vision described in *The Prophet's Camel Bell* which reappears in Laurence's later work. There is Asha, the eight-year-old child prostitute who returns in "The Rain Child" as Ayesha, and there is the young woman, already aging, forced to watch her child die of thirst. Of this latter figure, Laurence writes, "In all of life there was nothing worse than this."[4] Throughout the course of *The Fire Dwellers*, Stacey MacAindra will be haunted by similar visions of tormented mothers desperately trying to care for their dying children.

> Newspaper photograph. Some new kind of napalm just invented, a substance which, when it alights burning onto skin, cannot be removed. It adheres. The woman was holding a child about eighteen months old and she was trying to pluck something away from the scorch-spreading area on the child's face.[5]

The suddenness and prevalence of death, made so evident by her experiences in Somaliland, continued to preoccupy Laurence. Even when the setting of her novels changed from Africa to Canada, the images of death and decay persisted.

Predictably enough, *The Stone Angel*, the first of Laurence's Canadian novels, depicts a world of ruins. Hagar, her body already betraying her to decay, sees death in the landscape. Phrases such as "At the Shipley place the rusty machinery stood like aged bodies gradually expiring from exposure, ribs turned to the sun" (p. 169) or, "Crashing, I stumble through ferns and rotten boughs that lie scattered like old bones" (p. 190), create the impression that Hagar is in a world that is slowly being strangled by decay. Her body, its bones locked with arthritis beneath a coating of fat that swells in grim mockery of feminine proportion, its skin veined with blue and "the silverish white of the creatures one fancies must live under the sea where the sun never reaches" (p. 79), is obviously part of this world. Her mind is not.

In a world where machines are like corpses and tree stumps like dead bones, it seems appropriate that insects — creatures traditionally linked with decay — should predominate. In the first vision of the graveyard where the stone angel stands, we find that the peonies are infested with ants and later, when the marble angel lies toppled on its face amid these peonies, the ants scurry through the stone ringlets of her hair. Later still, Hagar will imitate the statue by placing dead june bugs in her own hair.

Hagar's world is infested with crawling things. As a child she had believed that a phantom lay hidden behind a closet door which was never opened. When she finally summoned the courage to open that door she found, instead, a pile of rags in which there nested small, frantic spiders. As a middle-aged woman, returning home to Bram after an absence of more than a decade, she discovers a kitchen strewn with filth, where, "On a larded piece of salt pork a mammoth matriarchal fly was labouring obscenely to squeeze out of herself her white and clustered eggs" (p. 170). And finally, as an old woman hiding from her children, she meets Murray F. Lees, who comes from a town called Blackfly.

It has often been noted that Laurence makes frequent use of Biblical imagery, but it is seldom recognized that these images are drawn almost entirely from two sections of the Bible: Genesis and the Revelation of Saint John the Divine, the tale of creation and the tale of destruction. The names Hagar and Rachel are drawn from Genesis, the story of birth. The references to the two-edged sword, the sequined heaven of St. John of Patmos and Mr. Troy, and to the skeletal horsemen, relate to St. John's vision of the death of the world.

This linking of birth and death mythology is particularly evident in Laurence's use of the sea. The short story, "The Perfume Sea," ends with Doree and Archipelago walking along the shore. This Side Jordan ends in a similar fashion, with Johnnie and Miranda, at last reconciled with one another and with Africa, walking along the shore of Sakumono beach. In the Canadian novels, both Hagar and Stacey retreat to the sea during moments of crises and return ready to face the environment from which they have fled. From this it might be concluded that the sea functions as a regenerative force in Laurence's novels.

Yet this regenerative function does not account for phrases such as, "those sea pebbles which as a child I used to think were the eyballs of the drowned"[6] or "all the broken machinery standing in the yard like the old bones and ribs of great dead sea creatures washed on shore" (p. 29).

The sea is also associated with death.

> I feel I may not be able to return, even if I open my eyes. I
> may be swept outward like a gull, blown by a wind too
> strong for it, forced into the rough sea, held under and
> drawn fathoms down into depths as still and cold as black
> glass. (p. 235)

In the Book of the Apocalypse, when Saint John first sees the throne of heaven, a sea of glass lies before it. This sea of glass represents the evil still present on the earth and, throughout the Revelation, the sea is shown to be a reservoir of evil, synonymous with the abyss itself. It is the birthplace of dragons and the refuge to which the evil forces return when defeated by the force of heaven. So long as it exists, it is impossible to have a complete victory over evil.

The sea is also linked with Hades as a refuge for the dead which, in the last stage of the Apocalypse, it is forced to yield up. Finally, when the New Jerusalem appears, we are told that the sea is no more.

It is in her Canadian novels that Laurence's reliance on Apocalyptic mythology is most pronounced and it is in *The Stone Angel* that the sea first appears in its more sinister aspect. During the night in the deserted cannery, when Hagar and Murray have both revealed their inner grief over the loss of a favourite child, there is a moment of silence in which they are made aware of a malevolent presence.

> We sit quietly in this place, empty except for ourselves,
> and listen for the terrible laughter of God, but can hear only
> the vapid chuckling of the sea. (p. 234)

Hagar feels the sea to be a trap, something that would lure her under and never release her:

> . . . a black sea sucking everything into itself, the spent gull,
> the trivial garbage from boats, and men protected from eter-
> nity only by their soft and fearful flesh and their seeing eyes.
> (p. 225)

In *The Fire Dwellers*, Stacey is also lured and repelled by the sea, feeling that it may strangle her or cage her beneath its surface:

> . . . nonentities of thoughts floating like plankton, green and
> orange particles, seaweed — lots of that, dark purple and
> waving, sharks with fins like cutlasses, herself held under-
> water by her hair, snared around auburn-rusted anchor
> chains.[7]

Luke will later call her merwoman, and ask, "Who held you down? Was it for too long?"[8]

Margaret Laurence has referred to Stacey as Hagar's spiritual granddaughter, and in her mermaid fantasies, Stacey does appear to be reliving Hagar's initial vision.[9] Alone in the cannery, Hagar imagines herself free of the bloated body which threatens to destroy her:

> . . . Now I could fancy myself there among them, tiaraed with starfish thorny and purple, braceleted with shells linked on limp chains of weed, waiting until my encumbrance of flesh floated clean away and I was free and skeletal and could journey with tides and fishes. (p. 162)

The fantasy ends abruptly and Hagar finds herself suddenly terrified. What she has longed for is death itself.[10]

But the sea in the Revelation is more than simply the sinister harbouring place of death. It is the home of monsters, spewing forth innumerable apparitions which delude and horrify mankind. In Laurence's work as well, the apparitions and the human grotesques are almost inevitably associated with the sea.

Stacey, in *The Fire Dwellers*, envisions the ocean as the dwelling place of giant beasts, of ships that "move in ponderously to be unladen like great sea cows swimming in to be milked,"[11] and other, lesser known creatures:

> How far out does it go? How many creatures does it contain, not just the little shells and the purple starfish and the kelp, but all the things that live a long way out? Deathly embracing octopus in the south waters, the white whales spouting in the only half-melted waters of the north, the sharks knowing nothing except how to kill.[12]

In *A Bird in the House*, Vanessa MacLeod recalls her fascination with Great Bear Lake, a mysterious "deep vastness of black water" which she had seen only on maps and had imagined to exist somewhere beyond the margin of civilization, where there was only ice and jagged rock, in a region devoid of warmth.[13]

Chris tells her that the lake was once filled with water monsters:

> Imagine them — all those huge creatures, with necks like snakes, and some of them had hackles on their heads, like a rooster's comb only very tough, like hard leather.
> . . . I could only nod, fascinated and horrified. Imagine going swimming in those waters. What if one of the creatures had lived on?[14]

At other times it is man himself, twisted and distorted by age, who can be likened to a monster from the sea. Throughout *The Stone Angel*, Hagar is confronted with women of immense proportions. Doris is likened to a "broody hen," a calving cow," "a sow in labour" (p. 29, 31, 55). Her body is plump and bulging under brown cloth, her sighs are brought "straight from the belly," and when nervous, she rasps like a coping saw (p. 33, 55). Bram's first wife is "fat and cow-like," his two daughters are "like heifers, like lumps of unrendered fat" (p. 173, 56). Murray F. Lees refers to his wife as "a big strapping girl . . . like a feather mattress," with "great white thighs" (p. 227). Even Lottie becomes a puffball of fat, looking as though "she'd either burst or bounce if you tapped her" (p. 209).

All of these stout, ponderous women echo Hagar's own fate. Her body too, is becoming layered with fat. Yet it is not until she reaches the hospital, in the final period of her life, that Hagar witnesses this physical distortion in its most extreme form. There she encounters Mrs. Reilly, "a mountain of flesh," and is told that, "they had to bring her in on a wheelchair, and took three orderlies to hoist her into the bed." There, on a neighbouring bed, a woman lies helpless, caged by her own "rolling and undulating" fat, "larded inches deep" (p. 259, 261, 267).

In *The Fire Dwellers*, Laurence returns to this vision in the form of Buckle's mother. Stacey is confronted with a woman of gigantic proportions, her flesh oozing out over the chair which surrounds it, the rings of fat around her throat trembling like eels, her arms like those of a kodiak bear. Adding to the grotesqueness of the creature is the fact that it is in a stupor, drunk on port which it has poured from a teapot.

The woman is a retired prostitute, blinded by acid which another prostitute had thrown into her face. Unable to see and with the rest of her senses numbed by alcohol, she lives encased in her body, entirely removed from the daylight and movement of Stacey's world. Her only link with the rest of humanity is Buckle, and when he dies, there is nothing.

> The way I heard it, they told her about the son and said they was coming back the next day to fetch her off somewheres, one of them homes, like, I guess. Well, she tries to cut her throat, see? Only she can't find the butcher knife. When they come in the morning there she was, still crawling around the floor, feeling everything, but she still hadn't

found it. Ever see her? Built like the back of a barn, she was. She must've looked real cute, crawling around on her hands and knees, with her great big tits bumping along on the floor, there.[15]

Stacey instinctively associates this human grotesque with the sea, calling her the "undersea giant woman" and the "she-whale."[16]

Johnnie Kestoe, in *This Side Jordan*, is preoccupied with a different form of female grotesque. As a boy he had witnessed the death of his mother, who had ruptured her womb in a bungled abortion attempt. The blood seemed to flow out endlessly from between her twisting, tormented thighs.

> The red stain spread and spread on the quilt, and it was quite a while before he realized it was her blood doing it. His father watched, too, sitting empty-faced while she cursed and prayed by turns . . . People must have heard his mother dying all the way up Kilburn High Road.
> So Mary Kestoe died, her black hair tumbling wild around her neck, her eyes open wide, as hard and bitter as they'd been in life, and staring her frantic fear of hell. And the high cold attic room grew silent at last.[17]

With jabbing, intolerable persistence, the apparition reappears, taking the form of a bleeding Negro girl whose circumcision scars had been reopened by his violation of her.

Rachel in *A Jest of God* shares in this vision, but for her it is more personal, for she imagines herself as the central figure:

> She is in the bathroom, and the door is locked, and she cannot cry out. The pain distends her; she is swollen with it. Pain is the only existing thing. On the floor, and all over herself, lying in it, and even on her hair, the blood.[18]

The tabernacle provides the setting for yet a third vision. Cornered at the back of the chapel, hemmed in on all sides by the walls which, through someone's macabre taste, have been painted greenish blue, "dense and murky, the way the sea must be, fathoms under," Rachel envisions a frightening world of sub-humans into which she has been suddenly thrust:

> The lay preacher is praying, and I can't hear the words, somehow, only his husky voice, his voice like a husky dog's, a low growling. Beside me, the hulked form of the farmer sits crouched over. They all seem to be crouching, all of

them, all around me, crouching and waiting. They are (of
course I know it) praying. It's not a zoo, not Doctor
Moreau's island where the beastmen prowled and waited,
able to speak but without comprehension.[19]

But Rachel's horror is real enough and gradually the deep green-
blue walls and the animal-men extend beyond the world of the tabernacle. The color blue reappears again and again, in the blossom on
the hyacinth, in the flashing neon sign of Japonica Funeral Chapel, in
the darkening night sky, in the organ room of the funeral parlor, even
on the walls of Calla's room. Each of the characters is likened to an
animal or a series of animals.[20] Calla is likened to a great horned owl.
Willard hunches like a vulture, his eyes like the "blue dead eyes of
the frozen whitefish."[21] Rachel's mother has a meadowlarking voice
and emerges from the house in the manner of a butterfly released
from winter. Rachel herself is a lean greyhound, a giraffe woman, "a
tame goose trying to fly,"[22] a Saint Bernard, an ostrich. In this world
of animal men, children climbing stairs are like fish swimming up-
stream and are ready to fall upon their teacher like falcons should she
show any weakness.

The situation in *A Jest of God* is that described in the opening paragraphs, of confident little Roman girls playing inside "some villa in
Gaul or Britain," unaware that outside the walls "blue-painted dog-
men"[23] await them. Invasion is imminent. Rachel, like those Roman
children, has been happily unaware of danger, living in a world composed primarily of illusions. It is only now, in her thirty-fifth summer, that she has begun to sense the dog-men around her.

Stacey's world in *The Fire Dwellers* is more complex. Newspapers,
radios, televisions — the media harass her, continually forcing an
awareness of the suffering human population which surrounds her.
There is an excess of distorted, twisted figures and, like Lemon, in
"The Merchant of Heaven" ultimately she can only turn away, ap-
palled "by the outrageous pain and need."[24]

Hers is a problem of survival, the solution appearing to lie in a
knowledge of which the two worlds is real; the one where she lives as
a housewife or the one which is continually thrust upon her senses by
newspapers, radios and televisions. "The program ends, and then the
News. This time the bodies that fall stay fallen. *Flicker-flicker-flicker.*
From one dimension to another."[25]

Universal destruction — the threatened holocaust of the Apocalypse
— appears about to overwhelm the world of daily quarrels and triv-

ialities that has comprised most of her life. Stacey looks at the Vancouver skyline and momentarily sees the city in ruins, scorched by atomic weaponry. She closes her eyes and feels that:

> The thin panthers are stalking the streets of the city, their claws unretracted after the cages of time and time again. The Roman legions are marching — listen to the hate-thudding of their boot leather. Strange things are happening, and the skeletal horsemen ride, ride, ride with all the winds of the world at their backs. There is nowhere to go this time.[26]

Frightened and indignant, Stacey faces a world where the apparitions have gained control. Like Hagar, as a child Stacey was haunted by the vision of a suffering animal — a gopher dying in the middle of a road, its stomach torn open by the impact of an automobile. And, like Hagar, Stacey has lived to see the suffering animal transformed into a suffering human.

Most of the visions Stacey has seen are still distant from her, captured by photographs taken in distant lands, brought by news media. But defining this distance becomes increasingly difficult. "I see it and then I don't see it. It becomes pictures. And you wonder about the day when you open your door and find they've been filming those pictures in your street."[27]

In this respect *The Fire Dwellers* continues a theme which has persisted in Laurence's work since the short story "Godman's Master" where Moses Adu frees the little godman from his box only to discover that he has bound him to a more subtle form of prison. Moses, who believes to be so far removed from the horrors of ancient Africa, finds the distance disappearing rapidly after his meeting with Godman, to whom he is bound by some intangible thread which threatens to tighten until it strangles.

"Godman's Master," though less than thirty pages in length, contains all of the motifs which were to recur in Laurence's Canadian novels. Indeed, the story's opening is much like that of a traditional horror tale. The hero, driving through the jungle at night in the midst of a rain storm, passes through a small village, which appears to be deserted. Then, with an explosive suddenness, a living form dashes out from the surrounding darkness, striking the automobile. An instant later the car is surrounded by villagers who demand payment for the slain goat. In an effort to pacify them, Moses agrees to be taken to the dwelling place of a local oracle.

The atmosphere thickens:

Moses' glasses were blurred by rain, so the carved door
and the blown moonflowers and the crouched villagers all
looked as though they existed in some deep pool, and he,
peering and straining, could see them only vaguely through
the shifting waters.[28]

At the house of the oracle there is a priest with "One gleaming
amber eye" and a voice rising out of a box which resembles a child's
coffin. Summoned by the creature in the box, Moses lifts the lid and
discovers a face.

. . . as old as Africa, as old as all earth. But it was not the
leathery oldness of health. The skin of this face was pouched
and puffy; it had a look of unpleasant softness, like skin
soaked too long in water.[29]

The image of the dead child, the mystery and terror rising from
deep murky water, the sudden vision thrust against calm surround-
ings, the opening of boxes, closets, doors which appear to hide some
mystery, and a view of rotting, sagging flesh, putrefied by the
elements and by age — all of these recur with sufficient frequency to
be regarded as characteristic of Laurence's work. She is an author
with a keen awareness both of the more horrifying aspects of this life
and of the shells of catch-phrases, rituals and trivial bigotries which
we build to protect ourselves from them.

Notes

[1] Margaret Laurence, *The Prophet's Camel Bell* (Toronto: McClelland and Stewart, 1963), p. 24.
[2] Margaret Laurence, *The Tomorrow Tamer and Other Stories* (Toronto: McClelland and Stewart, 1970), p. 56.
[3] Margaret Laurence, *The Stone Angel* (Toronto: McClelland and Stewart, 1970), p. 56. All further references appear parenthetically in the text.
[4] Laurence, *The Prophet's Camel Bell*, p. 66.
[5] Laurence, *The Fire Dwellers* (Toronto: McClelland and Stewart, 1969), p. 96.
[6] Laurence, *The Tomorrow Tamer*, pp. 50-51.
[7] Laurence, *The Fire Dwellers*, p. 33.
[8] *Ibid.*, p. 180.
[9] Margaret Laurence, "Ten Year's Sentences," in *The Sixties: Canadian Writers and Writing of the Decade*, George Woodcock, ed. (Vancouver: University of British Columbia Publications Centre, 1969), pp. 10-16.
[10] This death imagery also extends to birds associated with water (i.e. seagulls and loons). It is the seagull caught in the cannery that reminds Hagar of the saying "A bird in the house means a death in the house" and in the later works, Rachel,

Stacey, and Vanessa McLeod all remember the loons which were once found
around the lake and have now disappeared.

They rose like phantom birds from the nests on the shore, and flew out onto the dark still surface of the water.
No one can ever describe that ululating sound, the crying of the loons,
and no one who has heard it can ever forget it . . . those voices belonged to a
world separated by aeons from our neat world of summer cottages and the
lighted lamps of home. (Margaret Laurence, *A Bird in the House* [Toronto:
McClelland and Stewart, 1970], p. 121.)

Laurence appears to be drawing a parallel between the fate of the loons and that
of the Indians, both of whom are a dying race, forced to retreat before civilization. They too are caged, by their past and by a need for space and solitude.

[11] Laurence, *The Fire Dwellers*, p. 260.
[12] *Ibid.*, p. 298.
[13] Laurence, *A Bird in the House*, p. 62.
[14] *Ibid.*, p. 135.
[15] *Ibid.*, p. 262.
[16] *Ibid.*, p. 159.
[17] Margaret Laurence, *This Side Jordan* (London: Macmillan & Co., 1961), pp. 58-59.
[18] Margaret Laurence, *A Jest of God* (Toronto: McClelland and Stewart, 1966), p. 173.
[19] *Ibid.*, p. 30, 32.
[20] The one exception to this is Nick, who is associated with the sun. Sentences such
as "She is in the green-walled room, the boughs opening just enough to let the sun
in, the moss hairy and soft on the earth" and, "All I will ever remember is that he
arched over me like the sun" suggest that Laurence is alluding to the ancient myth
where the sun is equated with man and the earth is equated with woman. The frequent references to flowers throughout the novel, which also suggest the fertility
and femininity of the earth, is in keeping with this myth. (Laurence, *A Jest of
God*, p. 18, p. 150.)
[21] *Ibid.*, p. 23, 7.
[22] *Ibid.*, p. 40, 75, 130, 140, 177.
[23] *Ibid.*, p. 2.
[24] Laurence, *The Tomorrow Tamer*, p. 56.
[25] Laurence, *The Fire Dwellers*, pp. 58-59.
[26] *Ibid.*, p. 89.
[27] *Ibid.*, p. 305.
[28] Laurence, *The Tomorrow Tamer*, p. 139.
[29] *Ibid.*, p.143.

IMAGES OF CLOSURE IN *THE DIVINERS*

Cheryl Cooper

Margaret Laurence has said that *The Diviners* completes the cycle of the Manawaka books:

> . . . I think it's very doubtful that I'll write another book out of that background . . . it just seemed to me that those five books of Canadian fiction came out of that fictional prairie town, that the wheel had come full circle, that things had been completed.[1]

Each of the five Manawaka books can stand on its own, but *The Diviners* is enhanced by its relation to the other books as a work of summation and closure. *The Diviners* is a self-regarding fiction. Its overarching image is reflexivity. The conscious act of looking in a mirror or of watching "old films," this act of recollecting and ordering a personal history as a final testament, is an act of closure.

All Laurence's protagonists look at themselves in mirrors and, while what they see is an accurate subjective vision, it is often an inaccurate objective one. Rachel cannot succeed in avoiding mirrors. Her "glimpses of herself are almost always unflattering,"[2] although we are early cautioned against accepting her self-descriptions: "Do I see my face falsely? How do it know how it looks to anyone else?";[3] "Do I have good bones? I can't tell. I'm no judge."[4] Stacey's mirror-watching is a series of confrontations. She must learn to reconcile Stacey Cameron and Stacey MacAindra. Hagar, too, rages against her aging. Despite her "changing shell," she sees "the same dark eyes . . . the eyes change least of all."[5] Hagar, with her indomitable will, defies the mirror.

Only Morag, in *The Diviners*, is objective. When she looks in the mirror she sees:

> A tall woman, although not bizarrely so. Heavier than once, but not what you would call fat. Tanned, slightly leathery face. Admittedly strong and rather sharp features. Eyebrows which met in the middle and which she had ceased to pluck, thinking what the hell. Dark brown eyes, somewhat concealed (*good*) by heavy-framed glasses. Long, dead-straight hair, once black as tar, now quite evenly grey.[6]

Morag and her image are one. Unlike Rachel, Stacey and Hagar, the older Morag has the "more enviable mirror [self] image."[7]

For the "wordsmith," only through words can one come to terms with one's experience and find a measure of grace. Writing for Morag is an act of faith. Unlike the others, Morag realizes that who she is depends on more than what the mirror offers. She has a sense both of rootedness and freedom, not of limitation. Now she watches rivers, for her mirror is the river of time and memory, flowing "both ways."

The Diviners is a figural narrative akin to Joyce's *A Portrait of an Artist as a Young Man.* Although told in the third person, we see the world through the eyes of one character. As Clara Thomas writes, "we are captured by the illusion of Morag describing herself."[8] The difference between the experiencing and the experienced Morag is conveyed not through the manipulation of point-of-view, but through a consistent alteration of tense: past tense for the "present" or older Morag and present tense for the "past" or younger Morag.

The Diviners is a portrait of the artist on both its narrative levels. The younger Morag who eventually writes novels is portrayed by an older Morag writing a novel about her. The "Memorybank Movies" are in fact Morag's novel complete with chapter titles.[9] The first begins as Morag contemplates the last snapshot and "the totally invented memories" (p. 10). We move from a static photographic mode to a dynamic cinematic one. Appropriately, and somewhat ironically, this first Memorybank Movie opens like all "fairy tales": "*Once upon a time there was.*" It ends:

> Morag does not look back, but she hears the metallic clank
> of the farm gate being shut. Closed. (p. 17)

There is another ending: it is not the lives but the deaths of Morag's parents which are remembered and so it is the deaths which are recorded. Her parents remain "*Two sepia shadows on an old snapshot . . .*" (p. 18) and both the child and the writer hear the gate shut. "Home" is a concept which will be examined again and again as Morag seeks to re-establish that first lost home.[10]

Just as Morag sorts the snapshots into chronological order: "As though there were really any chronological order, or any order at all . . ." (p. 6), so, too, novelist Morag orders her material, the Memorybank Movies. Morag's "novel," her reconstruction of the past, is always ordered according to what she now knows. Just as she has been shaped by her past, she, in turn, shapes it to reflect what she has learned. The young experiencing Morag is unaware of a larger pattern, but the novelist selects and orders her memories because she has, in retrospect, perceived their importance. For Morag, aesthetic order is a way of resolving, through knowledge, her past.

The Tempest functions in The Diviners as another image of closure. Shakespeare's last complete play, written when he was approximately forty-seven and commonly taken as his farewell to his own art, concerns the artist, "the monster and magician of a thousand masks."[11] Morag, too, at the age of forty-seven is bidding farewell to her art. The young Morag chooses the theme of The Tempest for her novel, Prospero's Child, and describes it in a letter to Ella:

> It's called Prospero's Child, she being the young woman who marries His Excellency, the Governor of some island in some ocean very far south, and who virtually worships him and then who has to go to the opposite extreme and reject nearly everything about him, at least for a time, in order to become her own person . . . I've always wondered if Prospero really would be able to give up his magical advantages once and for all, as he intends to do at the end of The Tempest. That incredibly moving statement — "What strength I have's mine own/Which is most faint —" If only he can hang onto that knowledge, that would be true strength. And the recognition that his real enemy is despair within, and that he stands in need of grace, like everyone else . . . (p. 330)

Morag is speaking as much of herself, her "Black Celt" and her art, as she is The Tempest. She has rejected her Prospero, Brooke, and spurned the seclusion of "The Tower," an island in itself. She is now menaced by Chas, the brutal Caliban, and learns the price of becoming "her own person." As an artist, however, she hasn't yet reached the point where she will decide to give up her "magical advantages." Yet the reference to The Tempest foreshadows that time. As an image of closure, therefore, The Tempest works in a number of ways: Morag's life with Brooke has ended, but her career as an artist is just beginning; nevertheless, the image of the lone Prospero at the end of The Tempest prefigures the image of Morag at the end of The Diviners.

The young Morag, however, is still seeking islands. The letter to Ella ends with Morag's desire "to find a home, a real one," to visit Britain (another island) as "a kind of centre of writing," and to see Sutherland "where my people came from" (p. 331). Morag's "quest for islands" and "need for pilgrimages" is detailed in the movie sequence which begins, appropriately, with "Sceptr'd Isle." In the painter Dan McRaith, she recognizes a kindred restlessness, but she also sees Dan's best work is done not in London, but at his home in

Crombruach. He "'can't work anywhere else . . . It's the place that's important'" (p. 388) to him. She doesn't need to go to Sutherland after all for: "'The myths are my reality.'"

> "It's a deep land here, all right . . . But it's not mine, except a long long way back. I always thought it was the land of my ancestors, but it is not." (pp. 390-1)

Morag's home is "'Christie's real country. Where I was born'" (p. 391). The "Sceptr'd Isle" is not her artistic home nor the "Black Isle" her ancestral one. She returns to Canada, first to Manawaka to make her peace with Christie, and then to found her own home, the farm at McConnell's Landing.

> Land. A river. Log house nearly a century old, built by great pioneering couple, Simon and Sarah Cooper. History. Ancestors. (p. 414)

At McConnell's Landing, she is still thinking of islands:

> Morag, terrified of cities, comes out here, making this her place, her island . . . I've made an island. Are islands real? . . .Islands are unreal . . . Islands exist only in the head. And yet I stay. (p. 356)

It is then that Morag sees the Great Blue Heron:

> . . . A slow unhurried takeoff, the vast wings spreading, the slender elongated legs gracefully folding up under the creature's body. Like a pterodactyl, like an angel, like something out of the world's dawn . . . (p. 357)

In the vision of the heron, Morag glimpses the perfection she has been seeking in her life and art: certainty, serenity, mastery. The heron symbolizes wholeness, the cycle of life and death.

> That evening, Morag began to see that here and now was not, after all, an island. Her quest for islands had ended some time ago, and her need to make pilgrimages had led her back here. (p. 357)

I think that this is what led Clara Thomas to see in this vision an image of closure: "It is finally an image of acceptance and affirmation, central to the resolution of The Diviners and to the final and cumulative meaning of the Manawaka novels."[12]

The Manawaka books form a roman-fleuve and The Diviners consciously and effectively pulls them all together. "Margaret Laurence has said that she would like the five Manawaka works to be read, essentially, as one work."[13] In *The Diviners*, this intention is reflected in the reappearance and development of characters from the other Manawaka books. Echoes of *The Stone Angel* act in precisely this way, because *The Diviners* is concerned with the capacity of language to "get it right," to communicate and understand one's time and place. These echoes reverberate not only on thematic and structural planes, but also on a linguistic level. Certain key words in *The Stone Angel*, "bless," "release," and "mourning," become key words in *The Diviners*, modified by their new emotional context. These words have an extended meaning precisely because they recall *The Stone Angel*. The proud recalcitrant Hagar dying in her hospital bed reluctantly bestows her final blessing on her dutiful son, Marvin:

> Now it seems to me he is truly Jacob, gripping with all his strength, and bargaining. *I will not let thee go, except thou bless me.* And I see I am thus strangely cast, and perhaps have been so from the beginning, and can only release myself by releasing him.
>
> . . .
>
> "You've not been cranky, Marvin. You've been good to me, always. A better son than John."[14]

In *The Diviners* Morag returns from Britain to Manawaka and sits at Christie's hospital deathbed:

> "Christie — I used to fight a lot with you, Christie, but you've been my father to me."
>
> . . .
>
> "Well — I'm blessed," Christie Logan says. (p. 396)

When Hagar tries to recall "something totally free" she has done in ninety years, she thinks of the "lie" she told Marvin, "yet not a lie, for it was spoken at least and at last with what may perhaps be a kind of love."[15] Her selfless speech releases her from the petrifying bonds of pride. The roles are reversed in *The Diviners* where the living bless the dying. Morag acknowledges her debt to Christie as ancestor and first diviner, tale-spinner. He has given her "a place to stand on."[16] She has completed another "rite of passage" in the long journey home.

Hagar's dying wish is fulfilled in *The Diviners*:

> If I could, I'd like to have a piper play a pibroch over my grave. *Flowers of the Forest* — is that a pibroch?[17]

Morag hires a piper to play:

> . . . "The Flowers of the Forest," the long-ago pibroch, the
> lament for the dead, over Christie Logan's grave. And only
> now is Morag released into her mourning. (p. 403)

Until her encounter with Murray Lees, Hagar's concern for "proper
appearances" prevented her from being "released into her mourning"
for her dead, Bram and John. Only now at ninety does she see it
might have been otherwise. Like Hagar, Morag is a survivor. But she
has come to terms with her past to accept it and "be at peace with the
dead."[18]

Objects also migrate from one book to another. Hagar's clan pin
finds a home with Morag. Morag trades Jules his father's knife for
the Currie pin. Thus these ancestral objects are restored to those for
whom they still have power as talismans. And Pique will inherit
both knife and pin. Clan Gunn did not have a crest or coat-of-arms,
so Morag "adopts" the plaid pin with its war cry "Gainsay Who
Dare," a fitting cry for Morag, writer and inheritor.

Margaret Laurence's earlier Manawaka novels close with images
of continuance. *A Jest of God* ends with flight and promise. The bus
carrying Rachel and her mother to Vancouver "flies" along like a
"great owl through the darkness . . . What will happen . . . The
wind will bear me . . . Anything may happen, where I'm going."[19]
The Fire-Dwellers ends with a hesitant movement away from the
circles of hell. Stacey "feels the city receding as she slides into sleep.
Will it return tomorrow?"[20] *The Stone Angel* closes with "And then
. . ."[21] Hagar is dead but the novel is nonetheless open-ended.

The Diviners' last images are of closure. Royland, the old water-
diviner, accepts the loss of his powers. Yet the ability can be passed
on: ". . . quite a few people can learn to do it" (p. 452). This is what
Morag learns from Royland:

> The inheritors. Was this, finally and at last, what Morag
> had always sensed she had to learn from the old man? She
> had known it all along, but not really known. The gift, or
> portion of grace, or whatever it was, was finally withdrawn,
> to be given to someone else. (p. 452)

As Royland says, "'it's not a matter for mourning.' 'I see that now,'
Morag said."

Morag can both accept that her "gift" is "withdrawn" and that
others will continue the work; Pique will both sing Jules' songs and
create her own.[22] The natural process, the river, the willows chang-

ing with the seasons, the swallows and Canada geese, the generations who must find their own home and past, continue. Laurence affirms a larger pattern. Renewal intensifies Morag's personal sense of an ending.

This fulfills the theme of the novel introduced by the reference to *The Tempest.* Prospero-like, Morag is ready to give up her "magical advantages." We see the full implication of Prospero's last speech, "What strength I have's mine own,/Which is most faint." That knowledge, that "true strength," is now Morag's.

The last section of *The Diviners* bears the title of the whole and parallels the first called: "River of Now and Then." We have come full circle, with the river flowing "both ways":

> Look ahead into the past, and back into the future, until the silence. (p. 453)

The decisive difference between the opening and closing is in this word "silence." Morag's journey culminates in the renunciation of her art. What is completed in *The Diviners* is the struggle to understand and define a past. Morag's "silence" is full of the understanding she has achieved and the legacy she leaves. The last sentence of *The Diviners* is a fitting conclusion for all the Manawaka novels:

> Morag returned to the house, to write the remaining private and fictional words, and to set down her title. (p. 453)

Appendix

We are never explicitly told that Morag's movies form the chapters of the novel she is writing, but there are many hints. Morag explores her past as she writes about it. As Laurence states:

> For a writer, one way of discovering oneself, of changing from the patterns of childhood and adolescence to those of adulthood, lies through the exploration inherent in the writing itself . . . this exploration involves an attempt to understand one's background and one's past . . .[23]

Because Morag is writing about the past, she interprets, orders, changes, and imagines it. An early Memorybank Movie sequence is prefaced by Morag sitting down to work:

Alone, Morag sat still for another half-hour before she
could bring herself to get out the notebook and begin.
(p. 60)

But before the movie begins, i.e. before she actually begins to
write, in a section deliberately set off by italics and the use of the first
person, we move inside Morag's, the writer's mind:

A popular misconception is that we can't change the past —
everyone is constantly changing their own past, recalling it,
revising it. What really happened? A meaningless question.
But one I keep trying to answer, knowing there is no answer.
(p. 60)

Morag, the writer, ponders and directs her work and Laurence,
through her artifice, allows us to witness the thoughts of a writer
before, as it were, they are set down in fiction. Chapter Five opens
with Morag sitting down at the kitchen table "with a notebook in
front of her and a ballpoint pen in her hand" (p. 169).

Last night, sleepless until three a.m., long and stupen-
dously vivid scenes unfolded. Too tired to get up and write
them down, she still couldn't shut the projector off for the
night. Got up and jotted down key words, to remind her.
Staring at these key words now, she wondered what in
heaven's name they had been meant to unlock.
Jerusalem. Jerusalem? Why? Gone. What had she meant
by it? (p. 169)

"Jerusalem" is a key word for Morag only in the novel she is
writing and it is in that novel (the Memorybank Movies) that its
meaning is unlocked. A long series of movies is followed by "Work
over for the day" (p. 231). In Donald Cameron's interview with
Laurence, while she was working on The Diviners, she affirms,
"When I say 'work,' I only mean writing."[24] And in The Diviners "the
only meaning the word work had for her was writing" (p. 98).
Abrupt interruptions of the movies and a return to the present
Morag are always interruptions of Morag's writing:

"Hi, Ma. You working?"
. . .
"I'm not sure," Morag said, untruthfully, because she had
been. (p. 349)

The highly personal nature of her text worries Morag. She tells Pique, "'. . . I don't know if I'll want it published when it's finished'" (pp. 349-50). A long movie sequence is followed by writer's cramp (p. 404). Finally, the end of the Memorybank Movies heralds the end of *The Diviners*. The narrative levels merge and all that is left to Morag is "to set down her title."

Notes

[1] Bernice Lever, "Margaret Laurence Interview," *Waves*, 3, No. 2 (1975), p. 6.

[2] Leona Gom, "Margaret Laurence and the First Person," *Dalhousie Review*, 55 (1975), p. 241. Gom develops this motif more fully.

[3] Margaret Laurence, *A Jest of God* (1966; rpt. Toronto: New Canadian Library, 1974), p. 16. Hereafter cited as *JG*.

[4] *JG*, p. 17.

[5] Margaret Laurence, *The Stone Angel* (1964; rpt. Toronto: New Canadian Library, 1968), p. 38. Hereinafter cited as *SA*.

[6] Margaret Laurence, *The Diviners* (1974; rpt. Toronto: Bantam Books, 1975), p. 28. Hereinafter cited parenthetically.

[7] Gom, p. 244.

[8] Clara Thomas, *The Manawaka World of Margaret Laurence* (1975; rpt. Toronto: New Canadian Library, 1976), p. 134.

[9] This reading is not generally acknowledged. Only Leona Gom in her article "Laurence and the Use of Memory" (*Canadian Literature*, 71, p. 51) unequivocally declares "that the novel on which Morag is working is actually a verbal transcription of the movies she is playing." A few critics hint at this possibility. Clara Thomas in *The Manawaka World* comes very close when she says that "it is the very essence of Morag, the writer, that she remembers her past as stories" (p. 162) and again, "We are given the dramatized, 'fictionalized' Morag in the Memorybank Movies" (p. 171).

Bruce Salvatore in his review of *The Diviners* seems somewhat surprised by the notion: "Indeed, the end of the novel suggests that the book Morag is writing is *The Diviners*" (*Chelsea Journal*, 1, p. 38).

But most critics see the Memorybank Movies merely as moments of reminiscence and do not make the connection with Morag's novel. Barbara Hehner, for example, while asserting that *The Diviners* "uses the most sophisticated technique Laurence has yet attempted" nonetheless finds it "obtrusive" (*Canadian Literature*, 74, p. 41). She states that "Morag is not *really* telling us her own story. Similarly, Memorybank Movies are substituted for a smooth transition into reverie, because no one has memories so detailed and complete, with all past conversations intact" (p. 52).

I certainly do not believe that the Memorybank Movies act as an extended series of "substitutions." "Why Morag is a writer is not apparent" to Marge Piercy (William New, ed., *Margaret Laurence* (Toronto: McGraw-Hill-Ryerson, 1977), p. 212). Allan Bevan regards the Memorybank Movies only as "various selected episodes that throw light on Morag's wrestling with herself" (New, p. 217).

My interpretation is not central to the argument of this paper, but as there seems to be some problem over the function of the Memorybank Movies, I have attached a brief appendix presenting some of the "evidence" for seeing the movies as Morag's novel.

[10] Clara Thomas finds that *The Diviners* "incorporates many of the traditional epic techniques . . . To achieve a final pattern, Margaret Laurence has gone back to the epic, that most spacious of literary genres" (*Manawaka World*, p. 169). Within this larger structure, Thomas recognizes the "'Contained Epic' — the search for home" (p. 169). Morag has lost her Eden. Through her art, she attempts to regain it. In her novel about the journey of Piper Gunn and his people, she approaches only the *Shadow of Eden*. She hasn't yet regained paradise; that is the province of *The Diviners*.

[11] Henry James, "The Tempest," *Selected Literary Criticism*, ed. Morris Shapiro (New York: Horizon Press, 1964), p. 300.

[12] Thomas, *The Manawaka World*, p. 156.

[13] Thomas, p. 131.

[14] *SA*, p. 304.

[15] *SA*, p. 307.

[16] Margaret Laurence, "A Place to Stand On," *Heart of a Stranger* (Toronto: McClelland and Stewart 1976), pp. 13-18. "A Place to Stand On" was originally written in 1970 and titled "Sources" (it is reprinted in New's anthology under that title). As Laurence says in her brief introduction, it "deals both with my debt to African writers and my concepts of a writer's source." She quotes the lines from Al Purdy's poem, "Roblin Mills Circa 1842," which became the epigraph to *The Diviners:*

> but they had their being once
> and left a place to stand on

For the reader of *The Diviners*, *Heart of a Stranger* holds a special fascination as many of the essays reflect the themes of *The Diviners:* a writer's sources, survival, the imperialist subjugation of a native people, pilgrimage, ancestors, the river, home, "where one belongs and why."

[17] *SA*, p. 306.

[18] Laurence, *Heart of a Stranger*, p. 14.

[19] *JG*, p. 201.

[20] Laurence, *The Fire-Dwellers* (1969; rpt. Toronto: New Canadian Library, 1973), p. 308.

[21] *SA*, p. 308.

[22] Morag's career as a novelist is ending. This ending is intensified by Laurence's statements that she felt *The Diviners* to be not only her last Manawaka book, but her last novel. Many critics report this decision, but I assume that it originated in Margaret Atwood's article which first appeared in *Macleans* in May, 1974. Laurence tells Atwood: "I don't think I'll ever write another novel. It's not because I don't want to. I just have this knowledge, it's sort of a Celtic second sight — I always had it about my books — and I just don't think I will" (New, p. 40). *The Diviners* may not be Laurence's last book (rumour has it that she is in fact writing another novel); it nevertheless reflects a personal ending.

[23] Margaret Laurence, *Heart of a Stranger*, p. 13.

[24] Donald Cameron, *Conversations with Canadian Novelists* (Toronto: Macmillan, 1973), p. 101.

MYTH AND MANITOBA IN *THE DIVINERS*

Clara Thomas

For the past eight years, since she came back to Canada in 1969 as Writer-in-Residence at the University of Toronto, Margaret Laurence's work has been two-fold. Tens of thousands of people have read her books, and these will remain her timeless achievements in literature. Thousands of people have also heard her speak. Neither her readers nor her audiences could possibly doubt the sincerity of her convictions about Canadian nationality.

Since 1969 she has spoken on hundreds of occasions to clubs, classes and seminars, in public lectures and at university convocations. She has a powerful public presence, developed through intense self-discipline, for the solitude of writing, not the spot-light of speaking, is her natural preference. But from a sense of mission, she has made herself available to groups of all ages. Anyone who has watched her with students knows that her presence operates on them with the force of a benign psychic phenomenon. Always her message centres around the importance of our literature as a necessary foundation-link with generations of Canadians in the past, with one another in the present and with all the generations of the future.

Speaking at Simon Fraser's Convocation in the spring of 1977, she reiterated the convictions that are basic to her.

> The calibre and scope of our literature now is such that it can be read and taught simply because it is interesting, worth reading and worth teaching. But for us it has an added dimension as well. It is our own; it speaks to us, through its many and varied voices, of things which are close to our hearts; it links with our ancestors and with one another . . . [we do] have a great need to possess our own land, to know our own heritage, to value ourselves in relation to a world community.[1]

The words "ancestors" and "heritage" are keystones in that statement and their importance to individuals and communities is a basic premise in all of Laurence's work, the early *Tomorrow-Tamer* stories and the Ghana-set novel, *This Side Jordan*, as well as each of the five Canadian works. Her Scotch-Irish tradition and family background, her experiences in Somaliland, in the emergent nation of Ghana, and later with the great group of writers who first celebrated the independence of Nigeria, the strength of her own roots in Manitoba and her deep involvement in Canadian cultural nationalism, all these have combined to convince her that a writer's opportunity and responsibility includes weaving the past of his place and his people into a "a feeling of our own people, of our place of belonging . . . It is important to know that we all come from different sources, originally, but that in this diversity lies our true strength as a people".[2]

In a conversation with Irving Layton in 1970 she first recorded her belief in the close interweaving of history and myth in our literature.

> People like my grandfather, or like the character of Hazard Lepage in *Stud-Horse Man* . . . — These people are our myths. This is our history. And perhaps not consciously, but after awhile consciously, this is what we are trying to set down.[3]

In *The Diviners*, the most complicated and structurally complex of her novels, she writes out in full the process of Morag Gunn's education into her personal and cultural heritage — by implication the need of every child. To the adult Morag, remembering, her awareness widened in well-marked stages, from her early acceptance of outside authority to her revolt against it and finally to her confidence in her own inner integrity and sufficiency. The authority of Christie's voice, of the printed word, of the conventions of Manawaka, of her own age group, and of Brooke Skelton, is finally replaced by her own authority and her own truth. Similarly, Morag finally knows where her place is. She has escaped the town of Manawaka, but she carries it with her always. The true land of her ancestors is, finally, "Christie's real country. Where I was born."[4] As Laurence knows that writers must work out of their own roots in place and time, so for her both personal identity and nationality begin with place and region — any literature must, in this sense, reach the universal through first being local.

Christie Logan shows Morag the two large books of Ossian when she is twelve years old. In the narrative sequence of *The Diviners*, this incident occurs between Christie's telling of the first and second tales of Piper Gunn. This is a signal to the reader of one of Laurence's intents in *The Diviners*, the offering of an extended lesson on the transference of folk-lore into literature, history into myth and these into the development of a child. It happens when Morag is well into the hands of the public school system. — The printed word, not Christie's voice, has become her authority. When he finds her copying out Wordsworth's "Daffodils" (a poem which has become a cliché for British educational imperialism, especially as practised on children of the tropics who never saw a daffodil), Christie counters with his copy of James Macpherson's *Ossianic Poems*, a printed authority that he recognizes.

> "In the days long long ago," Christie says sternly, "he lived, this man, and was the greatest song-maker of them all, and all this was set down years later, pieced together from what old men and old women remembered, see, them living on far crofts hither and yon, and they sang and recited these poems as they had been handed down over the generations. And the English claimed as how these were not the real old songs, but only forgeries, do you see, and you can read about it right here in this part which is called Introduction but the English were bloody liars then as now. And I'll read you what he said, then, a bit of it." (p. 63)

There is a mountainous literature on James Macpherson and the probable authorship of the *Ossianic Poems*. Amongst all the controversy that has raged since their publication in 1760, however, no one has been able to deny their power and influence, not only in Scotland, but in Europe and America as well. Andrew Hook, a recent cultural historian, is well aware of these far-reaching effects, whatever the poems' ratio between folk-lore and individual imagination may have been.

> Genuine or fraudulent, a product of the Gaelic bardic tradition, or an artificial literary exercise, there is a note in these poems which found a response in contemporary readers everywhere, and which lingers there for the unprejudiced reader of today. Beneath the posturing and the rhetoric, the artificiality of language and style, there it remains: the elegiac note which so often characterizes a great epic poem, the lament for an age, a civilization that is passing, for the old way and the old way's order, which the present is destroying.[5]

In Margaret Laurence's work, however, this reference to Ossian indicates far more than nostalgia and regret. As her Manawaka heroines come to know that they carry their place and their past with them always, so it is one of Laurence's deepest beliefs that this is inevitable for everyone. The point of the past is its active function in our present, not a vanished reference point on which to focus fond nostalgia, resentment or regret. The book of Ossian in *The Diviners* thus signifies a printed authority that by itself is simply an artifact of the past. Transmitted through Christie to Morag, however, the work becomes a dynamic factor in Morag's search for her own identity. The sight of the books of Ossian, the mystery of their Gaelic and Christie's reading of the passage describing the great chariot of Cuchullin unlock Morag's imagination to a far, mysterious horizon and bring a proud community of the past right into her present. When, later, she writes in her scribbler about the chariot built by Piper Gunn's woman, she patriates it into her own setting:

the front shaped like a ship and a bird
birchbark scrolls around the sides
carvings of deer and foxes and bears
carvings of meadowlarks
carvings of tall grasses
carvings of spruce trees and spruce cones. (p. 86)

This chariot, developing in Morag's imagination from the Chariot of Cuchullin, is now part of her myth; and we, the readers, have been offered a lesson in myth's on-going, dynamic function in the development of the individual.

From the very first of Christie's tales, their function and power as myth are signalled in the text of The Diviners. Like all folk-literature, these stories, in the beginning, are orally transmitted; only some folk-literature, however, moves into the category of myth, and this depends on the need and belief of the listener. The tales of Piper Gunn are told to Morag to explain and illuminate her background and to engage and support her belief in her family's and her own pride and honour. When she accepts them they become, for her, powerful myths. She bases her identity on them and she acts out of her trust that they are a part of her.

Structurally, Margaret Laurence achieves her purpose with precision and finesse. There are three mythic sets woven into The Diviners: Christie's tales, which give Morag her distant past and also make her own father a hero and which she later passes on to Pique with the addition of Christie's own story; Jules (Skinner) Tonnerre's tales, told to Morag by Skinner, later passed on to their daughter with the addition both of the songs that Jules, personally, passes on to Pique and of Pique's own song; and the adult Morag's half-playful, half-serious myth-making of Catharine Parr Traill.

The sequences in which Morag hears Christie's tales and then Jules' tales begin with the child's own need. The first tale of Piper Gunn is featured in Morag's Memorybank Movies when she is nine though she knows that Christie had told her the tale before that. He is drinking red biddy and declaiming the valour of his Logan ancestors. *The Clans and Tartans of Scotland*, one of his four treasured books, is printed evidence of his ancestors' greatness, but there is nothing in it about the Gunns to give Morag pride: "When she first looked it up, she showed it to Christie, and he read it and then he laughed and asked her if she had not been told the tales about the most famous Gunn of all, and so he told her" (p. 48). This first tale is the story of the great Piper and his woman, Morag, who inspired the displaced Sutherlanders with his music and gave them the courage to endure and survive.

> What happened, then, to all of them people there homeless on the rocks? They rose and followed! Yes, they rose, then, and they followed, for Piper Gunn's music could put the heart into them and they would have followed him all the way to hell or to heaven with the sound of the pipes in their ears.
>
> And that was how they all came to this country, all that bunch, and they ended up at the Red River, and that is another story. (p. 51)

When she goes to bed after this first story, Morag tells herself her own tale of Piper Gunn's woman, Morag, and falls asleep comforted by a bravery that she begins to identify with herself: *Forests cannot hurt me because I have the power and the second sight and the good eye and the strength of conviction"* (p. 52).

Morag is twelve when Christie reads to her from the book of Ossian and they look at the Gaelic, "the strange words, unknown now, lost, as it seems, to all men" (p. 65). Shortly after, she and Skinner meet in the Nuisance Grounds and she begins to see that brushing him out of her mind with "he isn't anybody" is wrong. He, too, has a tradition behind him. It includes two hero-ancestors from long ago, his grandfather, Jules, and Chevalier "Rider" Tonnerre, and his tradition, too, involves a strange language. When she boasts of Piper Gunn he retaliates with some brief references to his two heroes, but he won't tell her his stories.

Christie's *Tale of Piper Gunn and the Long March* is next recorded. Morag is still in public school and as Christie talks she interrupts with questions and she also begins to doubt ("They walked? A *thousand* miles? They couldn't, Christie.") (p. 85). This tale tells of the march of the Sutherlanders, led by Piper Gunn and inspired by Morag, his woman: *"If we must live here in this almighty godfor-*

saken land, dreadful with all manner of beasts and ice and the rocks harsher than them we left, says Gunn's woman, *at least let's be piped onto it"* (p. 84). This story is about Manitoba and Morag is curious about its details, especially, out of her dawning respect for Skinner Tonnerre, about the halfbreeds: "(Did they fight the halfbreeds and Indians, Christie?) Did they ever? Slew them in their dozens, girl. In their scores. (Were they bad, the breeds and them?) What?" (p. 86).

Christie's first two tales have given Morag two heroic ancestors, Piper Gunn and his wife, Morag. It is after this second one, set in Manitoba, that Morag writes down her description of the chariot, built in the woods by the Red River, that the first Morag built for Piper, their child and herself. At this time, too, Morag starts a story about Clowny Macpherson, "A little scrawny guy" who was really very tough. She is intuitively and imaginatively beginning to fuse Christie's bardic role with the ancient bard's in Ossian.

At this time also Christie brings the tales of her ancestry right down to her own father and his heroism at the Battle of Bourlon Wood in World War I. This is set off by his accidental finding of his regimental book, *The 60th Canadian Field Artillery Book.* Again, this story answers Morag's need. Christie cannot identify her father's picture in the group and his memories of the action cannot tally with the book's bare prose: "Oh Jesus . . . don't they make it sound like a Sunday School picnic? . . . Well, d'you see, it was like the book says, but it wasn't like that, also. That is the strangeness" (p. 90). What Christie can do and does do is to make her father, Colin, into a hero for her: "Your dad saved my life that one time, then" (p. 89).

This is a hard story for Christie to tell and he only goes on with it as Morag urges him. She would like to have the book for herself but Christie keeps that. Instead he gives her the hunting knife that "some young twirp of a kid" had traded him for a package of cigarettes. Margaret Laurence has symbolically joined Morag to the Tonnerres by that knife. A reader who knows *The Stone Angel* knows that John Shipley traded his mother's plaid pin to Lazarus Tonnerre for the knife.   In the textual sequence of *The Diviners,* the adult Morag's first conversation with Catharine Parr Traill comes next. This is myth-making with a difference. Where the child Morag needed ancestors to admire, trust and function as her models, the adult Morag needs a kind of friendly adversary against whom to test the strength of her own identity and resolve. Beyond this, Morag's communings with Catharine Parr Traill are humorous in their tone, providing a leavener for Morag's anxieties and a periodic lightening to the tone of her anxious self-examination. In terms of Margaret

Laurence's illumination of the functions of history and myth, oral literature and written literature, however, the Traill-Morag episodes offer another level of instruction to the reader. Laurence is keenly aware of the authority invested in the printed word; she has already shown herself to be equally aware of its limitations ("It was like the book says, but it wasn't like that also. That is the strangeness").

To Margaret Laurence as to many of us, Catharine Parr Traill stands as the epitome of the benign, pioneer matriarch, "drawing and naming wildflowers, writing a guide for settlers with one hand, whilst rearing a brace of young and working like a galley slave with the other" (p. 95). Our evidence for Mrs. Traill's all-encompassing serenity and competence rests on her own printed books. When Morag, desperately anxious about Pique, finds "the pertinent text," she reads: "In cases of emergency, it is folly to fold one's hands and sit down to bewail in abject terror. It is better to be up and doing" (p. 97). In their ensuing dialogue, Morag honours the achievement of Catharine Traill, but she also argues the difference in her own situation: "*You* try having your own child disappear you know not where, Mrs. Traill. Also, with no strong or even feeble shoulder upon which to lean, on occasion" (p. 97).

The printed word, Laurence is saying — any printed word — must not be taken as authority in itself. It can be inspiration, it can also provide example, but in itself it must be recognized as inert. Only through translation into the needs and actions of its recipient can it become a dynamic and positive force. Therefore, Mrs. Traill is "lady of blessed memory" to Morag and subsequently "St. Catharine," but her canonization is done in affectionate and knowing irony: Morag's problems are ultimately to be resolved out of her own and no one else's strength.

There is another factor active in Catharine Traill's intermittent presence in the text of The Diviners. The adult Morag has moved to McConnell's Landing in Ontario and there she intends to stay. It is part of Margaret Laurence's own belief that to become truly a part of the place — any place — it is necessary to assimilate that place's history into one's own consciousness. This Morag does through the person of Catharine Traill and the pioneer tradition that she represents. It is a far different tradition from the Manitoba past that Christie's and Skinner's tales represent, but it is equally necessary to the process of Morag's new patriation.

Christie tells his third and last tale, "Piper Gunn and the Rebels," to Morag when she is fifteen, troubled and sexually frustrated by her meeting with Skinner in the valley and in need of comfort. Christie is surprised when she asks him for one of the stories he used to tell her: "Great Jumping Jesus, Morag, I thought you would've been past all of that" (p. 129), and Morag has gone beyond questioning to correcting his facts. This is the story of how the Sutherlanders were roused by Piper Gunn's music to take the fort and save their farmland from "Reel and his gang of halfbreeds." The story has lost its authority for her and she defends Riel and the Métis. Her thanks to Christie is a token only — he was right, she really is "past all that."

Morag hears Skinner's stories after they have fumblingly come together in his shack down in the valley: "But he puts an arm around her, and they walk the chill mudcarpeted streets beside the empty trees and the quiet half-dark houses, and he tells her. Stories for children" (p. 142). The next day, Skinner goes overseas with the Cameron Highlanders. After Dieppe, when Morag does not find his name among the long list of casualties from Manawaka, she tells herself his stories. It is here in the text that Lazarus' "Tale of Rider Tonnerre," "Rider Tonnerre and the Prophets," and "Old Jules and the War Out West" are recorded. The sequence ends with a fourth heading, "Skinner's Tale of Dieppe?", but no story follows. Now, when she is eighteen and ready to leave Manawaka for university, Morag possesses the tales of the two traditions. At this time, on the brink of adulthood, she also violently rejects them all.

Morag's passage from innocence to experience is, in one sense, gradually marked in the text, with her recollection of many incidents which hurt her and forced her growth ("Morag is twelve and is she ever tough"), and a few incidents, such as Christie's story-telling, which were a benign support to her growth. But her violent propulsion into the adult world comes with her experience of reporting the fire in the valley for Lachlan and the Manawaka *Banner*. After seeing the pitiful ruins of the shack where Piquette and her children died and watching the men, including Lazarus, carry out their charred remains, the world is all tragic cruelty for Morag: ". . . she puts her head down on the desk and cries in a way she does not remember ever having done before, as though pain were the only condition of human life" (p. 161). When next Christie starts ranting about his family and their proud past she rejects it all, not with rage, but with a weary, cynical hopelessness. All that is meaningless, she thinks, in the face of the awful reality she has seen and she stops Christie when he begins to explain to her why he used to tell her the old tales.

"What does it matter, Christie? It was all so long ago."

The Gunns have no crest, no motto, no war cry, at least
according to what it says in the old book Christie still hauls
out from time to time. Just as well. It's all a load of old
manure. (p. 162)

This is Morag's *non serviam*. She is going to leave Manawaka
"and I'm never coming back." All the past, her life with Christie and
Prin, her life in the town, the tales of her ancestors, are being shed
like an old skin and the new Morag will be free. Through the years of
her adult life, however, she will, reluctantly at first and then
thankfully, come to realize that she is not free, nor can she be, nor
does she want to be. And the past — all of it, including both her tales
and Jules' tales, — she will come to accept for what it must be to
her if she is to grow and if she is to give her daughter, Pique, the
myths she needs in order to grow.

So far, the story of the young Morag as recalled by the adult
Morag has been faithful to the basic conventions of the initiation-
novel. In *The Diviners*, however, the second part of the novel is as
carefully and explicitly charted as the first. Morag's reconstruction of
her past affirms a step-by-step growth to integration and acceptance
of herself and her place that is a world away from Huck Finn's
lighting out for the territories or *Lady Oracle's* compulsive escape-
artistry, or even Dunstan Ramsay's restless avoidance of social commitment and responsibility until very late in his life.[6]

She had to leave Manawaka in order to grow and, eventually, to
understand where she had been. She had to reject, temporarily, the
myths that had strengthened her childhood growth in order to learn
to understand them in a new way. After ten years of marriage, she
has to leave Brooke and the deepest reason for this is that she has
already grown in her understanding beyond the point at which he
first found her — the stage in which he needs and wishes her to remain. Even before her marriage, when she had gone back to
Manawaka for a few days, Prin had told her another version of what
happened to Colin and Christie at Bourlon Wood and she had begun
to understand what Christie had done for her.

Colin Gunn. Christie's tale of Gunner Gunn and the Great
War. How Colin saved Christie, staved off his dying, that
time away out there, on that corner of some foreign field
that is forever nowhere. It hadn't happened that way, then,
or probably not. It had happened the way Prin said. Christie
holding Colin in his arms. Colin probably eighteen. Eigh-

teen. Amid the shelllfire and the barbwire and the mud, crying. (p. 206)

As Christie and Morag talk later, Christie adds another element of
puzzle to be considered in her journey towards recovery from the
total rejection of all the past that she had vowed.

" . . . look here, it's a bloody good thing you've got away
from this dump. So just shut your goddamn trap and thank
your lucky stars."
"Do you really think that, Christie?"
"I do," Christie says, knocking back the whiskey. "And
also I don't. That's the way it goes. It'll all go along with
you, too. That goes without saying."
But it has been said. *The way it goes — it'll all go — that
goes.* Does Christie bring in these echoes knowingly, or does
it just happen naturally with him? She has never known. (p.
207)

Though at this point Morag denies that Christie is right, she has
already taken a step towards acceptance and understanding. When
she goes home to Prin's funeral she wants to ask Christie to tell all
the old tales to her but cannot, and when she goes back to Brooke
she rebels against the child-woman role that she has played with him.

"It's too bad you had to go back to the town this last
time," Brooke said. "You had effectively forgotten it. Now
it's all risen up again, and it's only upsetting you, Morag.
Can't you simply put it from mind?"
"I never forgot any of it. It was always there."
"When you first came to me," Brooke says, "you said you
had no past. I liked that. It was as though everything was
starting for you, right then, that moment. (p. 257)

Morag gradually comes to understand that Christie had made a
world of innocence for her and peopled it with heroes to answer her
needs. Her painful passage to experience began a complementary
process in which initial rejection of the heroes was only a clearing of
the ground before moving towards an adult's acceptance, understanding and positive use of the past. She moves from the need for heroes
to the recognition that endurance and community of spirit are the
true legacies of the past on which present generations must build.
Christie's comforting of Colin Gunn and his care for Morag; Lazarus'
indomitable "I'm going in, they're mine, there, them," at the time of

the fire, do not eradicate the heroic figure of Piper Gunn. That she
will always possess too. But her understanding both of the past and
its continuing presence and of her own responsibilities to it, to her
present and to the future, modulates and broadens.

With the advent of Pique, the pattern begins to repeat itself, this time
with a double heritage for the child and with Morag conscious of her
function as a selector and shaper of the past for her daughter.

> . . . Lazarus at the fire, Lazarus, snarling his pain, a stranger
> in the place where he lived his whole life. Lazarus, dead at fifty-
> one. Will Morag tell Pique all she knows of Lazarus, or of
> Christie, for that matter? How will the tales change in the tell-
> ing? (p. 338)

Jules visits Morag and Pique, when Pique is five, and again when she
is fifteen. On the first occasion, he sings his ballad for his grandfather,
Jules, and on the second, his songs for his father, Lazarus, and for
Piquette, his sister. Meanwhile, Morag has told her Christie's and
Lazarus' stories as well as the stories of Piper Gunn. Pique has her
mythic inheritance by the time she is fifteen. Because of the patterning of
the text, the alternating rhythm between Morag's present situation and
her memories, and because in the present time of the text Pique is a
young adult, we are shown her movement from childish acceptance to
questioning as a parallel movement to Morag's own remembered
development. At twenty-one Pique has it all but, like her mother at the
same stage, she questions its meaning to her.

> ". . . I never knew what really happened. There was only
> that one time, when my Dad was here — when I was fifteen,
> eh? And he said a lot of things. And the songs — I've got those.
> And he said some more, when I saw him in Toronto, this time.
> But some of those stories you used to tell me when I was a kid
> — I never knew if they happened like that or not."
> "Some did and some didn't, I guess. It doesn't matter a
> damn. Don't you see?"
> "No," Pique said, "I don't see. I want to know what really
> happened." (p. 350)

Morag comes into full, final adult understanding of the importance
of the myths to her and of Christie's dynamic part in giving them to her
when she and Pique visit Dan McRaith in Scotland. As she looks across
the sea to Sutherland, where she has always dreamed of going to find
her people, she knows, finally, that her own place is "Christie's real
country" (p. 391). Before Christie dies she is able to tell him that he has

been her father to her, to hear his reply, "Well — I'm blessed" (p. 396), and to give him the funeral that draws together all that he has given her both as father and as bard, the source of her ancestral inheritance.

> He swings the pipes up, and there is the low mutter of the drones. Then he begins, pacing the hillside as he plays. And Morag sees, with the strength of conviction, that this is Christie's true burial.
> *And Piper Gunn, he was a great tall man, with the voice of drums and the heart of a child, and the gall of a thousand, and the strength of conviction.*
> The piper plays "The Flowers of the Forest," the long-ago pibroch, the lament for the dead, over Christie Logan's grave. And only now is Morag released into her mourning. (p. 403)

Immediately after this in the sequence of the text, Morag releases herself from her half-humourous, half-serious connection with Catharine Parr Traill. She recognizes and claims her house and garden as her own, listing and naming its weeds and finally repudiating her imagined inferiority to the archetypal lady-pioneer.

> ". . . I'm going to stop feeling guilty that I'll never be as hardworking or knowledgeable or all-round terrific as you were . . . this place is some kind of a garden, nonetheless, even though it may be only a wildflower garden. It's needed, and not only by me. I'm about to quit worrying about not being either an old or a new pioneer. So farewell, sweet saint — henceforth I summon you not." (p. 406)

Margaret Laurence has demonstrated that for Morag, the functions of myth have been to give her strength to develop into her own person, to find her own place and finally, to rest easy in it. For Pique, as the book ends, her inheritance is sending her back to Galloping Mountain, to find out whether or not her place is there with Jules' brother Jacques and the family commune of the Tonnerres. Pique has achieved a greater degree of maturity at this stage than Morag had known at a similar age. Pique is without the bitterness that Morag carried with her from Manawaka; unlike the young Morag in Winnipeg, Pique does not hide her heritage but is eager to explore it; most important of all, at this early age Pique has already reconciled her heritage and put it into her own song.

> There's a valley holds my name, now I know
> In the tales they used to tell it seemed so low

There's a valley way down there
I used to dream it like a prayer
And my fathers, they lived there long ago.

. . .

I came to taste the dust out on a prairie road
My childhood thoughts were heavy on me like a load
But I left behind my fear
When I found those ghosts were near
Leadin' me back to that home I never knowed. (pp. 440-1)

In the text of *The Diviners* Margaret Laurence has, of course, written down the stories that were orally transmitted by Christie and Jules to Morag and by Morag to Pique, as well as the songs that Jules sang to Pique and Pique to Morag. Through Morag's writing as well as through her own, Margaret Laurence also demonstrates the carrying of the past into the present through literature. *Shadow of Eden*, Morag's fourth novel, is finished after she and Pique have come to McConnell's Landing and it too is the story of the highland clearances and the emigration of the Sutherlanders to the Red River. Writing to Ella Gerson after her book is finished, Morag indicates the intertwining of her myth and the facts of history into her fiction.

. . . The man who led them on that march, and on the trip by water to Red River was young Archie Macdonald, but in my mind the piper who played them on will always be that giant of a man, Piper Gunn, who probably never lived in so-called real life, but who lives forever. (p. 418)

The passing on of the authentic heritage of their people is a central preoccupation of writers of to-day, particularly of writers of the post-colonial nations. Laurence of Canada, Walcott of the West Indies, Soyinka and Achebe of Nigeria — these are preeminent among writers who accept a strong social and political, as well as artistic, responsibility in writing out of their own culture and primarily for their own people. Among contemporary Canadian novelists, Rudy Wiebe and Dave Godfrey are probably closest to Laurence in their interpretation of this challenge and responsibility. For Laurence, as for the others, a native Canadian literary tradition in no sense negates or ignores the total and continuing stream of all literature in the past and in the present.

Margaret Laurence's work is markedly "literary" in the conventional sense — *The Diviners*, for instance, is permeated with references to and resonances of *Paradise Lost, Paradise Regained* and *Samson Agonistes*. All of her work is also, of course, enriched by the spirit, the language and the rhythms of the Bible. But she is predominantly engaged in writing out of the experience of Canadians and in their accustomed speech patterns.

For her this begins in Manitoba. Until *The Diviners* it was possible to miss the uniquely Manitoban element in her work, for the town of Manawaka was not as relentlessly regionalized as was, for instance, Sinclair Ross's Saskatchewan town of Horizon. With the background of the Sutherlanders and the Métis, however, Morag's youth is unmistakably set in a Manitoba that has been given historical — and in Laurence's hand — mythological depth. She is very close to the historian, W. L. Morton, in what she has tried to do for her native province, beginning with the local and ultimately transcending it in her work.

There are many congruences between the works of W. L. Morton and Margaret Laurence, not only in the ideal towards which they write, but also in the circumstances of their careers. Professor Morton left the University of Manitoba to become Master of Champlain College at Trent University in Peterborough; while there he wrote an epilogue to his earlier *Manitoba: A History* (1957). Margaret Laurence returned from ten years in England to settle in Lakefield near Peterborough, and in *The Diviners*, set on the Otonabee nearby, Morag recalls and reconstructs her youth in Manitoba. In his *Manitoba: A History* Morton wrote of the Selkirk Settlers and the Métis society with a passion of understanding and sympathy that Laurence shares and develops in her personalized treatment of the Sutherlanders and the Tonnerres. To Morton, the historian and the novelist each have a myth-making function and responsibility and their basic problem is identical:

> The difficulty was to reconcile a landscape actually seen and realistically experienced with an internal landscape formed by reading. How could these be brought into a single, authentic vision in which neither would deny, but rather clarify the other? . . . I wanted, I think, that as the wilderness landscape had been remade by axe and plough into a cultivated landscape, that raw new landscape should be made into a human landscape of heightened tone and enriched association. I desired it to be seen not only as it could be seen, but as it might be seen.[7]

Margaret Laurence has expressed her sense of a common aim with Morton's in these words:

> I did in fact read, for the first time, Morton's *Manitoba: A History*, the summer that I began writing the first draft of *The Diviners*. I had, of course, read quite a lot of prairie history previously, but Morton's history gave me not only a great many facts that I needed (although few of these were actually used in the novel) but also a sense of the sweep of history, the overview which I think I share. I found this to be especially true of those parts of the history which deal with the Métis people. I subsequently had many conversations with him about the nature of writing history and fiction. I believe . . . as I think he does, too . . . that the two disciplines are very much related. The historian, like the novelist, must be selective and must necessarily write his own interpretation of the historical era with which he is dealing. The novelist (at least, this is true in my own case) seeks to bring characters to life as much as possible and to place these individuals within the historical context of their time and place. What I think I share, most of all, with Morton is the sense of my *place*, the prairies, and of my *people* (meaning all prairie peoples) within the context of their many and varied histories, and the desire to make all these things come alive in the reader's mind.[8]

Carl Berger speaks of Morton's wish "for a history of the West written with such fidelity to the inner texture of experience and so evocative of the sense of place that it would immediately trigger a recognition in those who had been molded by that history."[9] In *Manitoba: A History* Morton achieved the goal and the resolution that he strove for; in *The Diviners*, Margaret Laurence assimilated Morton's work with her own experience and past of her people to achieve her goal. They are the writers who, more than any others, have given Manitoba a powerful historic and mythic identity.

Notes

[1] *Simon Fraser University Week*, 8, no. 5, Spring, 1977.
[2] *Ibid.*
[3] "A Conversation about Literature: An Interview with Margaret Laurence and Irving Layton," *Journal of Canadian Fiction*, 1, no. 1, Winter, 1972. pp. 65-68.

⁴ Margaret Laurence, *The Diviners* (Toronto: Bantam, 1975) p. 391. All further
references to this edition are found parenthetically in the text.
⁵ Andrew Hook, *Scotland and America 1750-1835* (Edinburgh: Blackie, 1975), p.
119.
⁶ Wilfred Cude, "'False as Harlots' Oaths': Dunny Ramsay Looks At Huck Finn,"
Studies in Canadian Literature, II, no. 2, Summer 1977, pp. 164-187.
⁷ W. L. Morton, "Seeing an Unliterary Landscape," *Mosaic*, 33, 1970, pp. 7-8.
⁸ Correspondence with Clara Thomas, October 17, 1977
⁹ Carl Berger, *The Writing of Canadian History* (Toronto: Oxford University Press,
1976), p. 246.

ALICE MUNRO

ALICE MUNRO AND THE AMERICAN SOUTH

J.R. (Tim) Struthers

As a girl, Alice Munro lived in Huron County in rural Southwestern Ontario, and, after a twenty-year residence in Vancouver and Victoria from 1952 to 1972, she returned to live in Southwestern Ontario. In an interview with Graeme Gibson, Munro remarked that:

> . . . the writers who first excited me were the writers of the American South, because I felt there a country being depicted that was like my own. I can think of several writers now who are working out of Southwestern Ontario. It is rich in possibilities in this way. I mean the part of the country I come from is absolutely Gothic. You can't get it all down.[1]

Munro has discussed the relationship between the American South and her own country in greater detail with Mari Stainsby:

> If I'm a regional writer, the region I'm writing about has many things in common with the American South.
> *Your area is south Ontario.*
> RURAL Ontario. A closed rural society with a pretty homogeneous Scotch-Irish racial strain going slowly to decay.[2]

Thinkers like Allen Tate have recognized the individual, regional character of the dominant white society of the American South during the first part of the twentieth century and have sought to identify the features which defined it. Among these characteristics, which were reflected in the region's literature and which in turn impressed outsiders like Alice Munro, were:

i) the decay of an order, or what Tate, in a seminal essay entitled "The Profession of Letters in the South," called "the conflict between modernism and fundamentalism [which] is chiefly the impact of the new middle-class civilization upon the rural society;"[3]

ii) an almost religious belief in the land and in the old verities, the humanistic values, which it symbolized;

iii) a respect for family allegiances;

iv) a concern for manners and a commitment to a code of honour;

v) pride in race, religion, and class;

vi) a deep religious belief, marked by a sense of sin and a profound awareness of the Bible;

vii) a fusion of religious belief and social and political practice;
viii) a distinct sensitivity to the bizarre and the grotesque;
ix) a strong sense of the past and of the viability of tradition.
Several of these characteristics of the American South correspond
to the aspects of rural Ontario identified by Munro in the interviews
with Graeme Gibson and Mari Stainsby, and almost all of the rest
are equally applicable to rural Ontario, the location of most of
Munro's fiction. In "Heirs of the Living Body," the second section of
Lives of Girls & Women, Munro depicts the efforts of Del Jordan's
Uncle Craig to record his family tree and the history of Wawanash
County. Respect for the family and a sense of the past, two of the
most important features listed, are as essential here as they were to
Faulkner in his genealogies and history of Yoknapatawpha County.

Many of the features which defined the dominant white society of
the American South during the first part of the twentieth century
were characteristic of the blacks as well. It would be interesting to
expand the present comparison to include an investigation of possible further relationships between the American South and rural Ontario based on black and Indian experiences, over a longer period of
time, in the two places. A comparison of the societies and art of the
American South and of rural Ontario would somewhat resemble
Max Dorsinville's recent study of the cultures and novels of black
America and Quebec, *Caliban Without Prospero*.[4] Dorsinville's book
represents an admirable blend of imagination and careful, well-
digested research. Yet it is necessarily limited to a thematic and
psychological approach. Comparison of the art of the American
South and the art of rural Ontario, on the other hand, is more solidly
founded on the similarity of Scotch-Irish settlement patterns and the
intellectual patterns which they can determine.[5]

The profound influence of the writers of the American South on
Alice Munro rests on Munro's sense of kinship between the American South and rural Southwestern Ontario. On one level, their influence on Munro exists in terms of literary form. *Lives of Girls &
Women* has been called another collection of short stories, a story-
sequence, or a story-cycle; however, it may best be described as one
of a fairly wide-ranging variety of "open forms," organized books of
prose fiction made up of autonomous units which take on extra
resonance and significance when combined with other related units.
Such "open forms" are ones to which short story writers are especially attracted and which are usually created by the revising and the
structuring of separately composed, and sometimes previously published, short stories. Each organic whole which results has a greater

effect than one might expect a simple combination of its parts to have, since an "open form" is more unified than any miscellaneous collection of short stories by a single author, and as unified as, though formally different from, anything clearly describable as a novel.

Key works in this literary tradition of "open forms" are James Joyce's *Dubliners*, Sherwood Anderson's *Winesburg, Ohio*, and, in particular, two works by Southern writers, William Faulkner's *Go Down, Moses* and Eudora Welty's *The Golden Apples*.[6] The structure of *Go Down, Moses*, which was published in 1942, consists in moving twice from the past to the present, from "Was" to "Pantaloon in Black," then from "The Old People" (which opens, quite biblically, with "At first there was nothing"[7]) to the contemporary events of the concluding title story. *The Golden Apples*, which was published in 1949, is structured along the temporal axis of three generations. Its openness lies in having seven individually entitled sections told from different points of view.

As Eudora Welty moved from writing short stories and novellas to *The Golden Apples*, so Alice Munro moved from her first book, *Dance Of The Happy Shades*, a somewhat unified and loosely structured collection of short stories, to *Lives of Girls & Women*. The close similarity between the open, yet organically unified, structure of *The Golden Apples* and the structure of *Lives of Girls & Women* is largely the result of Alice Munro's natural inclination as an artist, not of any deliberate imitation of Welty's work: "I wouldn't say that I was conscious of the *structure* being modelled on hers . . . It wasn't really *modelled* but I have to acknowledge an enormous debt to her . . . I think more in this matter of vision."[8] Of course, Munro did know that this structure had worked, for she has spoken of *The Golden Apples* as one of her very favourite works of fiction.

Instead of the multiple points of view in *The Golden Apples*, Munro, in writing her second book, *Lives of Girls & Women*, elected to emphasize a single character. In this, *Lives of Girls & Women* is like James Joyce's *Stephen Hero* and *A Portrait of the Artist as a Young Man*, which succeeded his unified collection of short stories just as *Lives of Girls & Women* followed *Dance Of The Happy Shades*. Once again, however, Munro has adapted her inheritance. *Lives of Girls & Women* is distinct from the aforementioned books by Joyce, Anderson, Faulkner, and Welty, in that it is presented from a first-person feminine point of view. (In this and many other features, *Lives of Girls & Women* and Margaret Laurence's *A Bird in the House*, which was published a year earlier, in 1970, are remarkably

alike.) The unity of *Lives of Girls & Women*, then, arises from
Munro's focusing on the single consciousness of Del Jordan. *Lives of
Girls & Women* is a self-portrait of a young woman as a young artist
in rural Southwestern Ontario. *Lives of Girls & Women* is a
photographer's own documentary.

The title which Alice Munro originally chose for her second book
is suggestive: "I like the title of my next book, though, but nobody
else does. *Real Life*."[9] In a single description of real life, Munro can
evoke the complex moods of an entire story. Perhaps her most effective example of this kind of writing occurs in "The Time Of Death,"
which appears in *Dance Of The Happy Shades*. The story, as told by
an omniscient narrator, presents various responses to the death by
fire of eighteen-month-old Benny Parry. Then, at the close of the
story, we are offered the following sad, haunting description:

> There was this house, and the other wooden houses that had
> never been painted, with their steep patched roofs and their
> narrow, slanting porches, the wood-smoke coming out of
> their chimneys and dim children's faces pressed against their
> windows. Behind them there was the strip of earth, plowed
> in some places, run to grass in others, full of stones, and
> behind this the pine trees, not very tall. In front were the
> yards, the dead gardens, the grey highway running out from
> town. The snow came, falling slowly, evenly, between the
> highway and the houses and the pine trees, falling in big
> flakes at first and then in smaller and smaller flakes that did
> not melt on the hard furrows, the rock of the earth.[10]

This passage exemplifies Munro's characteristic adoption of a
straight, documentary style, her absolute rejection of the tendency of
many photographers to manipulate images. Here, in prose fiction,
she has presented a still photograph which, with the final detail of
the snowfall, evolves into a film.

Alice Munro possesses a visual or photographic imagination. She
has illustrated this fact in an interview with Kem Murch sometime
after the publication in 1974 of her third book, *Something I've Been
Meaning To Tell You*:

> K.M.: How do you remember the details of people's tics,
> speech patterns, walk and stride, dress, weather, shadows?
> Do you take notes daily or do they just come to you while
> you're writing?
> MUNRO: They just come to me when I'm writing. It's a

kind of seeing. Last year I saw a black-and-white photo of
my high school class that was taken in grade 10, and I *did*
remember the colour of everyone's clothes.[11]

In the attempt to create in prose fiction the effect of documentary
photography, Alice Munro was deeply influenced by James Agee and
Walker Evans. In a conversation with John Metcalf, Alice Munro
had already answered questions about literary influences on her
work and was discussing various painters when she interjected: "I
forgot to tell you a writer who influenced me enormously. It's James
. . . I think it's pronounced . . . Agee?" Metcalf replied: "The *Death
in the Family* man?", but Munro returned to answering his current
question.[12]

Munro's liking for *A Death in the Family*, and particularly for a
favourite scene in which Agee described the privacy which the young
boy and his father share while sitting on a limestone rock looking
across the darkness at the lights of North Knoxville, has been suggested by Munro's presentation of a comparable scene in "Walker
Brothers Cowboy," the opening story of *Dance Of The Happy
Shades*, where the young girl walks down to Lake Huron with her
father, sits with him on the rock-hard ground, gazes at the Lake, the
floats, the breakwater, and the lights of the town, and listens to her
father tell how the Great Lakes came to be. However, the work
which I suspect influenced Alice Munro as profoundly as Agee's
posthumously published novel *A Death in the Family* was the mon-
umental *Let Us Now Praise Famous Men*, the creation of two artists
— James Agee, journalist, and Walker Evans, photographer — from
their experience of living for several weeks in 1936 in Alabama with
three white, cotton tenant families. Agee insisted that the sixty-two
photographs by Evans which appear in *Let Us Now Praise Famous
Men* "are not illustrative. They, and the text, are coequal, mutually
independent, and fully collaborative."[13] The relationship between
photography and literature was central to Agee's aesthetic intention:

> I would further insist that it would do human beings, includ-
> ing artists, no harm to recognize this fact, and to bear it in
> mind in their seining of experience, and to come as closely as
> they may be able, to recording and reproducing it for its
> own, not for art's sake.
>
> One reason I so deeply care for the camera is just this. So
> far as it goes (which is, in its own realm, as absolute
> anyhow as the travelling distance of words or sound), and
> handled cleanly and literally in its own terms, as an ice-cold,

some ways limited, some ways more capable, eye, it is, like the phonograph record and like scientific instruments and unlike any other leverage of art, incapable of recording anything but absolute, dry truth.[14]

Agee's own enthusiastic description of the camera as an "eye" suggests the registration of an image of the object as object, a stylistic technique which he himself adopted in the purely documentary parts of *Let Us Now Praise Famous Men*. Yet, as Alfred T. Barson commented in *A Way Of Seeing*, *Let Us Now Praise Famous Men* is both an objective record and a personal response involving meditation, narration, association, and composition.[15] Its style, as Agee explained, is therefore varied:

But a part of my point is that experience offers itself in richness and variety and in many more terms than one and that it may therefore be wise to record it no less variously. Much of the time I shall want to tell of particulars very simply, in their own terms: but from any set of particulars it is possible and perhaps useful to generalize. In any case I am the sort of person who generalizes: and if for your own convenience and mine I left that out, I would be faking and artifacting right from the start.[16]

Consider, then, the similarity between Alice Munro's appetite for the details of the life and landscape of *rural* Southwestern Ontario and the precision at the beginning of Agee's section entitled "A Country Letter":

It is late in a summer night, in a room of a house set deep and solitary in the country; all in this house save myself are sleeping; I sit at a table, facing a partition wall; and I am looking at a lighted coal-oil lamp which stands on the table close to the wall, and just beyond the sleeping of my relaxed left hand; with my right hand I am from time to time writing, with a soft pencil, into a school-child's composition book; but just now, I am entirely focused on the lamp, and the light.[17]

Even Agee's diction, e.g. "focused," underlines his use of the camera-eye technique in this and other instances. (Here I am speaking of the registration of an image of the object as object. I am not alluding to "The Camera Eye" sections of John Dos Passos' *U.S.A.*, where, as Marshall McLuhan has said, "the development of one mind from childhood to maturity" is presented successively and "the author's political and social sense unfolds without comment."[18])

In *Let Us Now Praise Famous Men* there is a mutual dependence of subject, technique, and theme. As Agee explained, "The nominal subject is North American cotton tenantry as examined in the daily living of three representative white tenant families."[19] Yet, in truth, "the effort is to recognize the stature of a portion of unimagined existence, and to contrive techniques proper to its recording, communication, analysis, and defense. More essentially, this is an independent inquiry into certain normal predicaments of human divinity."[20] The theme is perception, the necessity of the recognition of the profound dignity of daily life. Agee's own feelings were, in a special sense, religious, and, for expressing his response, the camera-eye technique was insufficient:

> Here I must say, a little anyhow; what I can hardly hope to bear out in the record: that a house of simple people which stands empty and silent in the vast Southern country morning sunlight, and everything which on this morning in eternal space it by chance contains, all thus left open and defenseless to a reverent and cold-laboring spy, shines quietly forth such grandeur, such sorrowful holiness of its exactitudes in existence, as no human consciousness shall ever rightly perceive, far less impart to another: that there can be more beauty and more deep wonder in the standings and spacings of mute furnishings on a bare floor between the squaring bourns of walls than in any music ever made.[21]

It is the subject of *Real Life*, and the technique of the camera eye, but, more importantly, the theme that "everything that is is holy,"[22] as Agee said, echoing Blake, which so "enormously"[23] influenced Alice Munro. Her excitement for her subject was expressed in answering questions by John Metcalf:

> METCALF: . . . It seems that in all your writing you *glory* in the surfaces and textures. I don't know how to put this question to you without sounding philosophical or pompous but do you feel "surfaces" not to *be* surfaces?
> MUNRO: Yes. Yes. I know exactly what you mean. I feel that everything . . . Yes. I don't know how to answer your question without sounding pompous or . . . pseudo-mystical . . . It's very easy to sound this way when you're trying to explain what you feel about the way things look and the

tones in people's voices . . . and . . . it's probably . . .
there's this kind of magic . . . you know . . . about
everything.
METCALF: Is that a religious feeling on your part?
MUNRO: No. No. It's just an intense . . . well at least I
don't identify it as a religious feeling. It's just a feeling about
the intensity of what is *there*.[24]

Alice Munro shares this awareness not only with James Agee and
Walker Evans, but also with Eudora Welty. In *Lives of Girls &
Women*, Del thought:

It often seemed then that nobody else knew what really went
on, or what a person was, but me. For instance people said
"poor Mary Agnes" or implied it, by a drop in pitch, a sub-
dued protective tone of voice, as if she had no secrets, no
place of her own, and that was not true.[25]

The identical perception was expressed by Welty in *The Golden Apples:*

What Miss Eckhart might have told them a long time ago was
that there was more than the ear could bear to hear or the
eye to see, even in her.[26]

Such perceptions were stimulated by Welty's early experiences as a
photographer. Her first full-time job was with the Works Progress Ad-
ministration from 1933 to 1936. As publicity agent, junior grade, for
the State office, she travelled throughout the eighty-two counties of
Mississippi during the Depression. In 1971, Welty published *One
Time, One Place*, a collection of one hundred of the several hundred
photographs which she had taken on her own incentive, not for the
W.P.A., at that time. In travelling and in taking these photographs,
Welty, in her own words, was able "to see widely and at close hand
and really for the first time the nature of the place I'd been born into."[27]

Out of this experience came a lifelong desire which Welty would
seek to fulfill in writing fiction:

In my own case, a fuller awareness of what I needed to find
out about people and their lives had to be sought for through
another way, through writing stories. But away off one day
up in Tishomingo County, I knew this, anyway: that my
wish, indeed my continuing passion, would be not to point
the finger in judgment but to part a curtain, that invisible
shadow that falls between people, the veil of indifference to

each other's presence, each other's wonder, each other's human plight.[28]

As a photographer, Welty first learned to celebrate the dignity of the individual and of daily life:

> When a heroic face like that of the woman in the buttoned sweater — who I think must come first in this book — looks back at me from her picture, what I respond to now, just as I did the first time, is not the Depression, not the Black, not the South, not even the perennially sorry state of the whole world, but the story of her life in her face. . .Her face to me is full of meaning more truthful and more terrible and, I think, more noble than any generalization about people could have prepared me for or could describe for me now.[29]

Welty's experience as a photographer not only produced the dominant vision of her fiction, but also contributed a complementary technique, the Joycean epiphany:

> I learned quickly enough when to click the shutter, but what I was becoming aware of more slowly was a story-writer's truth: the thing to wait on, to reach there in time for, is the moment in which people reveal themselves.[30]

Welty discussed the close relationship between photography and literature in a magazine article entitled "Literature and the Lens,"[31] which she wrote before *The Golden Apples*. Like Agee, Welty took photographs with words:

> A red and bottle-shaped chimney held up all. The roof spread falling to the front, the porch came around the side leaning on the curve, where it hung with bannisters gone, like a cliff in a serial at the Bijou. Instead of cowboys in danger, Miss Jefferson Moody's chickens wandered over there from across the way, flapped over the edge, and found the shade cooler, the dust fluffier to sit in, and the worms thicker under that blackening floor.[32]

Like the closing description in Alice Munro's story "The Time Of Death," this passage from *The Golden Apples* is a still photograph which begins to move. The romance world of "cowboys in danger" is debunked by the realistic film of Miss Jefferson Moody's chickens, a film which Welty has presented through words. The exotic and gem-like qualities suggested by the name of the Bijou Theater are equally unrealistic in Morgana, Mississippi. This gentle and humorous irony is shared with Welty by Alice Munro, as seen in Munro's naming of towns — "Jubilee" in *Lives of Girls & Women*, and "Mock Hill" in "Something I've Been Meaning To Tell You," the introductory, title story from her second collection.

Alice Munro added an "Epilogue: The Photographer" to *Lives of Girls & Women*. Munro's choice of the photographer as a metaphor for the writer was an appropriate testimony to the enormous influence of James Agee and Walker Evans, creators of *Let Us Now Praise Famous Men*, and of Eudora Welty, author of "Literature and the Lens," *The Golden Apples*, and *One Time, One Place: Mississippi in the Depression/A Snapshot Album*.

In *Lives of Girls & Women*, when Del was still in high school, she had already recognized "that the only thing to do with my life was to write a novel."[33] In the novel which she began to construct in her imagination, a man known simply as *"The Photographer"*[34] visited the high school. His photographs of the region were false. They distorted life, instead of revealing it. The pictures he took turned out to be unusual, even frightening:

> People saw that in his pictures they had aged twenty or thirty years. Middle-aged people saw in their own features the terrible, growing, inescapable likeness of their dead parents; young fresh girls and men showed what gaunt or dulled or stupid faces they would have when they were fifty. Brides looked pregnant, children adenoidal.[35]

These fictive photographs are akin to those by Diane Arbus, about whose work and sensibility Susan Sontag has remarked:

> The camera has the power to catch so-called normal people in such a way as to make them look abnormal. The photographer chooses oddity, chases it, frames it, develops it, titles it. . . . The insistent sameness of Arbus's work, however far she ranges from her prototypical subjects [i.e. freaks], shows that her sensibility, armed with a camera, could insinuate anguish, kinkiness, mental illness with any subject.[36]

Like her imagined photographer, Del "changed Jubilee, too, or picked out some features of it and ignored others."[37] Her immature creation was unreal, grotesque:

> People in it were very thin, like Caroline, or fat as bubbles. Their speech was subtle and evasive and bizarrely stupid; their platitudes crackled with madness.[38]

In contrast, Del's Uncle Craig, whose household furnishings included several normal, commemorative photographs, had worked painstakingly at establishing his true family tree and at setting down the exact history of Wawanash County. The supposedly unremarkable actions of his family were precisely what made the family tree worthwhile to Uncle Craig. Similarly, in his history of Wawanash County, he did not value the "modest disasters" and the "three notable people;" rather:

> . . . it was daily life that mattered. Uncle Craig's files and drawers were full of newspaper clippings, letters, containing descriptions of the weather, an account of a runaway horse, lists of those present at funerals, a great accumulation of the most ordinary facts, which it was his business to get in order. Everything had to go into his history, to make it the whole history of Wawanash County. He could not leave anything out. That was why, when he died, he had only got as far as the year 1909.[39]

Much later, Del comments:

> It did not occur to me then that one day I would be so greedy for Jubilee. Voracious and misguided as Uncle Craig out at Jenkin's Bend, writing his History, I would want to write things down.[40]

As a fully mature artist, Del would strive, in the world of words, to be a true documentary photographer. Her aim in her art, like Walker Evans', would be to have:

> . . . every last thing, every layer of speech and thought, stroke of light on bark or walls, every smell, pothole, pain, crack, delusion, held still and held together — radiant, everlasting.[41]

Del's aim is being fulfilled by her creator, Alice Munro, who, in the final, climactic section of her second collection of short stories, *Something I've Been Meaning to Tell You*, emphasizes once again the essential relationship between photography and her own fictional style:

> Now I look at what I have done and it is like a series of snapshots, like the brownish snapshots with fancy borders that my parents' old camera used to take. In these snapshots Aunt Dodie and Uncle James and even Aunt Lena, even her chil-

dren, come out clear enough. . . . The problem, the only
problem, is my mother. And she is the one of course that I
am trying to get; it is to reach her that this whole journey has
been undertaken. With what purpose? To mark her off, to
describe, to illumine, to celebrate, to *get rid* of, her; and it did
not work, for she looms too close, just as she always did. She
is heavy as always, she weighs everything down, and yet she
is indistinct, her edges melt and flow.[42]

Notes

[1] *Eleven Canadian Novelists*, interviewed by Graeme Gibson (Toronto: Anansi, 1973), p. 248.
[2] "Alice Munro Talks With Mari Stainsby," *British Columbia Library Quarterly*, 35 (July 1971), 29-30.
[3] Allen Tate, "The Profession of Letters in the South," in his *Essays of Four Decades* (Chicago: Swallow Press, 1968), p. 521.
[4] Max Dorsinville, *Caliban Without Prospero* (Erin, Ontario: Press Porcépic, 1974).
[5] See John Kenneth Galbraith, *The Non-Potable Scotch: A Memoir on the Clansmen in Canada* (Harmondsworth: Penguin Books, 1967).
[6] Some might add Erskine Caldwell's *Georgia Boy* to this list; however, it lacks the structural unity and importance of the other works.
[7] William Faulkner, *Go Down, Moses* (New York: The Modern Library, 1942), p. 163.
[8] John Metcalf, "A Conversation With Alice Munro," *Journal of Canadian Fiction*, 1 (Fall 1972), 57.
[9] "Alice Munro Talks With Mari Stainsby," *British Columbia Library Quarterly*, 35 (July 1971), 30.
[10] Alice Munro, "The Time Of Death," in her *Dance Of The Happy Shades* (Toronto: McGraw-Hill Ryerson, 1968), p. 99.
[11] Kem Murch, "Name: Alice Munro. Occupation: Writer," *Chatelaine*, Aug. 1975, p. 70.
[12] John Metcalf, "A Conversation With Alice Munro," *Journal of Canadian Fiction*, 1 (Fall 1972), 57.
[13] James Agee and Walker Evans, *Let Us Now Praise Famous Men* (Boston: Houghton Mifflin, 1960), xv/xv. The page number following the diagonal refers to the Ballantine paperback edition.
[14] *Ibid.*, pp. 233-234/pp. 210-211.
[15] Alfred T. Barson, *A Way of Seeing: A Critical Study of James Agee* ([Amherst]: University of Massachusetts Press, 1972), pp. 78, 88-89.
[16] Agee and Evans, pp. 244-245/pp. 220-221.
[17] *Ibid.*, p. 49/p. 47.
[18] Marshall McLuhan, "John Dos Passos: Technique vs. Sensibility," in *Don Passos, the Critics, and the Writer's Intention*, ed. Allen Belkind (Carbondale: Southern Illinois University Press, 1971), pp. 234, 237.
[19] Agee and Evans, xiv/xiv.
[20] *Ibid.*
[21] *Ibid.*, p. 134/p. 121.

[22] *Ibid.*, p. 459/p. 418.

[23] John Metcalf, "A Conversation With Alice Munro," *Journal of Canadian Fiction*, 1 (Fall 1972), 57.

[24] *Ibid.*, 56.

[25] Alice Munro, *Lives of Girls & Women* (Toronto: McGraw-Hill Ryerson, 1971), p. 45/p. 38. The page number following the diagonal refers to the New American Library paperback edition.

[26] Eudora Welty, *The Golden Apples* (New York: Harcourt, Brace & World, 1949), p. 50/p. 57. The page number following the diagonal refers to the Harvest Books paperback edition.

[27] Eudora Welty, *One Time, One Place: Mississippi in the Depression/A Snapshot Album* (New York: Random House, 1971), p. 3.

[28] *Ibid.*, p. 8.

[29] *Ibid.*, p. 7.

[30] *Ibid.*, pp. 7-8.

[31] Eudora Welty, "Literature and the Lens," *Vogue*, 1 Aug. 1944, pp. 102-103.

[32] Eudora Welty, *The Golden Apples*, pp. 18-19/p. 21.

[33] Alice Munro, *Lives of Girls & Women*, p. 244/p. 203.

[34] *Ibid.*, p. 246/p. 205.

[35] *Ibid.*, p. 246-247/p. 205.

[36] Susan Sontag, *On Photography* (New York: Farrar, Straus & Giroux, 1977), p. 34.

[37] Alice Munro, *Lives of Girls & Women*, p. 247/p. 205.

[38] *Ibid.*, p. 247/pp. 205-206.

[39] *Ibid.*, pp. 31-32/p. 27.

[40] *Ibid.*, p. 253/p. 210.

[41] *Ibid.*

[42] Alice Munro, "The Ottawa Valley," in her *Something I've Been Meaning To Tell You* (Toronto: McGraw-Hill Ryerson, 1974), p. 246/p. 197. The page number following the diagonal refers to the New American Library paperback edition.

An early version of "Alice Munro and the American South" was read at the Canadian Association of American Studies conference at Ottawa in October, 1974. A revised version was published in *The Canadian Review Of American Studies* and won the first annual Marston LaFrance Memorial Award. The article is reprinted here with additional revisions by the author.

LIVES OF GIRLS AND WOMEN:
A CREATIVE SEARCH FOR COMPLETION
Miriam Packer

Del Jordan's pain and her moments of triumph, in *Lives of Girls and Women*, are related, not only to the trials of growing up female in an oppressive environment, but also to the development of her artistic vision. She aspires to both the social recognition that her mother wants and the sense of simple passive contentment which her maiden aunts appear to have — and still more. She needs sexual and creative fulfillment. One is reminded of Morag's words in *The Diviners*: "All I want is everything."

Models for Del's ideal of completion are not to be found among the girls and women in Jubilee. Where, from her perspective, are the women who do not feel burdened by, or cut off from, their bodies, women who live the whole cycle of life? It seems to me that Munro shows Del learning what she does *not* want to be, and formulating values in response which will enable her to live more fully than the women around her manage to do. At the novel's close, a developed sensibility is yet to come. Munro implies, however, that it is as inevitable as Del's need to come back to Jubilee, artistically and psychologically, to recall its every detail.

Lives of Girls and Women tells the story of a hopeful child who becomes a lonely adolescent and moves slowly towards acceptance of her isolation and ultimately to a celebration of the complexity of experience and of her own imagination. The warmth and humour in the telling never cancel out the essential seriousness, but the seriousness is not overburdening.

It is important to examine the exact quality of the narrator's childhood and adolescence, her childish perceptions of the world and the subtle ways in which those perceptions are altered. The changes never occur suddenly or dramatically; there is no sudden flash of light, although the adolescent may sometimes feel there is. Nor are the changes ever final; there is always the sense of something more to be learned and of the possibility of going back to an earlier belief — the possibility of fluctuation, of altering tentative perceptions.

The novel is divided into eight chapters, each recording one phase or aspect of Del's life and each clearly suggesting that the phase has not yet been "completed," but only temporarily set aside. Del's mother is presented through Del's eyes in the first chapter, "The Flats Road," where she is living with her husband, her two small children, and "Uncle" Benny, the eccentric assistant to her fox-farmer husband. The mother is seen as being still reasonably content, at ease with her husband. We even get a glimpse, through the nine-year-old Del's eyes, of occasional girlish affection in her mother.

But the most prominent features of her mother are her dissatisfaction with her social status and her ambition to get away from the Flats Road. She yearns to live in Jubilee, a more respectable place, she believes. She insists on withdrawing herself psychologically from this community, as she will continue to do later, in others:

> My mother corrected me when I said we lived on the Flats Road; she said we lived *at the end* of the Flats Road, as if that made all the difference.[1]

Del notices her mother's severe judgment of her neighbours' "haphazard lives and contented ignorance," and her deliberate use of a lofty voice and conspicuously good grammar in their presence.

> My mother was not popular on the Flats Road . . . my father was different. Everybody liked him . . . He felt comfortable here . . . (p. 7)

Nevertheless, there is still a closeness between them on which the child thrives. That closeness is not to last long, but while it lasts, Del feels secure and warmed by it.

> My mother sat in her canvas chair and my father in a wooden one; they did not look at each other. But they were connected and this connection was plain as a fence, it was between us and Uncle Benny, us and the Flats Road, it would stay between us and anything. (p. 22)

It is important to recognize the sense of safety she derives simply from hearing her mother and father talking together below after she has gone upstairs to bed:

> They seemed to be talking playing cards, a long way away in a tiny spot of light, irrelevantly; yet this thought of them, prosaic as a hiccup, familiar as breath was what held me, what winked at me from the bottom of the well as I fell into sleep. (p. 23)

The child's simple need for security, and her belief in a magically peaceful world, is sustained by innocence and hope.

Del is informed about the quality of life through the outsiders in her environment as much as through her immediate family. Chapter I is in part devoted to "Uncle" Benny, an outcast, a collector of debris, living in an old house and given at times to strange, ecstatic utterances. Uncle Benny's world is a microcosm of another bewildering world. Unwittingly, he teaches Del and her brother some of the frightening truth about life.

> So lying alongside our world was Uncle Benny's world
> like a troubling distorting reflection, the same, but never at
> all the same. In that world, people could go down in quick-
> sand, be vanquished by ghosts or terrible ordinary cities;
> luck and wickedness were gigantic and unpredictable;
> nothing was deserved, anything might happen . . . It was his
> triumph, that he couldn't know about, to make us see.
> (p. 22)

Uncle Benny's world makes the shelter of Del's early life all the more comforting. As yet, the garrison is a sustaining place — not a prison at all. She has no need to escape it.

The chapter, "Heirs of the Living Body," is devoted to the two spinster aunts, and their influence on Del. The aunts have designed a world of their own and they are quite content in it, but Del notices particularly the limiting values which set them apart from life's opportunities. She sees how quick these two women are to mock any individual (and especially any female) attempt to improve, any ambition to be publicly recognized. Underneath is the fear of appearing foolish:

> *Didn't he think he was somebody?* That was their final
> condemnation, lightly said . . . Not that they were against
> ability. They acknowledged it in their own family. But it
> seemed the thing to do was to keep it more or less a secret.
> Ambition was what they were alarmed by, for to be am-
> bitious was to court failure and to risk making a fool of
> oneself . . .
>
> There it was, the mysterious and, to me, novel suggestion
> that choosing not to do things showed, in the end, more
> wisdom and self-respect than choosing to do them. They
> liked people turning down things that were offered, mar-
> riage, positions, opportunities, money . . . (p. 32)

The aunt's values are defensive; to turn things down is to avoid the risk of failure, but it is also, as Del feels, to court stagnation.

The mother, "Princess Ida" of the third chapter's title, cannot turn anything down. Driven by ambition, she has moved away with her

children to her much-coveted town, Jubilee, leaving her husband and
Uncle Benny behind. The men, and Del's brother, have become outsiders together.

Jubilee, the promised land, is "the fort in the wilderness . . . a
shelter and a mystery." The shelter is in what the narrator calls the
"open pattern of the town," its code, its defined mores, its system of
proper behaviour. The wilderness is in its "secret pattern," clearly the
hidden life the girl perceives. She likes the "intricate arrangement of
town life," but she misses both the security and the wildness which
she associates with the Flats Road, with the time when her mother
and father were together. Her choice of words suggests this nostalgia:

> I missed the nearness of the river and the swamp, also the
> real anarchy of winter, blizzards that shut us up tight in
> our house as if it were the Ark. (p. 59)

In Jubilee neither Del nor her mother is protected from the town's
snobbery. And she is exposed to the frightening realization that the
"connection" between her mother and father is broken. Del is hungry
for some sign of her mother's love for her father, for some
acknowledgement that the father has not been forgotten in her
mother's blind fight for social respectability. She remembers a painting her mother has left in their Flats Road home, and she asks her
mother about it:

> "That one? Do you want that in here?"
> I didn't really. As often in our conversations I was trying
> to lead her on, to get the answer or the revelation I par-
> ticularly wanted. I wanted her to say she had left it for my
> father. I remembered she had said once she had painted it for
> him, he was the one who liked that scene.
> "I don't want it hanging where people could see," she said.
> "I'm no artist. I only painted it because I had nothing to do."
> (p. 60)

In Jubilee, Del sees her mother again withdrawing as every tactic
for social acceptance fails. And she learns more about her mother's
life. The stories her mother tells are all of her own heroic struggle
against great odds, and always she is left alone, the plodding
Cinderella figure, fighting to get an education, status and her just
rewards.

> I was troubled here by a lack of proportion, though it was
> hard to say what was missing, what was wrong. In the

beginning of her story was dark captivity, suffering, then
daring and defiance and escape. Struggle, disappointment,
more struggle, godmothers and villains. Now I expected as
in all momentous satisfying stories — the burst of Glory, the
Reward. Marriage to my father? I hoped this was it. I
wished she would leave me in no doubt about it. (pp. 66-7)

Del gradually learns that Princess Ida is no princess; in fact, the
more her mother insists on acting like a princess, the more she loses
her basic dignity and her child's respect. On the Flats Road, Del's
mother still gave the child a sense of security and wholeness.

Then, I had supposed her powerful, a ruler, also content.
She had power still, but not so much as perhaps she
thought. And she was in no way content. Nor a priestess.
(p. 62)

Now, she humiliates Del by her fumbling public gestures, her lofty
letters to the Jubilee newspaper, her hypocritically "decorative
descriptions" of the Flats Road, the very "countryside from which
she had fled." Del is pained by her mother's malaise — her inability
to accept herself, to accept the present. Del is more isolated than
ever, torn between two unsatisfying approaches to life:

Other people than Aunt Elspeth and Aunt Grace would
say to me, "I seen that letter of your mother's in the paper,"
and I would feel how contemptuous, how superior and silent
and enviable they were, those people who all their lives
could stay still, with no need to do or say anything
remarkable.
I myself was not so different from my mother, but con-
cealed it, knowing what dangers there were. (p. 68)

Del is aware that she cannot identify with the aunts' and the
town's repressiveness, but she is not yet brave enough to assert her
individuality and to confront their contempt.

In "Age of Faith," Del turns to the church. Her testing of the world
of the spirit is motivated in part by the need to defy her mother and
in part by the need to integrate her adolescent and artistic perceptions with a larger plan, here a design of God. At first she goes to
church mostly to assert her separateness from her atheistic mother
and to perform for the watchful town, hoping that "people would be
intrigued . . . by my devoutness and persistence, knowing my
mother's beliefs or nonbeliefs, as they did." The town functions as an
audience.

Later, Del's motivations change. She becomes intrigued by the possibility of real faith and she switches from the United Church to the Anglican Church, which is more foreboding from her mother's point of view. She goes secretly, and is impressed by the ceremony, listening carefully, hoping for a "scent of God," inspired to know more about a life transcending the limitations of Jubilee:

> Saints' days made me think of something so different from Jubilee . . . all quiet, a world of tapestry, secure in faith. Safety. If God could be discovered, or recalled, everything would be safe. Then you would see things that I saw — just the dull grain of wood in the floor boards, the windows of plain glass filled with thin branches and snowy sky — and the strange anxious pain that just seeing things could create would be gone. It seemed plain to me that this was the only way the world could be borne, *the only way it could be borne* — if all these atoms, galaxies of atoms, were safe all the time, whirling away in God's mind. How could people rest, how could they even go on . . . until they were sure of this? They did go on, so they must be sure. (pp. 83-4)

Del's need for God is related to her need for safety and her own creative need. An adolescent, she is curious and frightened. Part of her pain is the pain of seeing, and the pain of being unable to communicate her unique vision to others. It is the pain of isolation — the artist's isolation as well as that of the frightened young girl who seeks for a "world of tapestry secure in faith."

Her involvement in the church is temporarily abandoned when her younger brother challenges her god. In his desperation to save his dog's life, he asks her to pray. Prayers, she realizes, will not stop her father from shooting the dog. God is clearly not be seen in such simplistic terms. The frustrated little boy hits out at Del:

> He swiped at me with his clenched fists . . . With the making of his prayer his face went through severely desperate, private grimaces, each of which seemed to me a reproach and an exposure, hard to look at as skinned flesh. Seeing somebody have faith, close up, is no easier than seeing someone chop a finger up.
>
> Do missionaries ever have these times, of astonishment and shame? (p. 97)

Del's recognition is of human vulnerability, need, and humility. She is growing up quickly, testing life in her own way, groping for her own answers and always for consolation in her solitude.

The chapter, "Lives of Girls and Women," speaks not only of Del's sexual and romantic dreams, but of the distance between those dreams and the dissatisfied sexual lives of girls and women around her.

Sex is a taboo subject in Del's house. Her mother is afraid of any suggestion of it, though she writes urgent letters to the Jubilee newspaper advising birth control as a measure for social improvement. Fern Dougherty, the roomer, at ease with sex, serves as an interesting contrast. Fern is visited regularly by Mr. Chamberlain, and it is rumoured that she is a loose-moralled woman. Del is again initiated into two very different worlds: her mother's and Fern's. She finally rejects both — neither offers what she seeks.

Mr. Chamberlain is enticing — neat, well-dressed and given to suggestive teasing of the young Del. Her fantasies about exposing her body to him become deliciously decadent. Their real sexual confrontation is, by contrast, flat and perverse. Mr. Chamberlain engages Del in his plan to abandon Fern Dougherty; she is to make sure that none of his letters of promise to Fern are left behind. He "pays" her for her help morbidly, by driving out to the countryside with her, and masturbating while she watches. This is her first real-life confrontation with sex, and it is a potentially damaging and frightening experience.

Del's reactions are not the expected ones. The experience is not traumatic. She is the detached observer, perhaps already the artist, storing the details away.

Shortly after this, when Mr. Chamberlain has left town, Del watches Fern's reaction, her defensive cheerfulness about the desertion, and she listens in a removed way to her mother's words about vulnerable women such as Fern. Her mother's advice to Del closes the chapter:

> My mother spoke to me in her grave, hopeful lecturing voice.
>
> "There is a change coming, I think, in the lives of girls and women. Yes. But it is up to us to make it come. All women have had, up till now, has been their connection with men. All we have had. No more lives of our own, really, than domestic animals. *He shall hold thee, when his passion shall have spent its novel force, a little closer than his dog, a little dearer than his horse.* Tennyson wrote that. It's true. Was true. You will want to have children though."

That was how much she knew me.
"But I hope you will — use your brains . . . Don't be
distracted." (pp. 146-7).

But:

Her concern about my life, which I needed and took for
granted, I could not bear to have expressed. Also I felt that
it was not so different from all the other advice handed out
to women, to girls, advice that assumed being female made
you damageable, that a certain amount of carefulness and
solemn fuss . . . was called for, whereas men were supposed
to be able to go out and take on all kinds of experiences and
shuck off what they didn't want and come back proud.
Without even thinking about it, I had decided to do the
same. (p. 147)

Del does go on to "shuck off" what she doesn't want but she also
learns that she wants many of those things which she thought she
didn't. She moves from necessary blind rebellion and rejection
toward a more mature recognition of the worth of her environment.
At the end of the novel we are told that Del, who is concentrating
only on leaving Jubilee, is also becoming subtly aware of her need to
recreate Jubilee in fiction. Only later will she discover her hunger for
its every detail; only later will she be aware of the way in which
Jubilee has become part of her being.

She must first reject every value her mother espouses, and this she
does through her intense relationship with Garnet French — Jubilee's
outsider, everything her mother would *not* want for her daughter.
"Baptizing" concentrates on Del's first love affair, and on the new
awareness of self that comes with it. Del meets Garnet French when a
number of stabilizing features of her life are changing. Her mother is
ill and the protective partnership with her girlfriend Naomi is
dissolving. Naomi has moved out of school into the world of serious
working girls who concentrate with bewildering knowhow on
femininity, dating and weddings — as Naomi puts it, on living a
"normal" life. Del does not want to belong to the eccentric, asexual
world of her mother, but neither is she able to identify with Naomi's
"normal" life.

She reads a magazine article in which the psychiatrist-author states
that a normal boy looking at the full moon will think of the universe
and a normal girl will think only of washing her hair. Del is alarmed
by the article, presenting as it does the new conflict in her life. She

knows her mother would declare the article nonsensical male blackmail, and yet:

> That would not convince me; surely, a New York
> psychiatrist must *know*. And women like my mother were in
> the minority . . . Moreover, I did not want to be like my
> mother, with her virginal brusqueness . . . I wanted men to
> love me, *and* I wanted to think of the universe when I
> looked at the moon. I felt trapped, stranded; it seemed there
> had to be a choice where there couldn't be a choice. (p. 150)

The difficulty, the impossibility of making simple choices is to be seen again and again in a sensibility which needs to combine many worlds.

For a time, Del plunges into books, achieving high grades and a new area of stability, associating with the one eccentric intellectual boy in the school who is neutral ground; he keeps her safely out of the realm of sexual politics. The baptism of the chapter's title has yet to take place.

Garnet French is an outsider, mysterious, attractive and refreshingly inarticulate. Words do not interest him, and the first meeting between Del and him is a charged, spontaneous drawing together. Del is quickly caught up in Garnet, loving his body, loving his separation from the Jubilee world, and abandoning her scholarly ambitions. She wants for now only the excitement of a new dark world, an escape from her mother and Jubilee, and she chooses to concentrate on the qualities in Garnet French which she needs.

> I loved the dark side, the strange side, of him, which I did
> not know, not the regenerate Baptist; or rather, I saw the
> Baptist, of which he was proud, as a mask he was playing
> with, that he could easily discard. I tried to get him to tell
> me about being in jail. I would pay attention to the life of
> his instincts, never to his ideas. (p. 183)

Her baptism does not occur, however, in the meeting or in the love-making with Garnet French, but later, when they break apart. She discovers her own inner strength and resolve.

Garnet French, wanting more than his "strange darkness" to be recognized, intrudes on Del's beautiful escape world with a plan for permanence. He wants to get married, to have children, to have Del join the part of his life which she has chosen to avoid.

In an explosive scene, which begins in tones of light jest, the confrontation between Del and the reality of Garnet French takes place.

Sensing Del's resistance to baptism and to his marriage proposal, Garnet proposes to baptize her himself in the river in which they are swimming. The playfulness passes quickly and both are suddenly aware of the serious struggle for individual assertion which is taking place. As the tension becomes overt, and the fighting more frantic, Del realizes with sudden clarity that she has always had a firm sense of herself in this relationship.

> He pushed me down again . . . I held my breath and fought him. I fought strongly and naturally . . . But when he let me come up just long enough to hear him say, "Now say you'll do it," I saw his face . . . and I felt amazement . . . that anybody could have made such a mistake, to think he had real power over me. I was too amazed to be angry, I forgot to be frightened, it seemed to me impossible that he should not understand that all the powers I granted him were in play, that he himself was — in play, that I meant to keep him sewed up in his golden lover's skin forever, even if five minutes before I had talked about marrying him. (p. 198)

As she walks back home, away from Garnet French, she feels her isolation *and* her power, the loss and the gain side by side.

It is a painful victory. Freedom and possession of self are burdensome, as Del realizes. They mean that one is responsible for one's own life, that one has forsaken the easier, but finally less rewarding, possibility of letting another person take over and lead the way. Life has become possible now without her mother's values or Garnet French's.

> Cities existed; telephone operators were wanted; the future could be furnished without love or scholarships. Now at least without fantasies or self-deception, cut off from the mistakes and confusion of the past, grave and simple, carrying a small suitcase, getting on a bus, like girls in movies leaving home, convents, lovers, I supposed I would get started on my real life. (pp. 200-201)

The tone of this passage is adolescent in its simplistic conception of "real life." Del will obviously go on to discover that the divisions are not so clear, and the movie versions of new beginnings are misleadingly easy. For now, however, she goes out to meet the future with touching determination and a necessary sense of isolation.

The final chapter, "Epilogue: The Photographer," speaks of Del's commitment to an artistic recreation of Jubilee, and her eventual mature understanding that art is not that dramatically separated from reality. In fact, she learns that life as she has known it in Jubilee is full of the depth of mystery and drama which, as an adolescent, she associated mainly with gothic make-believe.

The novel which she had begun to write as an adolescent, based on the Sherriff family, is melodramatic, highly stylized and vividly separated from her daily life in Jubilee: "I did not pay much attention to the real Sherriffs, once I had transformed them for fictional purposes" (p. 206). It is only during her last summer in Jubilee when Del is invited into the Sherriff house for tea, that she is reminded of the link and the distance between her temporarily abandoned fiction and the life around her. She is still deliberately distanced from the town, too frightened and pained by her insights accumulated over the years. But now she is aware of the more profound and exact reality which has yet to be communicated.

It will be some time before Del has the courage to probe the depths of that reality, and to cherish the gift of her everyday experience. "People's lives, in Jubilee as elsewhere, were dull, simple, amazing and unfathomable — deep caves paved with kitchen linoleum" (p. 210).

But, just as the younger Del sought religion for "a scent of God" so that "life could be borne," the mature Del will seek for a reassuring integration of all things through art and the imagination. For now, Del guards her need, nurses her vision, until the time when she will have the strength and the maturity to express it.

Notes

¹ Alice Munro, *Lives of Girls and Women* (Scarborough: New American Library, 1974), pp. 6-7. All page references are to this edition.

MORDECAI RICHLER

THIRD SOLITUDE: CANADIAN AS JEW
Tom Marshall

> Vel, anyway, all I can say, is Tanks Gods, for Mordecai
> Richler. He is a bad Jew and a worse Canadian but he tells it
> as it is. Larry Zolf[1]

> What I am looking for are the values with which in this time
> a man can live with honour. Mordecai Richler[2]

Mordecai Richler has, it seems, been both embarrassed and obsessed
by his identity as Jew and Canadian. Though he offers little solid
evidence of knowing much about Canada beyond a few streets in
Montreal, he remains very Canadian. Feeling a strong (and natural)
affinity with American Jewish writers of his own generation, he
nevertheless chose — after his time in Paris — to live in London,
England, and not in New York. A man originally of the left, he expresses great admiration for the very English and very right-wing satirical genius of Evelyn Waugh. Surely rather a Canadian balance of
perspectives. Now he has come home again, though it was apparently quite unthinkable in the 1950s for him to do what Morley Callaghan and Hugh MacLennan had already done: live and work in
Canada.

The Apprenticeship of Duddy Kravitz and its companion piece
and complement, St. Urbain's Horseman, express in their own way a
return to Richler's roots in Jewish Montreal, to the third solitude of
that city. We are back in A.M. Klein's ghetto, at Fletcher's Field High
School, to be exact, where uncomprehending WASP teachers do battle with Jewish urchins. The model for this school, Baron Byng,
graduated Klein and Irving Layton (not to mention Klein's close
friend David Lewis) some years before it graduated Mordecai
Richler. No doubt it deserves a species of immortality.

One reads Duddy Kravitz, easily the funniest Canadian work of
fiction since Leacock's Sunshine Sketches, with increasing delight
and, at least initially, a certain degree of bemusement. It is pica-
resque, it has grotesquely eccentric characters and marvellous comic
dialogue, it concerns a very young man of extraordinary drive and
enterprise coming to — what? Not maturity, surely. What, finally, is
it all about? Love? Money? Survival? Tribe and family? Land?

Love or friendship that extend beyond his immediate family, his
own tribe, are luxuries Duddy cannot comprehend even while he has
them:

148   MORDECAI RICHLER

"I suppose," Mr. Calder said, pushing his plate away, "that
I should have expected something like this from you. I had
hoped we were friends."
"Sure we are," Duddy had replied, flushing. "But friends
help each other."[3]

White men, Duddy thought. *Ver gerharget*. With them
you just didn't make deals. You had to diddle. They were
like those girls you had to discuss God or the Book-of-the-
Month with so all the time they could pretend not to know
you had a hand up their skirt, but just try to take it away.
Just try, buster. He's offended, Duddy thought, but he made
the deal all the same. Two-fifty more a ton, sure. I suppose
he wanted me to play golf with him for eighteen years first
or something. I haven't got that much time to waste, he
thought. (p. 229)

"What do you want from me, Mr. Calder?"
"I enjoy your company."
"Come off it. I amuse you. That's what you mean."
"You're a friend of mine. I take a fatherly interest in you."
"Yeah," Duddy said, "then how come you never introduce
me to any of your other friends?"
"They might not understand you."
"You mean I might try to make a deal with them like I did
with you over the crap and that would embarrass you. I'm a
little Jewish *pusherke*. Right?"
"You're acting like a young man on the verge of a nervous
breakdown." (p. 261)

Whose side is Richler on in such cross-cultural exchanges as this? At
first, one is inclined to say: Duddy's, of course. Calder has cultivated
and patronized him for his entertainment value. But, on reflection,
one realizes that Hugh John Calder, the bored WASP businessman,
has a case too. No doubt Duddy amuses him, but Calder also admires (and perhaps envies) Duddy's spirit, his potential for accom-
plishment. There is no reason to doubt Calder's concern for Duddy's
welfare, especially when his diagnosis is so accurate. Probably these
two individuals of different class and religious background are incapable of understanding one another, or the forces that have shaped
the other, very fully, but human sympathy is offered to Duddy, and
he is unable to accept it. Like Stephen Leacock, like T.C. Haliburton,
like Susanna Moodie for that matter, Richler explores the comedy of

cultural tensions when he involves Duddy with an eccentric WASP businessman, a loving and honest French-Canadian girl, and an innocent, worshipful American friend. But Duddy fails every such test, from the initial encounter with the ineffectual liberal teacher MacPherson, on: he remains incapable of the transcendence of cultural barriers suggested by Klein in *The Rocking Chair.* He is fiercely and admirably loyal only to his own family.

Motherless, Duddy does not understand women or realize until he is driven to a kind of breakdown in her absence that he needs and loves Yvette without wanting to. The nature of their relationship is indicated in small exchanges such as these:

> Yvette wanted to wait, but Duddy insisted, and they made love on the carpet.
> "I don't get it," Duddy said. "Imagine guys getting married and tying themselves down to one single broad for a whole lifetime when there's just so much stuff around."
> "People fall in love," Yvette said. "It happens."
> "Planes crash too," Duddy said. "Listen, I've got an important letter to write. We'll eat soon. OK?"
> She didn't answer and Duddy began to type. (p. 191)

Duddy begins to realize his need for Yvette but eventually loses her because of the ruthlessness of his drive for property.

Money is the most important thing in Duddy's world, and it is easy for him to misunderstand his grandfather's saying that a man without land is a nobody. The old man of two ghettoes, one in the old and one in the new world, dreams ineffectually of a pastoral world, perhaps (as in Klein's Zionist poems) of Israel. Duddy dreams instead of development and exploitation and a vulgar but lucrative resort. The new world with which he must contend is the world of Jerry Dingleman, the Boy Wonder, and of Mr. Cohen:

> "Listen here, my young Mr. Kravitz, you want to be a saint? Go to Israel and plant oranges on a *kibbutz.* I'll give you the fare with pleasure. Only I know you and I know two weeks after you landed you'd be scheming to corner the schmaltz herring market or something. We're two of a kind, you know. Listen, listen here. My attitude even to my oldest and dearest customer is this," he said, making a throat-cutting gesture. "If I thought he'd be good for half a cent more a ton I'd squeeze it out of him. A plague on all the *goyim,* that's my motto. The more money I make the better

care I take of my own, the more I'm able to contribute to
our hospital, the building of Israel, and other worthy causes.
So a *goy* is crippled and you think you're to blame. Given
the chance he would have crippled you," he shouted, "or
thrown you into a furnace like six million others. You think
I didn't lose relatives? I lost relatives." (pp. 267-68)

Cohen, as Richler tells us, exaggerates his own ruthlessness and
crookedness, yet he does seem to have been guilty of criminal negli-
gence and of receiving stolen goods in his struggle to achieve material
security for himself and his family. Like most of Richler's characters,
he is far from being unsympathetic; indeed, he is rather likeable.
Richler's understanding and compassion are extended to the Cohens
and Harry Steins and Duddys and Virgils and Calders and Mac-
Phersons of this world at the same time as they are satirized. This is
the mixture of frailties that makes the human animal.

It is Richler's shifting perspective, his *concerned* and compas-
sionate criticism, that places him next to Leacock or Klein (even if he
has never read them), and separates him forever from Evelyn
Waugh, however much he may admire him. *The Incomparable
Atuk*, Richler's first attempt to function as a kind of Canadian
Waugh by manipulating Canadian caricatures and stereotypes in absurd situations, is funny and even instructive without ever being
very memorable or profound. The later *Cocksure* is somewhat more
successful in this vein, but neither book has the compassion and
depth of *Duddy Kravitz* or *St. Urbain's Horseman*, let alone the
savage Swiftian vision of Waugh. Richler is much kinder. His ambivalence, his irony, his ability to hold a number of perspectives and
attitudes in tension — these are Canadian.

I sometimes think (oversimplifying, to make a point) that there are
two kinds of Canadians, though I've only been describing one of
them. Firstly, there are the fanatics, of whom we've always had
heaps — all those fierce nineteenth-century Protestants and Catho-
lics who wanted to continue the religious wars in the New World.
Their twentieth-century spiritual descendants cling to one narrow
rectitude, creed, region, language, patriotism or another (and one
could include here those artists who cling to rigid aesthetic theories).
Secondly, there are those whose consciousness transcends cultural
barriers, those who seek compromise or synthesis, communication,
understanding, mutual respect — in a word, community: the crafty
Macdonalds and Lauriers and Kings and Pearsons who have held the
country together; the artists, such as Klein and Richler and Laurence

and Purdy, who also see that Canada is a coalition of minorities and regions that must, frequently, agree to disagree.

But it is inevitable that a writer like Richler, who depicts the faults as well as the virtues of his own immediate group, will be misunderstood and called anti-Semitic by those whose sympathies, like those of Duddy Kravitz, have narrow boundaries. All too often — in Scots, French, Jews, Indians or whatever — charity begins at home, and stays there. And, understandably, the Montreal Jewish community that endured subtle and not-so-subtle forms of anti-Semitism in earlier decades is very touchy about its public image, about providing ammunition to the potential enemy. But this is to miss the point in Richler's case; he is on record as saying that the working class Jew has more in common with the working-class Gentile than with the bosses of either persuasion, and his satirical account of rich, vulgar Jews is not primarily concerned with their Jewishness, nor is it without an element of affection.

Richler is a satirist and a moralist, a type of the Canadian small "c" conservative (consider Jake Hersh's reverence for "the late great Reb Shmul Johnson" in *St. Urbain's Horseman*). Both he and persons close to him have suggested that in another age he might well have been a rabbi. Duddy's Uncle Benjy, like the younger Richler a socialist and moralist, perhaps speaks for him when he says:

> "There used to be . . . some dignity in being against the synagogue. With a severe orthodox rabbi there were things to quarrel about. There was some pleasure. But this cream-puff of a synagogue, this religious drugstore, you might as well spend your life being against the *Reader's Digest*. They've taken all the mystery out of religion." (p. 146)

The complexity and apparent absurdity of the modern world encourages in Richler a vein of near-nihilistic parody: *Cocksure* is the most extravagant expression of it. But here we have Virgil's epileptic's newsletter, a devastating send-up of the over-sensitivity of minority groups, and the hilarious "avant garde" Bar Mitzvah film (even funnier, of course, in the film of the novel, and the only respect in which the film improves on the novel). Then there is this sort of black comedy:

> "You see," Virgil said, "it was a blessing in disguise. I'm glad you're not angry though. I mean well, remember I said you'd be remembered as the Branch Rickey like of the Health Handicappers? Well, what if Jackie Robinson had

turned out to be a two hundred hitter? That's what I turned
out to be, you know. A prize flop. But if not for the accident there'd be no *Crusader*. It might have taken me years
and years to get going. See my point?"
"Sure, Virgie. Sure thing."
There was a kind of flask attachment under the mattress
of Virgil's bed and it was gradually filling with urine. (p. 275)

All of this is meant to demonstrate an absurdist maxim (again enun-
ciated by Uncle Benjy, in his very important farewell letter to
Duddy): "Experience doesn't teach: it deforms" (p. 279). This saying
— which seems to be borne out by the development, physical and/or
moral, of Dingleman, Aunt Ida, Virgil and Duddy himself — would
be cause for despair, were it not for the balancing insistence on free
will and freedom of moral choice that comes later in the letter.

This brings us to two central and related questions about the
novel. It is genuinely "realistic" or "naturalistic," or is it a fantastic
parade of grotesques, a satiric fantasia aspiring to the condition of
Cocksure? Is it inexorably determined by brutal circumstances that
Duddy become a bastard, as monstrous as the monstrous Boy
Wonder himself, or can he choose to be something else? It seems to
me that ambivalence is once again the key word. Richler raises questions that he will not answer.

Consider the manipulation of time in the novel. In the early
chapters we get the story of Duddy and Mr. MacPherson, the well-
meaning but ineffectual teacher, a fussy WASP, a frustrated liberal
turned drinker, whose invalid wife collapses and dies after an
obscene phone-call from Duddy. Duddy does not come off very well
in this, and we are reminded of the MacPherson episode, perhaps
Duddy's first atrocity, at key points thereafter, including the novel's
penultimate page. But after this initial episode we are provided with
the extenuating circumstances of Duddy's family and background,
and then with the story of his mistreatment at the resort. These inspire considerable sympathy: nothing is simple or clear-cut.

"Where Duddy Kravitz sprung from the boys grew up dirty and
sad, spiky also, like grass beside the railroad tracks" (p. 46). This and
what follows beautifully enlists our sympathy for Duddy, who has
no mother, whose father is a highly likeable but not very bright cab-
driver and pimp, and whose favoured brother is a moral weakling.
He is loved well only by his pathetic old grandfather. He has, we
recall, invented an extra brother as a means of coping with his emotional deprivation. He is highly nervous, inwardly desperate, driven.

It is understandable that he becomes a gang leader among his friends. It is a world where one has to fight for survival, and Duddy is determined to be somebody, like the Boy Wonder, at any rate not a loser.

But the enthusiasm for Duddy's energy and ruthlessness evinced by such critics as Warren Tallman, is misguided in an "American" direction because it tells only half of the story and distorts the shape of the novel: Richler's intentions, as I've suggested, seem to have been more complex.[4]

MacPherson was, to a large extent, responsible for his own tragedy. But Duddy's treatment of Yvette and Virgil is a good deal nearer to being wholly reprehensible. He is indirectly responsible for Virgil's paralysis and cannot resist the temptation to swindle him in order to complete his purchase of land. In so doing, he loses the love of Yvette, Virgil and his grandfather, and is left only with the stupid admiration of Max and the sadistic satisfaction of having chased the physically and morally deformed Dingleman off his land. He chooses Dingleman as his enemy, a choice one might applaud, were it not so obvious that he is becoming more and more like him. His gesture is therefore an evasion; he has become his own worst enemy.

"Experience doesn't teach: it deforms." Is this then the book's lesson? Benjy also writes:

> There's more to you than mere money-lust, Duddy, but I'm afraid for you. You're two people, that's why. The scheming little bastard I saw so easily and the fine, intelligent boy underneath that your grandfather, bless him, saw. But you're coming of age soon and you'll have to choose. A boy can be two, three, four potential people, but a man is only one. He murders the others. (p. 280)

According to this notion, Duddy had (and perhaps still has) the potential to be more than another Boy Wonder or Sammy Glick. Richler leaves us with a balance of philosophies. He doesn't come out unequivocally for either the determinism of environmental pressures or the freedom of moral choice. He only suggests each possibility as it occurs in the confused mind of the dying Benjy. He refuses, ultimately, to judge Duddy (as Morley Callaghan refuses to judge his characters, as Leacock refuses to judge) since he cannot know whether Duddy has a choice or not. We have here neither a naturalistic novel nor a satiric fantasy, but something in-between: a realistic account with significant distortions, another Canadian hybrid. It is a marvellous book.

Jake Hersh, the hero of *St. Urbain's Horseman*, helps to reveal

Richler's most important concern: "the values with which in this time a man can live with honour." When he meets Duddy, after several years, in the earlier book, he is honest in his reaction to him:

> Duddy grinned. "Hoo-haw," he said, and he poured Hersh another drink. "It's so good to see you. We ought to have reunions like. When I think of all the swell characters I used to know at FFHS. Hey, remember the time that lush-head MacPherson accused me of killing his wife?"
> "He's in an asylum."
> "Wha'?"
> "He's in Verdun."
> "That's show biz, I guess," Duddy said, flushing. "I think I'd better be off. Thanks for the drink."
> "Aw, come on. Sit down."
> "Why pretend we're friends, Duddy? We hated each other at school." (p. 225)

Interestingly enough, the two do become friends. Hersh, like Richler himself, can see the good as well as the bad in Duddy. He is a kind of artist, a man struggling for moral vision — thus he is obviously much closer to his creator than most of Richler's other significant characters.

Hersh has a fantasy hero, an alter ego, in his mysterious cousin Joey, the Horseman of St. Urbain Street who (Hersh believes) tracks down Nazi war-criminals. Like Klein's Uncle Melech in *The Second Scroll*, the Horseman represents the heroic spirit of Jewry in a time of great moral confusion. But Jake, unlike Klein's narrator, has two alter egos: the other is Harry Stein who involves him in a sordid sex scandal. Jake becomes fascinated by the squalid Harry, a "little man" eaten up by spite and envy, one of Richler's most successful comic creations. If the Horseman is meant to be heroic, Harry is decidedly anti-heroic: they are the poles of Jake's possible self, and perhaps of the Jewish response to the terror of modern history. Ironically, it seems likely as well that the real Joey is not much better than a common thug, but Jake clings to his heroic fantasy as a remedy for his recurrent nightmares about Dr. Joseph Mengele and for his middle-aged obsession with, and disgust at, the ultimate facts of physical decline and death. *St. Urbain's Horseman* is an ambitious and impressive novel, funny, sad and powerful by turns, even if it lacks something of the exuberant freshness of *Duddy Kravitz*.

At this point, one is inclined to ask: why have so many of Canada's best and most significant writers in English been Jews? One thinks, for instance, of Klein, Layton, Cohen, Richler, Adele Wiseman and a number of younger poets and novelists. I have written before (in *A.M. Klein*) that there is a sense in which the Jews are the most Canadian of Canadians: history has forced them to experience the conflicts and tensions that all sensitive Canadians experience, but to an intense degree. The search for honour and for dignity in a world in flames, the prophets searching for vision in the desert of a new country: these themes are Jewish and Canadian and universal at once. Imaginative Zionism makes sense in a new country that is gradually discovering itself. In a sense, Canada — even Montreal, where so many of our Jewish writers grow up — can represent the confused modern world in microcosm, as Hugh MacLennan suggests in *Return of the Sphinx*, because it is a coalition of minorities: in this sense, an international country. The problem of identity is a problem of the diversity of Canada and the world.

The Jewish writer, because of the degree and the dramatic history of his own "different-ness," can see (paradoxically) that every Canadian is a "Jew," a stranger; everyone lives behind the barriers of his own cultural past, though some attempt to see over them. Thus Atuk, the Eskimo poet, is employed to demonstrate Jewish bigotry to the Jew by displaying his own, like a mirror-image. Richler carries this insight further in *Cocksure* where the true Jew, in the eyes of the trendy modern world-at-large, is seen to be your average decent WASP Canadian, one Mortimer Griffin. But it is in *The Apprenticeship of Duddy Kravitz* that the Jew as Canadian, the Canadian as Jew, receives its most balanced, its funniest and its most profound, expression.

Notes

[1] G. David Sheps (ed.), *Mordecai Richler* (Toronto: McGraw-Hill Ryerson, 1971), p. 114.
[2] "Interview with Nathan Cohen," *Mordecai Richler*, p. 38. This is obviously a very useful book, since I've quoted from it twice.
[3] Mordecai Richler, *The Apprenticeship of Duddy Kravitz* (Toronto: New Canadian Library, 1969), p. 228. Further references will be in parentheses in the text.
[4] Warren Tallman, "Wolf in the Snow," *Canadian Literature* No. 6, Autumn, 1960.

RICHLER'S HORSEMAN
John Moss

In morally absurd times identity becomes crucial to survival. If who
we are is confused or obscured, there is nothing to hang on to, no
solid vantage from which to watch and weather the storm. Duddy
Kravitz makes it, in *St. Urbain's Horseman*, as he did in his own
novel, because, bastard though he may be, he knows who he is. And
when he pretends to be something else, it is just that, conscious pre-
tence. Duddy can exploit moral anarchy because his own life is in
order: he knows his priorities and thereby himself.

In *St. Urbain's Horseman*, Jake Hersh's manifold identities bring
him into direct confrontation with a moral universe that has fallen
askew. Jake's quest is not for identity but for the self which the impo-
sitions of identity obscure. He is somewhat neurotic, but his sanity is
hardly in question. He does not achieve any profound or lucid insights into the nature of reality and his place within it. The social
pressures afflicting Jake are all too clearly defined, stemming from
his being a Jew, a middle-aged male, married and a father, a film director and an expatriate Canadian. Each category imposes criteria of
identity. He has been shaped and buffeted even by the evasions of
stereotype as he has struggled all his life with the anomalies of being
himself. All categories converge in the ruminations provoked by
charges of sexual misconduct laid against him. In his mind he leaps
from one identity slot to another, with only fantasies of the fabulous
St. Urbain's Horseman, his cousin Joey, for solace. Eventually his vision of Joey fails him, but by then he can go it alone.

Jake sees himself representative of his generation: "Young too late,
old too soon . . . Always the wrong age. Ever observers, never parti-
cipants. The whirlwind elsewhere."[1] Passing through the optimum
age for cannon fodder before Viet Nam and not soon enough for
World War II, his generation contributes to cultural history the fly-
speck era of the beatniks. Even his own life Jake experiences as a
scenario in his mind, accompanied in times of caustic consciousness
by a voice-over commentary which sometimes allows him the illusion of involvement, displacing his normal state of acute passive
concern.

St. Urbain's Horseman is confessional. Form does not arise inevitably from content. It is imposed by the author as a means of ordering his materials, the things that need to be said. Events might have
been arranged in quite a different way and the story could remain
much the same. Chronology is a convenience for Richler, rather than

a major plot device. Flashbacks and forward flow simply allow the author to work in the necessary details; Jake is never allowed to live in his own reality. Reader intertia, however, is countered by the dazzling clarity of Richler's prose and wit which skewer the attention and haul it along from paragraph to paragraph. By all rights *St. Urbain's Horseman* should be a bad novel, and possibly it is, but it is amazing and gut-wrenching confession.

Richler does not portray another world in his fiction but in chiaroscuro duplicates our own. He establishes a point of view from which we observe the frenetically passing scene. Many readers become annoyed with him for this, because he makes them see their own reality through his eyes, not his reality with theirs. In doing so, he is a threat and a serious satirist. Throughout, Richler explores identity as both quest and burden, always in the glare of moral indignation. Through his protagonist he is judge and victim both.

A more or less trumped-up sex charge which brings Jake into the Central Criminal Court of the Old Bailey in the summer of 1967 provides the motive force in *St. Urbain's Horseman*. Jake is charged with aiding and abetting sodomy, indecent assault and possession of cannabis. Acquitted of stashing pot and lending a hand to buggery, he is fined for indecent assault and the "folly, and sheer egoism" by which, in the judge's eyes at least, he has placed family and property in dire jeopardy through his association with the irrepressibly disreputable Harry Stein (p. 450). The novel attempts to answer the questions how has Jake's life come to this, and where does he go from here.

The mock violence of a sordid sexual game in which he was barely involved forces him into a confrontation with himself that has long been coming. Not until near the novel's end do we even learn what the charges specifically are — only that sex is involved — for it is the confrontation they provoke which is of high importance.

Sex has never played an overwhelming part in Jake's lifestyle. He has always coveted goals more than experience. The same self-consciousness that has made him a moderately successful and only partially compromised film director has forced him to play a wary hand in matters of sex.

Jake wavers between seeing his reticence as a moral advantage and a character flaw. Half in jest he sometimes assigns it to his nationality — *"Even in Paris, I remained a Canadian. I puffed hashish, but I didn't inhale"* (p. 13). Typically, in encountering a full-fledged orgy on Ibiza, Jake assumes non-combatant status — not because he is disinterested or disgusted but because he cannot overcome self-consciousness, even amidst a mass of writhing flesh.

When he marries and the marriage lasts and infidelity leaves him cold, he is embarrassed. Everyone else plays around, but he always goes home to Nancy. Brief flurries of satisfaction do not hold up against the humiliation to her, the anxiety for him, of an affair. When Harry involves him with the German au pair girl, Jake does not seduce but succumbs, and then reluctantly, only for a few short strokes before he ejects her from the house.

Neither his acquittal for sodomy nor his conviction for indecent assault have much significance for Jake. The obscene letters Harry sends to Nancy to undermine her faith in his relative innocence, he shrugs off. The whole affair with Harry and the British judiciary has been like the line at the bottom of a column of figures, the events of his life, and he has yet to work out the sum.

Instead he mopes. That is, until two things happen — Duddy Kravitz arrives on the scene, and Jake learns of the Horseman's death. Suddenly everything adds up. For the first time in his life Jake opens to Duddy, the vulgar, pushy, exuberant, proud, Jewish hustler, who is everything Jake isn't, except Jewish. Duddy comes on coarse and cocky — about short skirts, for instance: "I tell you, Yankel, if one of those chicks had a tampax inside, you'd see the string dangling." Jake's acquired gentility and innate sensitivity make him shudder.

Duddy sympathetically philosophizes: "All this new outspokenness in the arts is taking the kicks out of it for me. Gone are the guilty pleasures, the dirty secret joys." Jake assents, and denies his own iniquity. Duddy scolds him: "You mean to say, after the trial, all you've been through, the whole *tzimmis*, you didn't even get laid out of it?" (p. 458). Jake nods.

Duddy writes him a cheque from petty cash for ten thousand dollars to tide him over. And Jake accepts, overwhelmed by Duddy's unabashed glee at holding the upper hand. Such vulgar directness and honesty and his own acceptance of them as valid ways of coping give Jake a tremendous lift. Joey's death, however, sets him free.

St. Urbain's Horseman is a novel of personal triumph but the triumph is a long time in coming, and meanwhile a zany, sardonic and sometimes touching account of a man's life is allowed to unfold. Jake Hersh's life is where the story happens, although it is the author's voice that tells it. The Hershes are a Montreal Jewish family, still largely immigrant, in the second and third generations, whose first domestic residence was the St. Urbain Street ghetto. Some of them remain there. But most have graduated to Outremont or elsewhere, carrying much of the ghetto with them as a protective barrier against assimilation. Some, like Jenny, disclaim their heritage. Most have joined that amorphous middle-class union known as the Montreal Jewish Community. A few, like Jake, try to straddle two worlds, being a non-Jewish Jew as it were. And then there is Joey, Jake's imaginal alter-ego, a *golem* for his people, an elusive scoundrel.

Jake's parents divorce when he is a child. He and his sister Rifka are brought up by their mother, abetted by various uncles, ranging from pious to prosperous. Rifka marries Herky, whose main line is toilets. After Jake makes a false start to New York, on money extorted from Herky by confessing to homosexuality, for a one-way ticket, he moves to Toronto. He shares an apartment with Luke Scott, the product of an advantaged home. They both aspire to careers in theatre and cinema, Luke to write and Jake to direct. Typical of their recent generation, they find Toronto limiting and provincial and head off for the bright lights of London, England, themselves too provincial to stay home and change things. In England they make good — particularly Luke who is lauded for his talent and charm. Jake makes money, at one point even being paid not to direct a picture, and marries a gorgeous passionate Gentile with whom he has beautiful children. But recognition, fame, satisfaction elude him.

Richler moves through Jake's earlier years quickly, in chronological sequence. When he reaches Jake's marriage and the conditions of his life in the last decade or so, he allows the narrative to slow down and the covert purpose of the novel to emerge. It is essentially twofold: to show the crass and amoral society in which Jake lives and to show Jake's ambivalence about his role within it. Close-up views and long-shots are continually juxtaposed to reveal both. For example, Jake ruminates about "war and rape. Famine. Rats gnawing at the toes of black babies. Outside, bestiality. Fire raisers." But still he enjoys the comforts of the "shelter he has provided for his family":

> The persistent whirring from the kitchen is the nocturnal Mr. Shapiro, Molly's hamster, racing nowhere on his wheel. Jake's responsible for the stained wallpaper in the dining room, a champagne bottle's eruption. The sideboard was Nancy's folly. Her first auction. There's food in the larder, wine in the pantry, money in the bank. His wife is the woman he wants. He enjoys the children.
> — So, Yankel. How are you doing?
> — I can't complain.

Then there obtrudes the familiar photograph of a bewildered little Jewish boy, wearing a cap, a torn pullover, and shorts, his eyes aching with fear as he raises his arms over his head. There are other Jews huddled together on this narrow street in Warsaw. Wearing caps, supporting bundles. All of them, with arms raised. Behind them, striking a pose for the unseen photographer, are four German soldiers. One of them casually points his rifle at the petrified little Jewish boy. (p. 72)

Jake's "Jewish nightmare" persists. And the refrain echoes through his head, from post-war testimony about Nazi atrocity:

"Mengele cannot have been there all the time."
"In my opinion, always. Night and day."

At one of his bleakest moments, he adds, "If God weren't dead, it would be necessary to hang Him" (p. 272). In Jake's running fantasy about his cousin Joey, he sees the Horseman on a white stallion thundering into the Doktor's Paraguay retreat to avenge six million murdered Jews.

Richler also brings broad and personal perspectives together through Jake's responses to the widely celebrated achievements of the handicapped, which he sees as quasi-freak shows. He is fascinated and repulsed by the inane praise heaped on the girl who cooks from an iron lung, amputee painters who use their toes or teeth to wield the brush, the colostomized actor who profoundly declares his victory over cancer. Jake is dismayed at the obscured fact that a healthy body would surely be preferable in each case. It is just this attitude that credits God with the Holocaust because out of it was born the state of Israel. And, sadly, there is perhaps a touch of jealousy in Jake's response, from one who has not been able to surmount obstacles within his own personality of a much less dramatic nature.

In the middle distance, Richler focuses on Jake's contemporaries and the lifestyle he shares with them. Probably the most memorable scene in this respect is the Sunday morning softball game on Hampstead Heath, a weekly ritual through the summertime for the expatriate cinematists. Richler begins his account in a mood of high camp, and slowly lets the sad reality take over. At one point, Gordie Kaufman, a formerly blacklisted writer now making spectacular films and money, is on the mound facing Tom Hunt, a black actor and former semi-pro ball-player:

If he homered, Hunt felt he would be put down for

another buck nigger, good at games, but if he struck out,
which would call for rather more acting skill than was required of him on the set of *Othello X*, what then? He would
enable a bunch of fat, foxy, sexually worried Jews to feel
big, goysy. Screw them, Hunt thought.

But Kaufman, too, has problems:

> I must bear down on Hunt, Gordie thought, because if he
> touches me for even a scratch single I'll come off a patroniz-
> ing ofay. If he homers, God forbid, I'm a shitty liberal . . .
> Gordie gritted his teeth, his proud Trotskyite past getting the
> best of him, and threw a fast ball right at Hunt, bouncing it
> off his head. Hunt threw away his bat and started for the
> mound, fist clenched, but not so fast that players from both
> sides couldn't rush in to separate the two men, both of
> whom felt vindicated, proud, because they had triumphed
> over impersonal racial prejudice to hit each other as individ-
> uals on a fun Sunday on Hampstead Heath. (p. 245)

Still comic at this stage, though biting, by the chapter's end Richler
shows them all to be small-minded and humourless men, typical in
so many ways of their times and place.

Jake's London life is characterized by incipient paranoia. When
things go well, he feels badly. He is guilt-ridden over the tranquility
of his domestic situation. He rages at the mindless pleasantries of a
society which will not acknowledge the evil it spawns, or hides. In
his attic aerie Jake has tacked pictures of Nazi leaders to the wall. If
he does not hate, if he does not sustain indignation, he will vanish,
be no one. His personality has been shaped by the void between the
over-zealous moral consciousness and his overbearing cynicism.

Into the void leaps Harry Stein. Harry is as inventively nasty a
character as one is likely to meet. He is a bright, vicious and thoroughly obnoxious deviate. Jake takes to him, in spite of himself.
Harry's specialty is obscene phone calls, often exploiting inside information about clients of the accounting firm where he works. When
he tries to collect a debt of Joey's from Jake, he is refused: "It was only after Harry left that Jake noticed the large round hole burned into
the fabric of the new winged armchair from Heal's. Why, the
bastard, Jake thought, with sneaking admiration, he did it on purpose" (p. 340).

Although there is no reason why Jake should be responsible for
Joey's debt, this is only the beginning of Harry's campaign for resti-

tution. He repeatedly phones in the middle of the night; orders various goods delivered C.O.D. to the Hershes; reports Jake to the tax investigators ("I see in the same fiscal year you paid another advance, also of £1,000, to one John A. MacDonald") (p. 351); and to top things off, anonymously reports a bomb stashed aboard Jake's flight to Cannes, forcing a landing and search in Paris. Jake pays up. They become occasional friends: Harry uses Jake as a contact with the glitter-world; Jake thrills to see a human disaster fight back. Eventually their association leads to the Old Bailey. Harry is sentenced to seven years in prison.

Meanwhile, from the time he was a child on St. Urbain Street, Jake's interior world is dominated by his cousin Joey Hersh, the avenging Horseman. He has not seen him in person since the time during World War II when Joey disappeared, shortly after exhorting Jews to fight the anti-Semitism rampant in Quebec. It was the Jews, Jake's own uncle Abe in the vanguard, who got rid of him. Thenceforth, Joey turns up in Jake's experience mostly through hearsay and the residual evidence of his having passed by — at least one wife, a child, ex-mistresses, debts, rumours and enemies. Jake thinks of him obsessively, urgently: "Joey Hersh, Jesse Hope, Yosef ben Baruch, Joseph de la Hirsch, St. Urbain's one and only Horseman where are you now?" (p. 377). Where is he ever, but in Jake's mind? The real Joey Hersh whom Jake can never catch up with may be a scoundrel indeed. But Jake conceives of him as the *golem*, the legendary avenger of his people, whose greatest achievement will be the assassination of the notorious Josef Mengele. If he appears wicked, that is as it should be, for the *golem* has no soul: that way he can battle evil on its own mundane ground.

As long as Joey exists in Jake's mind, there is no need for himself to be a moral agent, despite his suffering from an awareness of the depravity which is so readily overlooked by everyone else. Joey seems to range about the world, avenging injustice everywhere on Jake's behalf, and urging Jews to fight for themselves. When Jake hears of Joey's death, after the trial, he is crushed. "He wept because the Horseman, his conscience, his mentor, was no more." Jake is forced, perhaps for the first time in his life, to be only himself. He wonders "if the Horseman was a distorting mirror and we each took the self-justifying image we required of him" (p. 464). Jake has imposed most upon him for he wanted Joey not only to bear his guilt but absolve it as well. Recognition of this snaps the bonds of passivity. Jake determines to become the Horseman himself, within his own mind. It is a metamorphosis which leads him to possession of himself, no longer the vicarious cynic but alive and active in earnest.

Suddenly, at the novel's end, Jake has made a "belated return to the land of the living" (p. 466). For years, morbidly concerned with the deterioration of his body, the colour of his urine, the condition of his piles, the possibility of cancer, stroke, *et al*, Jake has lived closer to the regions of death than he would care to admit. His obsession with Mengele and the Nazi atrocities signals the same morbidity on a broader scale. When his father dies of cancer of the kidney, Jake returns to Montreal for the funeral. Rather sadly, he sees the family from which he has sprung as a corpse:

> The Hershes, all of them, seemingly one cherished decomposing body to Jake now. Like him, susceptible to germs. Wasting. Shivering together in spite of the blistering heat. Diminished by one.
>
> Suddenly, the enveloping black birds began to twitter. All manner of rabbis, young and old, blackbearded and clean-shaven, rocked in prayer, heads bobbing, competing in piety. For each, Hersh buried paid dividends above ground. Every expired Hersh was bound to be commemorated by a rabbi's study or additional classroom for the yeshiva, a *sefer torah* donated here or an ark paid for there, a parochial-school library or a fully equipped kindergarten. In Everlasting Memory of . . .
>
> "Oy, *oy*," Rifka wailed.
>
> "Issy! My Issy!" Fanny put in, outreaching her. (p. 389)

Seeing himself and reality always in terms of death and dying, Jake remains the prisoner of his cynicism even at his father's funeral. He is finally freed by the culminative effect of the trial and word of Joey's death, with a crude assist from Duddy Kravitz.

Since so much of Jake's self-consciousness stems from his being a Jew, Richler's satiric thrust is directed sharply at Jews. Since Jake is a Canadian, although it is of less consequence to him, national pretensions are pricked as well. Since Jake is above all a person fully conscious of his time and place, his time and place take an almost unrelieved drubbing. And Jake is human, therefore subject to raillery applicable to most of his species. But all this does not make Richler a misanthrope, as many too quickly conclude.

Jake's outrage over the past and future of the Jews, combined with Richler's devastating wit and passionate invocations of shame and blame, suggest the author's profound concern. Richler is condemned mostly by bigots who cannot comprehend the exposure of bigotry as conquest, and not a public disgrace. Like those who for years found

Swift contemptible because they confused him with Gulliver, Richler's readers often fail to see the ironic detachment between himself and his creation. The problem is compounded because so much of the fiction draws from known autobiographical facts. To think Jake and Richler are the same, however, is to miss the point of the satire altogether, and to prove the accuracy of its thrust. Yet the confessional mode of the novel invites just such confusion. It is a problem Richler has been unable, or perhaps unwilling, despite his great technical skill, to resolve.

Richler cannot be accused of excessive clarity of intent. Otherwise he would not be so often misread, or unread and abused. He is a moral writer but this is expressed in his fiction by attitude, not a coherent moral system. He shows hurt and outrage, and perhaps less of peace or ecstasy, and invariably he passes judgments. These are not rationally worked out but they are deeply felt and expressed with conviction, perhaps most emphatically when he is being most satirical. He is the Canadian writer people love to hate; particularly Jews despise him — not all, of course, but many. Why? The answer seems to me founded upon two realities, one Richler's, the other Jewish. Clearly his Jewish heritage bears strongly on him. He is intensely critical of the distortions of Jewish identity, religious and secular, in modern Western times. He laments the lost ferocity and innocence of the Chosen People. Without being orthodox, he is a conservative; without forgiveness, he is a romantic. But Jews whose world is bilateral — in all affairs there is the Jewish side and there is the other — see his naive cry against the worst he perceives among them as an attack against the whole of them, holding all things Jewish up to the judgment and ridicule of the other side. Such a bilateral outlook, which has given Jews their special history in the world, does not readily admit criticism, particularly in public. Particularly by someone who is not clearly one with the world he judges — the licence of so many Jewish comedians in the popular media.

Richler is no less unsparing about Canada and Canadians: things are not as he feels they should be and therefore come under his skewering gaze. Similarly, he takes on popular culture, mass media, stereotypes of all sorts, numberless things that offend him. Ultimately, none of us are spared, even those who piously struggle to agree with him. He is a threat to the very least among us. So long as his judgments are couched in fiction, projected with the ambiguity and resonance of art, he is on solid ground. We, the judged, feel the world move beneath us, unsettling evidence that his art is effective. Unfortunately, Richler does not confine himself to fiction. In articles and public addresses his moral conviction becomes merely the stuff of petty diatribes, of confused and rhetorical bitchiness. He has picked up many detractors along this route, but of course many readers as well.

Notes

[1] Mordecai Richler, *St. Urbain's Horseman* (Toronto: McClelland and Stewart, 1971), p. 87. Further references appear parenthetically in the text.

RUDY WIEBE

A MIGHTY INNER RIVER: "PEACE" IN THE EARLY FICTION OF RUDY WIEBE

Hildegard E. Tiessen

Rudy Wiebe's *Peace Shall Destroy Many* (1962) and *The Blue Mountains of China* (1970) function within the Canadian literary context not only as works of Prairie fiction but also as documents that illuminate Mennonitism, a particular religious and ethnic orientation which has impressed itself upon the Prairie landscape for the past one hundred years. In each novel the material used is Mennonite, and the thematic framework in which it is cast is a theological one, tempered primarily by the author's own interpretation of Anabaptist teaching. Wiebe briefly describes the Mennonites in the Foreword to *Peace Shall Destroy Many* as "Anabaptists of the sixteenth century . . . the extreme evangelical wing of the Reformation movement":

> . . . The name "Mennonite" was early attached to them, after Menno Simons, their sole early theological leader to survive persecution. Because the group's literal biblicism expressed itself in believers' baptism, a life of discipleship, separation of church and state, non-participation in war or government, the "Brethren," as they preferred to call themselves, were savagely martyred by Catholic and Protestant alike. Restrained from open proselytizing, they could do no more than teach their faith to their children; what in 1523 began as a religious movement became in time a swarming of a particular people from various nationalities bound together by a faith.[1]

In this same Foreword, Wiebe anticipates a major motif in *The Blue Mountains of China*: "they were a religious nation without a country. They were driven from Switzerland to America, from Holland and northern Germany to Prussia, then Russia, finally to North and South America" (p. [7]).

The characters of both of Wiebe's Mennonite novels are representatives of the group of Mennonites that originated in Holland and northern Germany and began to emigrate to the Steppes of Russia in 1789. By 1914, approximately 100,000 had settled in over two hundred villages spread across the south and east of Russia, even though many had already begun to move to Canada from Russia in 1874. The migration to the New World was undertaken when the

privileges originally offered to the Mennonites by Catherine II —
religious toleration, exemption from military duty, freedom to
establish private educational institutions — were jeopardized; it continued as long as a way out of Russia could be found. The experiences of the fugitives in Moscow, as described in Chapter 4 of
The Blue Mountains, are representative of what these people had to
face when, during the 1920s, they fled from the Communist regime
which at that time further stifled their religious and social liberties.
The story Wiebe tells of the Mennonites in *The Blue Mountains* —
although the details make it a mixture of what he would choose to
call "layers of fact" and "prisms of fiction"[2] — is a genuine physical
and spiritual history of these people. A sense of the authenticity of
Wiebe's account is provided in an individualistic "folk-response" to
the novel:

> Brother Wiebe has torn us up by the roots with the black
> earth still clinging, and for all our people, let us pray.
>
> . . .
>
> The facts of our history we, many of us, know tolerably
> well.
> It is the truth of our history that we have never learned.
>
> . . .
>
> Our history is a history of fragments; God has torn the veil
> of our people; He hath scattered us in remnants abroad.
> Wiebe has gathered up the fragments: often, he has grappled
> with us clumsily, or violently, as we ourselves are a clumsy
> and a violent people . . . often, he has taken us gently like
> children by the hand, as we also may be gentle and like
> children. One would think that, gathering fragments from so
> many diverse places — from Winnipeg to Siberia to South
> America — Wiebe should be left with a patchwork quilt.
> But truly, we are all of the same cloth. Truly, gathered
> together in our kulak boots and our blistered feet and our
> imported alligator shoes, we are all one family.[3]

In an interview, Wiebe once stated that he would like to think of
himself as "someone who's trying to live what the original Ana-
bapists were about."[4] The early Anabaptist fathers had stressed in
their teachings a literal application of Jesus' concept of the brotherhood of man. In his fiction Wiebe attempts to demonstrate that the
man who would seriously wish to express that principle, and so live
at peace with his neighbour, must first find peace within his own soul
— specifically, the peace Jesus spoke of so often, "such as the world

cannot give."[5] Wiebe's theology, as he provides it in *Peace* and *The Blue Mountains* is concerned above all with a definition of this inner peace and with a fictional exploration of some men's discovery of it:

> In a way I see that as the main thing that Jesus is all about, you know, the conscious knowledge of being at peace, in a state of rest in relation to everything around you, because somehow you are in a state of rest in relation to the God that has made it all. You don't have to be perturbed even if you are violently assaulted, because basically you're still at peace. In Jeremiah's images, it's like a moving stream, irresistibly moving on, but, in relation to its environment, perfectly at rest.[6]

Following the publication of *Peace Shall Destroy Many*, most critics expressed an apprehensive, casually dismissive attitude towards Wiebe. The initial reviews, which appeared in newspapers and periodicals that ranged broadly in interest and sophistication, were relatively insensitive to the novel, and were ready to dismiss it altogether. Apparently somewhat embarrassed by Wiebe's explicitly religious themes, reviewers failed generally to receive the novel on its own terms — as a serious attempt to deal aesthetically with a way of life dogmatically sustained by the Mennonite Prairie settlers — and acknowledged the work simply as a token of a new author's "promise." Numerous influential members of the Mennonite community itself were unable to approach the book from a detached perspective, and so further obscured its merits with heated and prolonged controversy.

Critical consideration thus remains confined to these early reviews, in which the novel is frequently perceived as flawed by undue moralizing. Reviewers remain oblivious to young Hal Wiens, who is both thematically and structurally a central figure. *Peace* is not primarily his story, yet Hal, whose name is an abbreviated form of Helmut (from the German: "bright spirit"), represents the positive force sustained throughout the novel which finally points toward a renewal of the life of the Wapiti community.

The story begins with Hal and Jackie Labret, one of the local "half-breeds," looking for frogs' eggs while playing hooky from school on a spring morning:

> Brandishing his empty pail, the fair boy edged farther,

eyes wild with the pushing life of spring.
"The eggs should be out today — oogh!" he gasped, the
water numbing his knees.
"Yah!" The dark boy pushed gurgling by towards the
sprouting grass of the slough-flats. The frogs were croaking
loudly. (p. 10)

It is significant that this young Mennonite boy should be exploring
the countryside with one of the "half-breed" children. Friendly association with the "breeds" is not condoned among the adults, a fact
made evident with regard to the relationships between Herman
Paetkau and Madelaine Moosomin, Elizabeth and Louis, Thom and
the Indian children. Hal's attitude to the "breeds" is distinct:

> You couldn't tell the difference between Jackie Labret and
> Johnny Lepp by the way Hal talked about them. (p. 222)

> "Half-breed" to Hal was merely a species of being that did
> certain things he himself was not allowed to do because they
> were "bad." (p. 15)

Hal appears in three of the four lyrical preludes that define the
cyclical structure of the novel. Spring, Summer and Autumn. Significantly, he does not appear in the prelude to Winter, a season which
the narrator himself indicates bears a direct relationship to the
"spiritual winter" of man. It is only when the heart of Winter has
passed that Hal's older brother, Thom, and other members of the
community, begin to realize the folly of their life of avoidance and to
reconcile themselves to a mode of acceptance already practised by
this simple child who innocently embraces the world. Young Hal
symbolically prefigures the state of inner peace, the reality and significance of which others are made to comprehend only at the end.
He is the agent who announces in the last pages of the book that the
community's isolation will end, by his denying the notion that the
bush — which, as the central metaphor, represents the barrier between Wapiti and the world — defines its physical and spiritual
borders.

As the world of Wapiti begins to disintegrate and the superficially-
accepted formulae by which the people of the Mennonite community
have structured their existence fail to sustain them, Thom Wiens
comes to a fresh awareness. On Christmas eve he begins to perceive
how Deacon Block's attempt to maintain an old, external order in a

new land has strained the concept of Christian brotherhood and the pacifist stance, so central to the early Anabaptist faith. Thom, whose call into military service is imminent, has already begun to question the working out of the beliefs of his forefathers against the demands of war. He is struck now by what meaning the Christmas pageant might have for him as a member of a traditionally non-resistant religious group. As he watches and listens, the barn adjacent to the Wapiti school becomes a grotesque parody of the scene of the nativity. The violence he witnesses makes him realize that he must consider the question of non-resistance in a context that extends far beyond the immediate conditions of the war:

> . . . a long forgotten statement by Joseph rose to his
> memory. 'We are spared war duty and possible death on the
> battlefield only because we are to be so much the better
> witnesses for Christ here at home.' Comprehending suddenly
> a shade of those words' depth, he realized that two wars did
> not confront him; only one's own two faces. And he was
> felled before both.
>   No. If in suppression and avoidance lay defeat, then vic-
> tory beckoned in pushing ahead. Only a conquest by love
> unites the combatants. And in the heat of this battle lay
> God's peace. (p. 238)

Thom, equipped with Joseph Dueck's knowledge about the meaning of peace, suddenly realizes the significance of the words boldly displayed at the front of the Wapiti school: "Peace on Earth, Goodwill towards Men." The discovery of peace as an inner state is central to the working out of Thom's mental and spiritual struggle. Similarly, in *The Blue Mountains of China*, the recognition that peace is not an outward condition allows David Epp and John Reimer to affirm their own unique responses to their world.

Because the theology of *Peace Shall Destroy Many* is consistent with that of *The Blue Mountains of China*, the first novel, which is mostly concerned with defining the nature of what Wiebe regards as the peace Jesus spoke of, serves as a valuable introduction to *The Blue Mountains*; the latter is concerned with the practical experience of this peace in man's life. Central to an understanding of the theology of both novels are Joseph Dueck's lengthy comments on the several meanings of the term "peace," comments making up a treatise rather too awkwardly presented within the context of *Peace* in the form of a letter from Dueck to Thom Wiens. Wiebe will not be misunderstood here. Dueck, who acts as the author's mouthpiece, delineates in a very straight-forward manner several of the traditional ways of apprehending and applying the term "peace." He begins by saying:

> . . . "peace" is often used in a general statement "to hold one's peace" — that is, a state of restfulness which includes silence. . . . As long as everything goes smoothly and they themselves cannot be blamed, "peace" is being maintained. (p. 162)

The "peace" Dueck speaks of here is, as he himself states, the form "frequently applied in our church meetings when a difficult point arises." This is the quiescence Thom refers to when he speaks with his mother about Block: "he is Deacon; everyone's quiet and peaceful when he speaks" (p. 218). Similarly, it is what the Deacon himself refers to when he approaches Herb Unger about the running of the latter's farm: "we all want to live at peace together. That is best" (p. 77).

By its very nature both superficial and threatening, it is a kind of whitewash which harbours decay underneath. Like the second use of the word "peace" which Dueck defines, its presence is a symptom of the impending destruction of the community: "As long as God gives us good crops and we don't have to fight in any war we are at peace. We can squabble with our neighbour as much as we please. Or we can neglect him entirely" (p. 162). Not peace but meretricious good order is what the people of Wapiti experience in their relationship with the neighbouring "half-breeds," whom Dueck refers to at the *Gemeindestunde:* "They know that when war was declared, we all, on the instant, professed a love for our fellow man, men thousands of miles away whom we had never seen, a love which they, living beside us for fourteen years, had never felt" (p. 61).

The overriding desire, among the people of Wapiti, for such a public tranquility, makes Thom Wien's thought that perhaps "it would be better living in a community with a man named Two Poles than with a man named Unger" strike him as the "strangest thought [he] could imagine" (p. 39). The desire for the maintenance of this kind of peace provides an excuse for the fact that no one ever visits Herman Paetkau, the rationale for buying out all the English and "half-breeds" in the area, and, finally, the grounds for Thom's question to his mother: "And why must we in Wapiti love only Mennonites?" (p. 215).

Dueck defines near the end of this letter what he perceives to be the peace of which Jesus spoke; it is the peace which allows him to leave Wapiti.

. . . Peace is not a thing static and unchanging: rather a
mighty inner river . . . that carries all outward circumstances
before it as if they were driftwood. This was the peace
Christ brought; he never compromised with a sham slothful
peace, as we want to. He said, "Do not think that I have
come to bring peace on earth; I have not come to bring
peace, but a sword." He brought no outward quiet and comfort such as we are ever praying for. Rather, he brought inward peace that is in no way affected by outward war but
quietly overcomes it on life's real battle field: the soul of
man. By personally living His peace, we are peacemakers.
(pp. 162-3)

Dueck is responding here to Wapiti's avoidance of everything that
does not relate directly to the well-being of the immediate community. For the Mennonites here, apathy and retreat had become a vul-
garized expression of the social and political passivity which had
been adopted by the Anabaptists during and after their many years
of persecution. Although they had originated as the forceful left wing
of the Reformation, the Mennonites, driven relentlessly by their pur-
suers into the far corners of the continent, had been early forced to
withdraw from all forms of public life. They came to be known, and
to regard themselves, as *"die Stille im Lande"*; that is, "the quiet in
the land." Their passivity was most obviously demonstrated in their
doctrine of non-resistance, a belief initially respected by the govern-
ments of the countries in which they chose to settle. In his message to
Thom, Dueck insists that the Mennonites must begin to express their
pacifism not by turning away from the hatred and warfare in the
world, but by combatting it with positive action. This idea is more
violently reiterated by the inwardly tormented Samuel U. Reimer
when he replies to the psychiatrist in Chapter 12 of *The Blue Mountains of China.*

"Maybe one man can't change the way the world runs. But
can't he do something, anything, just some little thing maybe
about what he thinks is worst? Can't he?"

. . .

"You were in the big war and you say it's terrible. Okay, I
wasn't. I was a Mennonite C.O. In 1943 the church worked
it out for me and I worked in a camp, but that doesn't mean
I'm not really a C.O."

. . .

"I did, well, mighty little then — dirt jobs, that was the way

to live for others in World War II; I guess. I'll never be sorry
for planting a tree rather than shooting a man. Anyway
that's the way I did, then, and less ever since. Nothing really. But now — now . . . now such nothing isn't enough . . .
For me war, mutilation, starving people, that's the worst,
now."[7]

Sam Reimer stands somewhere between those characters whom
Wiebe presents as people able to move forward positively, enthusias-
tically embracing an existence to which a faith in God has given
meaning, and those in whom irrepressible guilt has brought about a
complete rejection of life. Beside Sam on the one hand is David Epp,
"reckless of anything save his reckless faith"; (p. 137) on the other
Jacob Friesen V, so driven by fear of an omnipresent God that he can
cope only temporarily with his existence by repeating mechanically
the bed-time prayer common among Mennonite children: "Lieber
Heiland, mach mich fromm, dass ich in den Himmel komm" —
"Blessed Saviour make me pure that I may get to Heaven."
During the time that Sam encounters all the social obstacles that
prevent him from going to Vietnam to "proclaim peace" he continually recalls the story of David Epp, of whom his brother John
had told him. David had received God's call as abruptly as Sam had,
but despite his misgivings he had responded at once: "David . . .
such a dreamer such a wonderful dreamer who even when they were
in China already, over the border with their whole skin and not a
Communist in two hundred miles to touch them he still keeps right
on dreaming" (p. 55). On the other side of the blue mountains,
David Epp suddenly had recalled with a troubled spirit what his
father once had said about there being peace over every hilltop, and
he had recognized that he had been deceived. Overwhelmed with the
realization that his personal peace did not lie across the mountains,
he had resolved to return to his Russian village and to those friends
and relatives whom he and the others had betrayed. For Sam Reimer,
however, the realization that he should have gone anyway, gone to
Vietnam, somehow, despite all the obstacles which had been thrown
in his way, came too late:

> "It was a mistake. When I heard the voice, I should of
> gone. Left a note and gone. When you know like that, are
> chosen, you shouldn't wait, talk. Go."
> "Sam," [Emily] said. "Sam, what would it have helped?
> What?"
> "Maybe not a thing, nothing. Like that Epp that went

back." He thought a little. "Yes. It would have helped
nothing. But do it, that's it. Some of it, just do it," he added
heavily. (p. 179)

David, "that Epp" to whom Sam alludes, is never heard of again
after he crosses the mountains back into Russia, yet Wiebe makes it
very clear that if David had to die, he would have done so as a man
at peace with himself, free from the anguish Sam suffers for not
knowing if he might indeed have been able to proclaim peace in Vietnam. The prose passage which expresses David's emotions when he
arrives in Russia, after crossing back alone over the blue mountains
of China, contains one of the most explicit allusions to the title of the
novel and illuminates its thematic significance. The phrase, "the blue
line . . . of the mountains," is interrupted by a significant short interior monologue — a narrative mode which, throughout the novel,
renders the most personal responses of a character to his immediate
condition — *"over every hilltop is peace now every treetop moves
through you: every breath cease the nestlings hush in the wood now
only wait you too will soon have peace"* (p. 140). David realizes the
multiple ironies that accompany his father's belief that peace can
mean anything anywhere else but in man's own soul.

The final scene of David's story shows him sitting at home before
"the dishes from their last eating." The description is reminiscent of
the last supper of Christ. David, a betrayer, has been unable to wrest
his mind from the fact that *"the Lord Jesus the same night in which
he was betrayed"* offered the first communion, and said *"but let a
man examine himself and so let him eat of that bread and drink of
that cup for he eats and drinks unworthily eats and drinks damna-
tion to himself"* (pp. 126, 130). The only peace that David Epp can
finally experience — the peace that was denied Sam Reimer — is the
peace of reconciliation with God, documented by Joseph Dueck in
Peace Shall Destroy Many. While he sits in his deserted Russian
home, David sees the mountains again, but recognizing the irony in-
herent in what the blue mountains of China had actually come to
represent to him, he sees them in a significantly new light: "he
thought he could see the blue line . . . of the mountains far away,
beautiful as they had ever been from there. But he knew now that
was only his imagination. Or romantic nostalgia" (p. 140).

As it is the language of a visionary dream that provides the title for
Peace Shall Destroy Many,[8] so it is the action of a dreamer. David

Epp, which becomes — indirectly at least — the inspiring force directing the peace missions of David Epp, Jr., and John Reimer, and the would-be pilgrimage of Samuel U. Reimer.

All these men demonstrate a principle already articulated by Thom Wiens in *Peace Shall Destroy Many*, that it was "not reasonable," for example, "for Menno Simons to give up a fat priesthood to become a hounded minister" (p. 47). It is not "reasonable" for David Epp to cross back into Russia, nor for his son to live with the wildest Indians in Paraguay, nor for Sam Reimer to want to go to Vietnam to proclaim peace, nor for his brother John to carry a cross from Winnipeg to Edmonton. "But Joseph keeps questioning," says Annamarie Lepp in *Peace* "can a Christian cast off responsibility by mere refusal — by mere avoidance?" (p. 46). Jesus said, "If anyone wishes to be a follower of mine, he must leave self behind; he must take up his cross and come with me. Whoever cares for his own safety is lost; but if a man will let himself be lost for my sake, he will find his true self."[9] The peace which Jesus brought to man, as Joseph defines it in *Peace*, is the peace John Reimer experiences, symbolized by his taking up an actual cross. Like David Epp, he finds the "inward peace" that "quietly overcomes" external disturbance on what Wiebe refers to as "life's real battle-field: the soul of man."

Inspired by his brother Sam, who, in turn, was inspired by David Epp, John Reimer takes a walking tour toward the mountains. He is a Mennonite Everyman, but he is not rushing from persecution nor toward the peace that his fathers so erroneously sought over and over again beyond mountain ranges. A boy from Nabachler,[10] John is just walking: "I am not going anywhere; at least not in Canada. That's the whole point, and I have to carry something that shows that . . . I am a human being, walking. That's all." When he reaches Calgary he perceives the mountains, as David Epp had observed the mountains of China after he had returned to Russia, in ideal terms: "sharp, beautiful, clean." But both men regard with irony any promise of peace on the other side. Like David, John realizes that "usually when you get over there's always more of what you climbed them to get away from." So he decides to go north instead of west, a decision affected primarily by his own interpretation of Jesus' teaching. John feels no need to cross over the mountains: "On the mountain Moses said, 'Go over that river, there's the land God has given you forever,' but Jesus just said, 'I'm going to make a place ready for you and then I'll come and get you. You wait'" (pp. 225-7).

The most prominent theme of *The Blue Mountains of China* is that Mennonites are New Testament Christians whose promised land

"isn't anywhere on earth." Their role, according to Wiebe, is not to '
seek the peace which they variously and erroneously have interpreted as quiescence, good order, or public tranquility. Peace, Wiebe
insists, is an inner state. Nor are they to become passive and apathe-
tic at home, as Reimer says accusingly, "growing fat off the land."
According to Wiebe's theology, Jesus came not to bring man
Gemütlichkeit, but, as John Reimer says, He came "to lead a revolution" for social justice.

The new society John describes is composed of peace-makers like
Joseph Dueck and David Epp, for example: those who choose first to
live His peace.

Of all Wiebe's mature characters — that is, those who have passed
beyond the time of childhood innocence and the accompanying
"peacefulness" demonstrated by Hal Wiens in *Peace Shall Destroy
Many* — it is Frieda Friesen who stands out as the one who expresses
most completely that perfect state of being. Like Thom Wiens, Sam
Reimer and David Epp, Frieda is confronted quite abruptly with a
crisis situation during which she chooses the way that leads to inner
peace:

> It was a little later, November, 1906, when we already had
> two nice children, Johann and Esther, that God sent me great
> temptation and doubt. My nerves were very bad; I could
> not be alone. The devil stood right beside my bed with red
> horns and said, "Do it, do it!" though he never said what.
> Twice the elders had to come to pray. Then I learned to
> know our Lord Jesus. Through many prayers and sleepless
> nights and God's grace I found forgiveness of all my sins and
> came to the true quiet faith. I was teaching our little Johann
> the night-prayer I had learned as child, but I had to learn
> to pray it again then, like a grown-up who knows has to
> pray to God:

> > Tired am I, go to rest,
> > Close my eyes, hands on my breast.
> > Father, may your eye divine
> > Watch above this bed of mine.
> > Where I did some harm today,
> > See it not dear God, I pray;
> > For your grace and Christ's red blood
> > Makes all of my evil good. (p. 46)

Jesus said "I have told you all this so that in me you may find peace. In the world you will have trouble. But courage! The victory is mine; I have conquered the world."[11] Frieda, in her "true quiet faith," is satisfied that her life is in God's hands. In her gentle first-person narratives, which are effectively interspersed throughout *The Blue Mountains of China*, she emphasizes in her quiet way the value of her own experiences, and by implication, the ultimately coherent, meaningful nature of experience in general. While telling of her life she has counsel for her listeners, wisdom passed down to her from her own father. " 'But think always like this,' he said, 'it does come all from God, strength and sickness, want and plenty'" (p. 10).

Frieda bears a name that suits her most appropriately. "Frieda" is a derivative from the German word, *"Friede,"* which means "peace." "When my father came to get us in the evening," she relates to her listeners, "I said right away that the teacher had said in school I was Frieda. My father laughed. 'Yes, yes. You aren't home now. You aren't Fritzchi like at home and just watch out that you're *friedlich* at school, like your name'" (p. 8).

Frieda's *Friedlichkeit* is such that Wiebe is able to use her life as a fictional exploration of what it might mean for a human being to experience peace, such as the world cannot give, and trust in God that allows him to accept both the easy and the hard of life with goodwill and enthusiasm. Wiebe has created in Frieda a completely believable and engaging character living out an ideal freedom from that inner tension which has come to be called the existential *angst* and thriving as a spiritual being regardless of the nature of external circumstances. Simply to affirm the truth of a promise of God is for many of Wiebe's characters the most significant gesture of their lives. To be able to live day by day in quiet faith, with the conscious knowledge of being at peace because, in the words of Frieda Friesen, "some things in this world only God has to understand," is the promise realized.

Notes

[1] Rudy Wiebe, *Peace Shall Destroy Many* (Toronto: McClelland and Stewart, 1962), p. [7]. All subsequent page references are to this edition.
[2] Ruby Wiebe, "Passage by Land," in *the narrative voice: short stories and reflections by Canadian authors*, ed. John Metcalf, (Toronto: McGraw-Hill Ryerson, 1972), p. 257.

3 David Toews, "Rudy Wiebe — *The Blue Mountains* . . .", a forum for exploration, dialogue, and information published by and for Mennonites in the university (April 1971), p. 4.
4 Rudy Wiebe, "Rudy Wiebe: The Moving Stream is Perfectly at Rest", *Conversations with Canadian Novelists.*, ed. Donald Cameron, (Toronto: Macmillan,
   1973), p. 148.
5 John 14:22 (*New English Bible*)
6 Wiebe, "Rudy Wiebe: The Moving Stream is Perfectly at Rest," p. 156.
7 Rudy Wiebe, *The Blue Mountains of China* (Toronto: McClelland and Stewart,
   1970), p. 172-74. All subsequent page references are to this edition.
8 The title comes from the narrative of a dream vision, recorded in Daniel 8:23-25.
9 Matthew 16:24-26.
10 Wiebe derived the name Nabachler from the endings of the names of the three
   most prominent Mennonite settlements in Manitoba: Gret*na*, Stein*bach*, and
   Wink*ler*.
11 John 16:33

RUDY WIEBE'S APPROACH TO HISTORICAL FICTION: A STUDY OF *THE TEMPTATIONS OF BIG BEAR* AND *THE SCORCHED-WOOD PEOPLE*

Allan Dueck

In *The Temptations of Big Bear* (1973) and *The Scorched-Wood People* (1977), Rudy Wiebe explores a crucial period in the history of the Canadian prairies. *Big Bear* relates the story of the settling of the Canadian West from 1876 to 1888 as seen from the Indians' perspective, and portrays vividly the transformation of the prairie from its wild state into an ordered land. *Scorched-Wood*, which covers roughly the same time period, from 1869 to 1885, re-creates history from the viewpoint of the French Métis, themselves relative newcomers to the prairie but with a unique identity shaped by their dual Indian and French ancestry. This second novel focuses particularly on the historical events culminating in provincehood for Manitoba and Saskatchewan, and in the collision of Métis' values and beliefs with those of the incoming white settlers.

Several distinctive aspects of Wiebe's approach to historical fiction emerge from a careful reading of *Big Bear* and *Scorched-Wood*. His strong sense of the past and his honesty in incorporating the religious elements of life into his art permeate both novels, as they do all of Wiebe's fiction. Wiebe's own Christian world view provides the basis for his radical reinterpretation of Canadian prairie history from the perspective of the defeated outcasts. It also enables him to incorporate into the stories the intensely religious world views of both the River Cree and the Métis peoples. In these novels, the peoplehood — identity and self-respect — of the Indians and Métis becomes a primary focus. As in all of Wiebe's fiction, the people whom he presents most successfully are the primitive peoples who retain close contact with the elemental aspects of life. These novels demonstrate most convincingly Wiebe's surpassing abilities as storyteller, for the stories of Big Bear and Louis Riel are intensely alive.

A sense of the past infuses all Wiebe's work, yet his historical fiction is not mere documentary history. Wiebe rejects the common conception that historical facts are knowable and objectively verifiable by reference to historical data. In his view, the objective rendering of an historical story is impossible because both those who initially recorded the "facts" and those who subsequently interpret them are biased. The narrator in Wiebe's "Where Is the Voice Coming From?", after he has ostensibly attempted to re-create objectively a story from Indian history, realizes that "if ever I could, I can no longer pretend to objective, omnipotent disinterestedness. I am no longer *spectator* of what *has* happened or what *may* happen: I am become *element* in what is happening at this very moment."[1] That is, history does not happen in a vacuum "back there" somewhere, but is imaginatively re-created by the artist. A corollary of this idea is that because people are biased, different people may interpret even the same "facts" differently.

How to present the "facts" is a central concern in *Big Bear*. As Wiebe explains in a headnote to the novel, the material for the story is historically accurate in the sense that it is founded upon real events and real personages. But the story of the "opening up" of the Canadian West, which from the point of view of white history is the glorious story of the indomitable pioneers, is, from the point of view of Indians, anything but glorious. Rather, it is the story of promises made, but not kept, by white invaders, promises of hardship and starvation, and — although there is the poetic promise of a new day — of the death of a culture. In telling the story from the Indians' viewpoint, Wiebe accomplishes what is difficult indeed: he convinces the white reader that the Indian perspective makes infinitely more sense than the white view.

In the collision of the cultures this difference in point of view is readily evident. While the Indian culture values freedom and a close relationship with the land, the white culture values the domination and exploitation of the prairie "wilderness." The whites' tremendous drive to exploit the land is incomprehensible to the River Cree. Big Bear cannot conceive of ownership of the land because, as he says, "No one can choose for only himself a piece of the Mother Earth. She is. And she is for all that live, alike."[2] In contrast Governor Laird happily thinks, "Not quite $53,000 for a bit more than fifty thousand square miles of grass and hills. A down payment actually, but complete with rivers, valleys, minerals, sky — everything, forever!" (p. 69). These fundamentally different understandings of the natural world pervade the whole novel, and Wiebe's empathy with the Indians' more elemental attitude towards the land serves as a basis for criticism of the whites' preoccupation with control and exploitation.

Through the differences in point of view between Indians and whites during Big Bear's trial for treason, Wiebe's reinterpretation of prairie history surfaces most forcefully. When the presiding magistrate asks Big Bear for his own defence, the chief only remarks that he obviously is innocent of contributing to the 1885 Indian uprising because he did not even wear war paint during the turmoil (p. 395).

From his point of view this is a significant argument, but Big Bear immediately recognizes that the court so preoccupied with its "white things" will not seriously consider his view. For that reason he devotes most of his defence to an indictment of the whites for their destruction of the Indians' way of life and an eloquent demand for help; he says, for example, "you have taken our inheritance, and our strength. The land is torn up, black with fires, and empty. *You have done this.* And there is nothing left now but that you must help us" (p. 398). As a final plea, he asks the court "to print my words and scatter them among White People" (p. 400). Clearly, then, one of Wiebe's central concerns in *Big Bear* is to repudiate the biased white view of prairie history and to rectify its errors.

Despite the fact that neither historian nor artist can possibly know how an historical event actually happened, the writer who is creative in his sympathies can, by imaginatively re-creating historical events, get much closer to the "truth" than by attempting to render an exact snapshot. The very mode of presentation, fiction, implies that the writer knows that his way of looking at things is not the only way. Thus, as Wiebe says in his interview with Donald Cameron, "He goes in and shows you, This is the way I see it, as it could have happened."[3] Herbert Butterfield has described this sort of truth in historical fiction as a faithfulness to the spirit of a past age.[4]

Because this imaginative re-creation involves the interpretation of historical "facts," it will inevitably reflect the author's world view. As Wiebe says in his interview with Cameron, an artist can shape the raw materials of history "according to some kind of world view that he has, some kind of concept of what people are like."[5] Without doubt Wiebe's Christian world view contributes to his capacity for dealing meaningfully with historical materials. In *Big Bear,* as in *The Blue Mountains of China* and "Voice," Wiebe can unify the isolated bits of history into an artistic whole because he holds that history *has* meaning. For the many contemporary artists who hold to a relativism no such interpretation is possible, only collage.

Although *Big Bear* is not religious in any formal sense, in contrast to Wiebe's earlier novels, in fact the religious impulse is fundamental to the novel. The whites may speak platitudes about God's goodness and about their religious belief, but their Christianity has no effect on their everyday lives. The Indians, on the other hand, live always in intimate awareness of the Only One (one of Wiebe's several translations of the Indians' term for the Supreme Deity) and assume the Only One's relevance. The most striking evidence of the Indians' intense religiosity comes in Big Bear's own visionary orientation, similar in many respects to Louis Riel's in *Scorched-Wood*. Metaphorical in style, each vision shows the chief's intimacy with the spiritual world and at the same time foreshadows events yet to come in the novel. In the bundle vision, Big Bear encounters a Little Man who shows him six River People, "their hands behind their backs and their heads twisted to the side as if their spirits had been jerked out at their necks and their necks frozen" (p. 65). That vision points years ahead to the hanging of Wandering Spirit and five other Cree warriors for their parts in the uprisings against white Canada. In a vision Big Bear receives after his last buffalo hunt, Coyote shows the chief a fountain of blood that turns the whole world richly red, a vision that anticipates the Rattlers' bloody attack on Frog Lake which not even the old chief's frantic "*Tesqua, tesqua!* Stop! STOP!" can squash (p. 258). While these visions play an important role in the novel's narrative structure, their primary significance lies in their testimony to Big Bear's spirituality.

The Indians' religiosity is apparent also in their approaches to everyday life. When the chiefs smoke together or the community gathers for a Thirst Dance, the Indians celebrate their peoplehood and also their relationship to a larger reality. Despite the strong hierarchy within the Indian community it is more egalitarian than white democracy because, as Big Bear says, the "[Great] Spirit is above all, and under His eye every person is the same" (p. 17). Whether stealing horses, hunting buffalo, or fighting, the Indians always pray for the blessings of the Main One and thank Him for His help. Big Bear addresses even the problem of evil in religious terms; although he doubts the goodness of the Only One in sending the whites and taking away the buffalo, he thinks the "Spirit must have sent these whites to us so we must find the way He wants us to live with them" (p. 105). Subsequently, in terms reminiscent of Frieda Friesen's stoic acceptance of all things as from God, Big Bear says that "it is good in one way I am cheated, for now I begin to understand what great good The Only One had given me. Now I can truly worship the kindness of That One" (p. 196). That the Indians in *Big Bear* share with the best Christians in Wiebe's other fiction an intense awareness of transcendent reality and a strong sense of peoplehood and equality suggests not that they are thinly disguised Mennonites, but that Wiebe recognizes the validity of other varieties of religious experience than his own.

The importance of peoplehood — foundational in the unique self-

understandings of Old Testament Israel and the Christian Church —
infuses Wiebe's historical fiction. In none of his historical fiction does
Wiebe's use of historical rather than contemporary materials indicate
a merely antiquarian interest in the past. As Wiebe remarks in his
interview with Donald Cameron, the past is relevant because it is
part of each person's present.[6] For Wiebe, therefore, stories are in a
sense explorations of today.[7] In *Blue Mountains* the leitmotif of "the
knowledge of / our origins, and where / we are in truth, / whose
land this is / and is to be"[8] implies this use of history. The critical
exploration of Russian Mennonite history in *Blue Mountains* takes
an important step towards defining who the Mennonites are today.
Before a people can know who it is today, it must know who it was
in the past.

Indeed, for any culture seeking its identity, a knowledge of its origins is essential. Canadian Indians, many of whom know nothing
about their past except perhaps the white misconception that they
are the "bad guys" in a television western or the "drunken bums" of
the prairie depression novel, must know that they are more than
that. And one of Wiebe's achievements in *Big Bear* is surely that he
depicts the Indians as a people that can look back upon moments in
its past with pride. This portrayal is not a call for Indians to return to
primitive ways, for that is, even if romantically desirable, impossible. It is rather the assertion of their peoplehood that must precede
any recovery of cultural vitality. Specific themes, such as Big Bear's
call for unity among all Indian people in opposing the white menace,
are obviously topical in today's redefinition of cultural roots among
Canadian Indians. But the awareness which the novel brings that the
Indians have had a dynamic culture with a strong sense of transcendent reality, intimate ties with the land, a genuine sense of community and, of course, great leaders such as Big Bear, is crucial.

Wiebe says in "On the Trail of Big Bear," the "stories we tell of our
past are by no means merely words: they are meaning and life to us
as *people*, as a *particular* people; the stories are there, and if we do
not know of them we are simply . . . memory ignorant, and the less
are we people."[9] Big Bear's final words at his trial underscore this rich
understanding of voice and story as life-blood of a people. He says,
"A word is power, it comes from nothing into meaning and a Person
takes his name with him when he dies. I have said my last words.
Who will say a word for my people? Give my people help! I have
spoken" (p. 398). Who will speak for his people? His own voice, his
story as told now by Wiebe, becomes the word that can contribute to
a renewed sense of peoplehood among the Cree and other Indian
peoples.

Although ideas are important in *Big Bear*, this is not finally an "idea-novel"; it is a superb story. Despite the novel's considerable length and the diversity of the characters, the reader remains engrossed throughout. The novel is not, of course, flawless. Both the segment presenting the series of battles between the Indians and the whites and the one reconstructing the trial of Big Bear seem overly long, although in each case some justification for the length is plausible. At times in *Big Bear*, as in Wiebe's earlier fiction, some of the characters towards whom Wiebe obviously is not sympathetic seem to be caricatures. Sometimes, however, caricature is an effective means of satire as, for example, in the story of the "grand pursuit of Big Bear" where General Middleton becomes a jam-eating Falstaff who avoids confrontation with the River Cree in battle, but hurries back to Fort Pitt to receive praise for his "victory" when the Indians surrender. And, although some characters with whom Wiebe does not sympathize are caricatures, others such as the missionary McDougall are quite credible.

Despite these flaws, *Big Bear* demonstrates Wiebe's ability to use symbol and metaphor effectively; it demonstrates further that Wiebe now trusts the symbols enough not to have to explain them. The prominent motif in *Big Bear* of the gradual transition from buffalo to train confirms this sureness in Wiebe's artistry. Initially the buffalo roam the prairies — although ominous signs of their depletion are evident — but as the white encroachment continues the buffalo give way to the railroad until, finally, Big Bear receives a vision of the world "slit open with unending lines, squares, rectangles . . ." (p. 409). This extended metaphor emphasizes the inexorable destruction of the Indian culture. Another motif that dramatically reinforces the downfall of the culture is Big Bear's gradually diminishing stature among his people. While initially he is an eminent and respected leader, he slowly loses his influence until eventually the young warriors in his following, Little Bad Man and Wandering Spirit, begin to dictate policy. His voice no longer respected in the community councils, Big Bear becomes Lear in rags as he walks about wearing only a shabby old blanket. In the sense that Big Bear is not merely an individual but a representative of the River People, his humiliation parallels and reflects the decline of the culture.

Throughout his fiction, Wiebe has shown a tremendous empathy with the primitive mind. Writing primarily about Indians, Eskimos, and rural Mennonites, Wiebe has:

. . . a truly admirable feel for the obscure, deep-seated

drives that motivate people who have not yet made their life-experience artificial and alien by conceptualizing and intellectualizing it. He knows what really matters to most people — the simple facts of existence from birth to death — and beyond. He knows that man is not self-sufficient and that he needs to believe in a force above and beyond his control or comprehension if he is to find meaning in life.[10]

Big Bear encompasses the lives of just such primitive people. An old man's calling the children to sleep with the Sun, the "coned warmth of the lodge" (p. 51), delight in the taste of warm buffalo blood and milk, exuberance at the Thirst Dance, and the security of sexual companionship: these are the everyday activities and emotions that matter to the River Cree. Not all experiences are happy, of course. Big Bear loses his good name unjustly, the Cree are often hungry, and death becomes a frequent intruder into the Cree camps. But whether happy or distressful, the experiences that pervade the novel are not intellectual abstractions.

In his historical fiction, Wiebe tries to get past mere reportage to what Butterfield calls the "human story" behind past events.[11] Wiebe himself describes the quest for authenticity in the following terms:

> Trusting the "quintuplet senses", the story teller, too, has been tutoring them, to be his guide through the maze of life and imagination. Through the smoke and darkness and piled-up factuality of a hundred years to see a face; to hear, and comprehend, a voice whose verbal language he will never understand; and then to risk himself beyond such seeing, such hearing as he discovers possible, and venture into the finer labyrinths opened by those other senses: touch, to learn the texture of leather, of earth; smell, the tinct of sweetgrass and urine; taste, the golden poplar sap or the hot, raw buffalo liver dipped in gall.[12]

In the characterization of Big Bear, Wiebe succeeds in getting at the human side of historical events, for the chief is one of the most intensely human characters in all of Wiebe's fiction. Having a reverence for the earth and for deep human relationships, and an awareness of the transcendent, Big Bear knows what is truly important in life. He is, as Kitty McLean recognizes, a "Person" not only in the sense of being one of the River People but in the sense of being fully human.

One of the most positive aspects of *Big Bear* is its powerful ending.

In Wiebe's previous novels, particularly *Peace Shall Destroy Many* and *First and Vital Candle*, a somewhat heavy-handed melodrama tends to mar the conclusions. In this novel Wiebe creates a poetic evocation of Big Bear's "trail to the Sand Hills" that unifies the central threads of the novel and culminates in an affirmation of life that makes the story more than a monument to the death of a culture. Despite the undeniable realities of the Indians' degradation, Big Bear retains a faith in the Only One and the land that He has given. In this tremendous affirmation of life and in the symbolism of the rising sun, the novel transcends the pathetic plight of the Indians to affirm a faith that the values and spirit of the Indian peoples will survive.

As Big Bear is in many ways the embodiment of his people, so is Riel, in Wiebe's vision, a focus for Métis history and cultural identity. Permeating *The Scorched-Wood People*,[13] as it pervades *Big Bear*, is Wiebe's incisive reinterpretation of Canadian prairie history, here, involving the so-called Riel Rebellions. At the heart of this reinterpretation lies Wiebe's fresh approach to the motivations of leading personalities in the historical scenario, particularly Louis Riel and John A. Macdonald. If white historians have tended to depict Louis Riel as a fanatical, though perhaps eloquent, madman who made preposterous political claims for the Métis as a means of blocking the white Canadian push westward towards a vast Canadian confederation, Wiebe, in marked contrast, portrays Riel as a religious visionary who makes tremendous efforts to advance the cause of his people always in reasonable and humanitarian ways. In fact, in *Scorched-Wood*, Riel's honesty and generosity appear almost to be handicaps that ultimately allow unscrupulous whites, headed by Macdonald, to deprive the Métis not only of all their just rights but of their human dignity as well. By sharp contrast, John A. Macdonald, whom white history has affectionately regarded as a pillar of integrity and the grandfather of Canadian confederation, emerges as a dishonest and shrewd political schemer who preaches morality and justice, but who lives a continuous lie. In dealing with the Métis' reasonable causes for discontent on the prairies, Macdonald's characteristic responses are bribery, dishonesty, and evasion; if these fail, then guns.

Wiebe's reinterpretation of prairie history is apparent not only in his portrayal of leading personalities in that history, but also in his incisive juxtaposition of the moralities and attitudes of the invading and indigenous peoples. One such juxtaposition occurs in terms of the two sides' ethics of war. The catalogue of white atrocities at the Battle of Batoche is long. In contrast to the Métis' use of old guns, the

WASP army tests the new Gatling gun, a "patented killing machine" against the few Métis trying to protect their farms and families (p. 247). The whites loot Métis property indiscriminately (p. 280), and General Middleton himself falsely accuses and arrests a Métis individual in order to steal his furs (p. 302). In comparison with the Métis' careful self-defence, many of the whites seem intent on the torture of Métis life and the destruction of their property almost as ends in themselves. Thus, in terms of the ethics of war, Wiebe clearly offers a new perspective on prairie history; in Scorched-Wood the adjective "savage" fits the "democratic," "humanistic" whites much more appropriately than it fits the Métis.

The portrayals of leading Canadian statesmen, such as Macdonald and Laurier, as charlatans and amoral political opportunists, and of supposedly savage rebels such as Riel and Dumont, as honest, humanitarian, and democratic persons illustrate Wiebe's radical vision of prairie history. In his portrayal of such historical incidents as Riel's hanging and in his comparison of Métis and WASP Canada in terms of the ethics of war and the morality of land ownership, Wiebe's new perspective on "the facts" is further apparent. The reinterpretation of history in Scorched-Wood reinforces Wiebe's aesthetic premise in "Where Is the Voice Coming From?": that several stories about the same historical events can take very different forms when seen from different perspectives.

Talking with Donald Cameron, Wiebe defines himself as "someone who's trying to live what the original Anabaptists were about. . . . To be an Anabaptist is to be a radical follower of the person of Jesus Christ . . ."[14] Many readers can readily discover Wiebe's Anabaptist-Christian perspective in Peace or Candle in which Joseph Dueck and Josh Bishop use specifically Christian language, and speak against war and in favour of nonresistant love. But, although the characters in Scorched-Wood do not share Wiebe's own stripe of Christianity, Wiebe's fundamental religious perspective informs the entire novel. In Scorched-Wood, as in Big Bear, Wiebe's reinterpretation of the history itself reflects the author's world view. But the religious dimensions of the novel go much further. The Métis' Catholic Christianity, particularly as expressed by Riel, provides the vantage point from which the Métis interpret all their experiences. Riel's political actions grow out of his Christian beliefs. The issue of Riel's sanity or insanity revolves around the varying views about the validity of his religious claims. And, finally, the nature of Riel's role as visionary prophet of his people merges into a saintly Christ-like calling that further underscores the religious orientation of the novel.

That Wiebe's reinterpretation of Indian and Métis' history reflects his Christian world view is clear. From the point of view of Anabaptist Christianity, Christ's mission was that of being a servant, particularly to oppressed and underprivileged peoples. Two Mennonite scholars, Perry and Elizabeth Yoder, refer to several New Testament passages (among them Mark 10:42-45 and Luke 22:24-29) to support the Anabaptist theology of Christian life as servanthood. The Yoders summarize their analysis in these words: "In the kingdom of God social structures and roles are different. Greatness in the kingdom is evidenced not in dominance, but in service of others."[15] Furthermore, Anabaptist Christianity affirms the ultimate worth and dignity of each human life. This viewpoint reflects itself today in Mennonite nonresistance, which receives forceful expressions in each of Wiebe's first three novels. These fundamental religious perspectives go a long way to explain Wiebe's thoroughgoing reinterpretation of prairie history in *Big Bear* and *Scorched-Wood*. In both novels, Wiebe examines historical events from the perspective of suffering underdogs instead of from the viewpoint of the conquerors and dominators.

Another pervasive indication of Wiebe's religious orientation lies in the profoundly religious outlook in terms of which the Métis understand all experiences in life. This quality stamps all the major characters in Wiebe's fiction from Thom Wiens to Frieda Friesen to Big Bear to Louis Riel. As does Big Bear, Riel lives every moment of his life by the visions he receives, though Riel's language for the source of these visions — the Holy Spirit — is Christian. In his commitment to lead the Métis people, Riel is guided by visions that call him to his mission. At St. Anthony's before declaring the formation of the new Provisional Government, Riel explains:

> "The Spirit of God fell upon the sainted Bourget of Montreal, blessed be his named, who knew us and knew our prayers, who told me my grand commission for our people of the North-West, and hear his words: 'You have a great mission to fulfil, which you must complete in every respect.' And God's glory has broken like lightning from the vaulted domes of golden cathedrals, his voice has rolled thunder to us in a wooden church: 'Hear me! My son, why do you fight against me? Have I not called you, Louis David Riel? To the great mission of the Métis people? Rise! Call your people to that mission with which I will bless the earth!'"
> (p. 223)

Not only in terms of his life-long mission but also in terms of his daily intercourse, Riel lives by his visions. Before the Battle of Batoche, for example, the Métis leader "cannot see [in his prayers] ambush and night raids" (p. 255), and soon afterward he receives a vision that tells him the battle is to take place on the hill above Batoche (pp. 263, 277). Riel's interpretation of the Métis' experience in terms of Old Testament patterns further reflects his fundamentally religious viewpoint. When in 1869 Riel prays the Israelite prayer from Deuteronomy 26:5-10 (p. 24) as the invocation for Métis nationhood, he clearly sees Métis experience in terms of Israel's experience in biblical times. In terms of his prayers and visions, and interpretations of everyday realities in his life, then, Riel reflects a profoundly religious viewpoint.

Much like the issue of Samuel U. Reimer's sanity in *Blue Mountains*, the issue of Riel's sanity arises in connection with doubts about the validity of his religious experience. Most white Canadians in the novel consider Riel mad because of his religious visions. General Middleton, for example, considers him "sane enough in general everyday subjects," but finds his eyes "mad . . . quite mad" (pp. 314-15). Even his friend, Dr. Lachapelle, who regards Riel with great tenderness, cannot accept Riel's religious claims as valid.

> Such a clear case of megalomania, of messianic paranoia, overheated on Bible-reading and persecution, the world in the clutch of evil, take the flaming sword of God and destroy it in judgement. Father Bolduc saw too much religious problem here; Riel's political ambitions on earth finished forever, and now clearly he was making himself a role so unreal that actual events would never prove him wrong; destroy Protestant London, papal Rome. Oh, poor Louis! . . . [A] brilliant mind, a charismatic personality destroyed, destroyed. (p. 166)

Yet, Riel's followers, notably Gabriel and the members of the Exovedate, confirm the validity of Riel's religious claims and, hence, his sanity. Confirmation of Riel's sanity, and, by implication, of his religious views, comes most articulately from Dr. Augustus Jukes, senior surgeon of the North-West Mounted Police, who says that "we are too likely to call men whose understanding of life goes counter to the usual opinion, insane. Sanity becomes then a mere matter of majority opinion, not a test of the wisdom of what is spoken" (p. 330). The novel as a whole, then, reflects the viewpoint of the narrator who thinks "Riel the most sane man in that courtroom in Regina, the most saintly man in the North-west . . ." (p. 331). Religious experience, Wiebe asserts, is a mark of sanity — not evidence of insanity.

The centrality of the religious impulse in *Scorched-Wood* characterizes all Wiebe's fiction. As Wiebe explains in a recent interview with Brian Bergman, "It seems to me that the religious and spiritual dimensions of the human being are of almost supreme importance in understanding the humanness of a character . . . I couldn't possibly write a novel about a character who didn't, to some extent at least, have a spiritual orientation towards his world and himself."[16] Although Wiebe's intensely religious world view is exceptional in today's fiction, it has an authenticity that commands respect.

As in *Blue Mountains* and *Big Bear*, Wiebe's use of history in *Scorched-Wood* is forward-looking. In each novel, Wiebe gives the people who are its subject a voice: a voice that helps to define the identity and self-respect of the people whether Mennonites, River Cree, or Métis. Herbert Butterfield describes the highest potential for the historical novel in these terms: the historical novel "becomes the consciousness of belonging to a place and a tradition . . . In this way it becomes itself a power in history, an impulse to fine feeling, and a source of more of the action . . . which it describes. The historical novel itself becomes a maker of history."[17] In *Scorched-Wood*, as in all his historical fiction, Wiebe helps a people know who they are.

Primary among the obstacles to peoplehood for the Métis is the whites' prejudice. This is reflected, for instance, by Judge Black's condescension for the moccasins on Riel's feet (p. 64), or Macdonald's dismissal of the Métis as "nothing but pemmican-eaters" (p. 115). Prejudice becomes overt discrimination when the WASP settlers disregard Métis' land claims, the Hudson's Bay Company trades unfairly with them, and even nuns such as Sara receive dehumanizing treatment. White definitions of Métis people can all too easily become the Métis' own definitions of themselves. Thus, people such as the young Joseph Delorme cannot "look a big white like Schultz in the eye" (p. 37), and even Riel himself has "lived through the blur of youth and guilt so totally other than his own he never knew the right connections, the correct behaviour as even the most ignorant white did instinctively . . ." (p. 80). A more insidious barrier than white prejudice and discrimination is the transfer of Métis' loyalties to the whites, which indicates the loss of the Métis' self-worth. Remarks such as Riel makes about Joe McKay, a Métis "sell-out," form a recurring refrain through the novel: "McKay was exactly the kind of half-breed the Saskatchewan did not need: a man who used his Cree wits and his Cree body to carry about negotiation demands for the police" (p. 227). The ultimate obstacle to people-hood is, as narrator Pierre Falcon says, the loss of pride in oneself and one's past. For the Métis, this loss of pride results in their utter degradation, as they become "known simply as 'road allowance people', having no place whatever except in their clanking wagons, their rusted cars on the placeless public roads" (p. 328).

Narrator Falcon, in terms similar to Wiebe's remarks about cul-tural identity in "On the Trail," points to the precondition for a positive Métis identity. Falcon recalls Métis' dreams "of a peculiar people and the pride of yourself as a self . . ." (p. 276). Such pride is precisely what most Métis in the novel lack. Not only the sell-outs, but even many of Riel's faithful followers lack such self-understanding. In the rifle pits at Batoche, for example, Patrice and Napoléon define Métis identity in negative terms. Napoléon admits he is not Sioux or Cree, and Patrice returns, "You're not French Canadian either" (p. 286). Moïse Ouellette shows a more profound self-understanding when he says, "We are who we are" (p. 286), but Moïse speaks for a minority.

In the vacuum of self-identity, Riel emerges as the voice of the Métis people in the same way that Big Bear is the voice of the River Cree. Just as the narrative technique in "The Naming of Albert Johnson" reflects Wiebe's notion that a person or idea is not "real" until it has been named,[18] so here Riel becomes the voice that "names" the Métis people and thereby helps to shape their identity. Always when he speaks in public, his voice holds the "crowd's atten-tion with his first word" (p. 27), as it does when he addresses the celebrating Métis at the Red River. And, as the skeptical Madeleine Dumont learns, Riel's voice exerts even greater power in interper-sonal situations; she confirms Gabriel's observation that when you "hear him alone, there's no way to shake him" (p. 264). Wiebe's em-phasis upon Riel's voice is not merely an affirmation of the leader's oratorical eloquence, but also of his speaking the story of the Métis so they can gain the self-respect necessary for survival as a people. In this sense, Riel repeatedly describes his incessant writing as "writing . . . to give his people a voice" (pp. 131, 159). This voice always tells them the same story, though in different words: that they are not merely "road allowance people," but a people with a unique heritage and a worthwhile identity.

Riel's calling as the voice of his people merges subtly with his saint-hood in the novel. At the end of his stay at the Grey Sisters' hospital in Quebec, Riel rededicates himself to the cause of his people in religious terms: "if the sacred cause of the Métis reclaims me, could I, their brother, refuse them my life, my blood?" (p. 167). Subsequently Riel prays repeatedly for strength "to love my people according to your mercy" (pp. 187-88). Through his suffering love for his people, he becomes, as Bishop Grandin realizes, the Métis' saint (p. 218). Riel himself recognizes that his execution promises redemptive possibilities for his people; he reports that the spirit has told him Macdonald has to hang him so "the people can make me a saint" (p. 337). At the end, Gabriel confirms Riel's saintly role as voice of the Métis people. Not only does Gabriel assert the validity of Riel's vision, but he points to Riel as a voice for the Métis in the future: "you think Riel is finished? He said a hundred years is just a spoke in the wheel of eternity. We'll remember. A hundred years and whites still won't know what to do with him" (p. 351). "We'll remember." To the extent that the Métis can recover a view of themselves as Riel saw them and as Riel himself lived — to that extent, Wiebe suggests, they can recover their cultural vitality and self-respect. As in *Big Bear*, the ending of *Scorched-Wood* is thoroughly positive. Though it does not gloss over the present realities of Métis degradation, it points the way to a recovery of their peoplehood in the future.

Speaking about the Eskimo Higilaq's song, Wiebe in the "Introduction" to *The Story-Makers* remarks that the fact that "we encounter her journey almost a century later" indicates that "story *is*, much longer than the fact."[19] In *Scorched-Wood*, as in all Wiebe's historical fiction, historical accuracy is not the primary goal despite Wiebe's meticulous concern for precise historical data as a basis for his novels.[20] Wiebe's real goal in his historical fiction is to "shape facts and events" with such skill as "to show the human meanings behind them . . . , [to] move us to understand 'what happened' in a profounder human way."[21] *Scorched-Wood* exemplifies Wiebe's achievement in reaching this goal, for the story moves us to a deeper understanding of the events in prairie history and their meaning for all Canadians today.

Despite a few rough edges, *Scorched-Wood* convincingly demonstrates Wiebe's masterful storytelling. One notable strength lies in the narrative technique itself. Wiebe's use of old Pierre Falcon as narrator is both appropriate and effective. Pierre, a wise person whose experience dates back to the days when the Métis fought for Cuthbert Grant but who outlives the events of 1885, spans a wide sweep of Métis experience and reflects authentically and sagely on it. He is, furthermore, Riel's grandfather (p. 35), and so is credible as a spokesperson for Riel's own experience. A particularly suitable aspect of Pierre's characterization is his role as poet-singer of his people. At the Métis' Red River celebration of the first Provisional Government, Pierre leads the celebrants with "The Sad Ballad of King Muck" (pp. 38ff.), a satire of William McDougall, the appointed Governor of the North-West. Although occasionally narrator Falcon explains that his songs are earthy and humourous and that he must leave the exact story for Riel's own more accurate words, Falcon as singer of his people's songs merges into Riel, as voice of his people, and even into Wiebe, himself the voice of the Métis in the novel.

Another effective aspect of the story is Wiebe's emphasis upon the cyclical pattern of the Métis' experience. The larger pattern of Wiebe's novels is always a clue to their meaning. In *Peace*, for example, the movement of the action through four seasons indicates Thom Wiens' progressive growth from blindly following traditional Mennonite faith in spring to the winter of his and the community's spiritual dissolution and the promise of rebirth with the return of spring. And in *Candle* the seven sections of the novel alternate between the present and the past, each successive section from the past delving more deeply into Abe Ross's personal history until Abe is able to find the essence of his spiritual desolation and launch the process of healing. In *Scorched-Wood* a predominant motif is the cyclical pattern of Métis experience between 1869-70 and 1885. The causes of Métis' discontent before each rise of their defiance are virtually identical. As Riel remarks in 1885, "It's Red River all over . . . land, abuse of human rights, and hunger — it was all 1869 . . ." (p. 184, cf. p. 33). Prior to each so-called rebellion, the Métis hold a buffalo hunters' trial: the first time to try Tom Scott (pp. 79ff.) and the second time, Ballendine and Whitford (pp. 145ff.). Both before being chased out of Manitoba and before being defeated in Saskatchewan, the Métis rise to celebration of their new nationhood only to be destroyed soon afterward. The twice-repeated cycle of Métis experience gives way only in the promise of a third cycle through the person of Louis Riel who, as the novel's ending affirms, may become the voice for new life.

As in *Big Bear*, Wiebe's use of imagery and symbolism in *Scorched-Wood* is masterful. Often Wiebe succeeds in evoking the mood of an upcoming scene by means of effective imagery. Consider, for instance, the imagery of swarming bees to suggest apprehension in the following description of the mood in St. Anthony's just before Riel shunts aside Father Fourmond to deliver his own harangue:

ALLAN DUECK   197

Father André sitting below Fourmond sensed something in
St. Anthony's, a murmur perhaps, or the gradual waver of a
beginning keen; he could not say he heard it but he looked
at Vegreville beside him and the other was already looking
at him, eyes arched in question. Beyond him Nolin stirred as
if he sat on a burr. Something wrong. André glanced at the
window, half open to the chilly spring air: as of bees,
swarming. (p. 221)

As in *Big Bear*, the intrusion of the railroad in *Scorched-Wood* also
concisely symbolizes the whites' advance across the prairie. The
horses' revolt against crossing the tracks when Gabriel and his men
return from Montana with Riel contrasts the whites' and Métis' ways.
An unnatural "monolith," the railway characterizes the whites' trying
to subdue nature even at nature's expense (p. 193). Riel senses the
sharp opposition between this symbol of whiteness and the "unaf-
fected prairie and sky" over grazing buffalo — natural symbols of
the Métis' way of life. Not only does the railroad-crossing episode
contrast white and Métis approaches to life, but it suggests the difficulty the Métis people will have in coping with the whites' invasion.

A major strength of Wiebe's approach to historical fiction is his
ability to help the readers see the "human side" of history. Historical
fiction differs from history books in that story focuses on the lives of
particular people, and attempts to get readers to see the events in a
profounder way without pretense of objectivity. Wiebe's depiction of
John Kerr, a young Ontario private in Wolseley's army reflects
Wiebe's approach. Rather than relate in general newspaper style the
Toronto recruitment rally, Wiebe focuses on John Kerr's perceptions
of John and Anne Schultz's harangues and the young man's response
(pp. 91-94). And when Wolseley's army reaches Manitoba, Wiebe
commences the portrayal of the army through the interplay of Kerr's
fear and lust and righteous hatred (pp. 118-19). On the Métis side,
minor characters such as Will O'Donoghue remain relatively flat;
however, again the reader sees not merely an abstract account of
their deeds, but their inner motivations. O'Donoghue, for example,
transfers his Irish hatred of British rule to a Métis hatred of Ontario
WASP rule. Gabriel Dumont emerges as a well-rounded character
with a highly pragmatic approach to life, a lusty love of dance and
sexuality, brilliant military strategies, the capacity for intense friendship with Riel and commitment to a cause, genuine though inarticulate religiosity, and the capacity to change from buffalo chieftain to
military strategist to crack performer in Buffalo Bill's Wild West
Show.

But Wiebe's finest effort lodges in the portrayal of Riel himself. Wiebe succeeds in capturing Riel's complex personality so that the Métis leader becomes a person whom the reader knows and sympathizes with, not just an historical figure. Riel's religious self is credible even for nonchristian readers precisely because it is not simplistic. From the time of his religious training in Montreal to the end of the novel — Riel moves through stages of accepting the Catholic Church to rejecting its authority, through knowing certainly the reality of his calling to doubting it and even his faith itself, through praying unendingly to not knowing how to pray, through furiously brushing dusty sacred objects from a church altar to meekly recanting his rebellion against the Catholic Church. In his political leadership of the people, Riel fluctuates from being a brilliant negotiator decisively active to being utterly indecisive. He can flee in fear from Wolseley in Fort Garry, and later insist that the crucial battle must be fought at Batoche against Gabriel's better judgment. Riel can hate the enemy enough to pray for "hearts of steel, that our knives may find their bones" (p. 225), and at another time insist that his men not shoot until the other side has fired. He is equally at home leading the Exovedate, speaking with women and children, carrying a cross fearlessly behind the Batoche battlefield, and addressing a large political rally. Riel is a lucid thinker, a voracious reader and prolific writer, and an idealistic and charismatic leader. Not just a visionary or thinker, however, Riel also expresses deep love for his sister Sara, Gabriel, his mother, and his son Jean. He experiences sexual love almost as religious ecstasy. Perhaps most significant are Riel's love for, and his selfless leadership of, his people. Out of these complex motivations and characteristics emerges Wiebe's Riel: a richly human person who can indeed become the saint of the Métis people.

From the foregoing examination of *Big Bear* and *Scorched-Wood*, four distinctive qualities of Wiebe's historical fiction emerge. Both novels involve a reinterpretation of prairie history from another perspective than that of the white Canadian majority. Both novels reflect the author's own religious perspective, first in the historical reinterpretation and secondly in the centrality of religious experience in the lives of the characters. In both novels, Wiebe's perspective on history affirms the cultural heritage and identity of a demoralized and oppressed people. And, finally, both novels reflect Wiebe's preeminence as storyteller.

At one point in *Scorched-Wood*, Pierre Falcon says,

I have prayed, give me to make this song of Riel. You

gave me so many songs of people, of Cuthbert Grant and
Lépine and Gabriel hunting McDougall, even of silly
Dickson. Give me this song too so that when in the century
to come our people lie in the miserable trenches of poverty
and humiliation and disease and perhaps despair, when
troubles surround them like automatic rifles they can sing a
song of faith, of belief in vision for which the mud on their
feet gives them no evidence. I prayed that for some years,
and that song of Riel was not given me until I lay on my
deathbed. (p. 140)

In *Big Bear* and *Scorched-Wood* Wiebe himself becomes the singer of
songs, the teller of stories that give a voice and an identity to the
River Cree and Métis peoples.

Notes

[1] *Where Is the Voice Coming From?* (Toronto: McClelland & Stewart, 1974), p. 142.
[2] Rudy Wiebe, *The Temptations of Big Bear* (Toronto: McClelland & Stewart, 1973), p. 28. All subsequent references to *The Temptations of Big Bear* are to this edition, and are indicated in parentheses after each quotation.
[3] "Rudy Wiebe: The Moving Stream Is Perfectly at Rest," *Conversations with Canadian Novelists.* Part Two (Toronto: Macmillan, 1973), p. 152.
[4] Herbert Butterfield, *The Historical Novel* (Cambridge: Cambridge University Press, 1924), p. 50.
[5] "Moving Stream," p. 152.
[6] An Unpublished Interview by Donald Cameron (Edmonton, 1972), p. 23. I refer here to the unpublished transcript of the taped interview because Cameron does not include this comment in the final version of the interview.
[7] See Lion Feuchtwanger, *The House of Desdemona: the Laurels and Limitations of Historical Fiction*, trans. Harold A. Basilius (Detroit: Wayne State University Press, 1963), pp. 129-31. Feuchtwanger argues that the best writers of historical fiction use stories from the past in order to help elucidate the present. Historical materials are especially useful for this because, by providing distance, they allow the artist a greater objectivity in dealing with contemporary materials.
[8] Rudy Wiebe, *The Blue Mountains of China* (Toronto: McClelland & Stewart, 1970), p. 2.
[9] "On the Trail of Big Bear," *Journal of Canadian Fiction*, III, No. 2 (1974), p. 46.
[10] E.E. Reimer, "Rudy Wiebe's 'Steel Lines of Fiction': the Progress of a Mennonite Novelist," *Mennonite Mirror*, 1, No. 1 (September 1971), 28-29.
[11] *Historical Novel*, p. 29.
[12] "On the Trail," 45.
[13] Rudy Wiebe, *The Scorched-Wood People* (Toronto: McClelland & Stewart, 1977). All references to *The Scorched-Wood People* are to this edition, and are indicated in parentheses after each quotation.
[14] "Moving Stream," p. 148.
[15] *New Men/New Roles: A Study Guide for Christian People in Social Change* (Newton, KS: Faith and Life Press, 1977), p. 23.

16 "An interview with . . . Rudy Wiebe: Storymaker of the Prairies," *The Gateway* (November 10, 1977), 9.
17 *Historical Novel*, p. 42.
18 *Where Is the Voice Coming From?*, pp. 145-55. Cf. Rudy Wiebe, "Introduction," *The Story-Makers* (Toronto: Macmillan, 1970), pp. ix-x.
19 *Story-Makers*, p. xi.
20 See Wiebe's comments about the need for historical exactness in "On the Trail," 47-48.
21 *Story-Makers*, pp. xiii-xiv.

ABOUT THE CONTRIBUTORS

John Lauber has taught American literature, modern poetry, and Shakespeare at the University of Alberta since 1965. He has published works on Jane Austen, Byron, Melville, William Stafford, and most recently on Pound's *Cantos*. He became a Canadian citizen in 1974 and is presently making himself bilingual.

Catherine McLay teaches Canadian literature at the University of Calgary. She has published articles on Shakespeare, Willa Cather, Margaret Laurence, and W.O. Mitchell, as well as Margaret Atwood. She is currently working on an anthology of Canadian women poets and a study of fiction by Canadian women.

Wilfred Cude teaches Canadian literature at the University of British Columbia. He has published numerous articles on Canadian writers, including Sinclair Ross, Robertson Davies, and Mordecai Richler.

Gordon Roper taught Canadian literature at the University of Toronto and is now a Professor Emeritus at Trent University. He contributed three chapters to the *Literary History of Canada*. He brought together the Massey College Collection of Canadian fiction and is building the Shell Canada Collection at Trent.

Ellen D. Warwick has lived and studied in various countries, including Peru, Mexico, and Canada. While in Toronto she did graduate work in Canadian literature at York University, publishing articles on Robertson Davies and Gwendolyn MacEwen. She presently resides in Boston.

Clara Thomas teaches Canadian literature at York University. She is the author of *The Manawaka World of Margaret Laurence* and several other studies of Canadian writers. She has published numerous articles and reviews on Canadian fiction in a variety of periodicals.

Frank Pesando teaches English at Georges Vanier Secondary School in Toronto. He is currently writing a book on the nocturnal wildlife of urban and suburban North America.

Cheryl Cooper, originally from Regina, now lives in Vancouver. She divides her time between studying Canadian literature at the University of British Columbia and assisting a rare book dealer specializing in Canadian literature.

J.R. (Tim) Struthers of London, Ontario, is the author of various bibliographies, reviews, interviews, and articles dealing with Canadian literature and with its relation to British and American literature. He has written two articles on Alice Munro, and is currently editing a volume of criticism about Hugh Hood.

Miriam Packer is a native Montrealer who has taught English at Sir George Williams University and at l'Université de Montréal, and is now at Dawson College in Montreal. Her doctoral thesis on the fiction of Laurence, Munro, and Atwood has been revised for publication.

Tom Marshall teaches Canadian literature at Queen's University in Kingston. He has published five books of poetry and three critical works, including *Harsh and Lovely Land*, forthcoming from University of British Columbia Press. He was chief editor of *Quarry* during its formative years and was poetry editor of *The Canadian Forum*.

John Moss teaches Canadian literature at Queen's University. He was editor of the *Journal of Canadian Fiction* for five years and is the author of two critical books, *Patterns of Isolation* and *Sex and Violence in the Canadian Novel*. He is presently completing a third, entitled *A Reader's Guide to the Canadian Novel*.

Hildegard Tiessen has taught English at Wilfred Laurier University for the past four years. She is completing her Ph.D. dissertation from the University of Alberta. She has recently become involved in publishing and is the president of Sand Hill Books.

Allan Dueck teaches literature, communication, and the Bible at Hesston College in Kansas. He holds a Master of Divinity degree in the Bible and theology from Mennonite Biblical Seminary in Indiana and he received an M.A. from the University of Alberta, with a thesis on "Rudy Wiebe as Storyteller: Vision and Art in Wiebe's Fiction."

ACKNOWLEDGEMENTS

Grateful acknowledgement is made to the following:
John Lauber for "Alice in Consumer-Land: The Self-Discovery of Marian MacAlpine."
Catherine McLay and the *Journal of Canadian Fiction* for "The Divided Self: Theme and Pattern in *Surfacing.*" Reprinted by permission.
Wilfred Cude and *The Fiddlehead* for "Bravo Mothball! An Essay on *Lady Oracle.*" Reprinted by permission.
Gordon Roper and the *Journal of Canadian Fiction* for "*Fifth Business* and 'That Old Fantastical Duke of Dark Corners, C.G. Jung.'" Reprinted by permission.
Ellen D. Warwick for "The Transformation of Robertson Davies." This is a greatly expanded version of an essay that originally appeared in the *Journal of Canadian Fiction*. Reprinted by permission.
Clara Thomas and the *Journal of Canadian Studies* for "Myth and Manitoba in *The Diviners.*" Reprinted by permission.
Frank Pesando and the *Journal of Canadian Fiction* for "In a Nameless Land: Apocalyptic Mythology in the Writings of Margaret Laurence." Reprinted by permission.
Cheryl Cooper for "Images of Closure in *The Diviners.*"
J.R. (Tim) Struthers and *The Canadian Review of American Studies* for "Alice Munro and the American South." Reprinted by permission.
Miriam Packer for "*Lives of Girls and Women*: A Creative Search for Completion."
Tom Marshall for "Third Solitude: Canadian as Jew."
John Moss for "Richler's Horseman." This is an adaptation of a chapter from *Sex and Violence in the Canadian Novel*, published by McClelland and Stewart, Ltd., Toronto. Reprinted by permission.
Hildegard E. Tiessen for "A Mighty Inner River: 'Peace' in the Fiction of Rudy Wiebe." This is an adaptation of an essay that originally appeared in the *Journal of Canadian Fiction*. Reprinted by permission.
Allan Dueck for "Rudy Wiebe's Approach to Historical Fiction: A Study of *The Temptations of Big Bear* and *The Scorched-Wood People.*" This is a greatly expanded and altered version of a piece that originally appeared in the *Journal of Canadian Fiction*. Reprinted by permission.

PHOTO CREDITS

Margaret Atwood by Graeme Gibson
Robertson Davies by Paterson
Margaret Laurence by Eedie Steiner
John Moss by Stan Dragland
Rudy Wiebe by Shirley Glew, *The Gateway*